Seductive Surfaces

Studies in British Art 6

Seductive Surfaces:
The Art of Tissot

Edited by Katharine Lochnan

Published for
The Paul Mellon Centre for Studies in British Art
The Yale Center for British Art

Yale University Press, New Haven & London

Typeset in Adobe Garamond
Printed in Great Britain by BAS Printers Limited, Over Wallop, Hampshire

Library of Congress Catalog Card Number 99–65333
ISBN 0-300-08184-7

A catalogue record for this book is available from the British Library.

Contents

Preface

The Art Gallery of Ontario has had a long and continuing interest in the work of the remarkable nineteenth-century narrative painter and printmaker, James Joseph Tissot. This interest and commitment, marked by the acquisition of two major paintings in the late 1960s and the mounting of a retrospective exhibition in 1968, was reactivated in the early 1990s by the remarkable gift and partial purchase of the most important collection of Tissot prints in private hands, the Gotlieb collection. The Gotlieb collection had already been published by one of the leading Tissot scholars, Willard E. Misfeldt, in the exhibition catalogue *J.J. Tissot: Prints from the Gotlieb Collection*, which accompanied the travelling exhibition organised by Art Services International in 1991. This valuable contribution to Tissot literature is the definitive reference work on the Gotlieb collection. With the acquisition of 152 prints, and the support of the Gotlieb family through continuing purchases for the collection, the Art Gallery of Ontario now takes its place as a major international study centre for the art of Tissot, and for printmaking of the later nineteenth century.

In celebration of this acquisition, and in the spirit that the Gallery carries an obligation to push always towards new ways of seeing and thinking about its collection, the Gallery decided to present a symposium in the autumn of 1996 which highlighted some of the new scholarship being undertaken on Tissot and his times. 'Unmasking Tissot' was an interdisciplinary look at Tissot's production in the light of expanding contexts for understanding his activity. The symposium was organized in the spirit, and with the belief, that the content of Tissot's work, the stories it told for late twentieth-century audiences were yet to be unmasked. The symposium was begun quite simply in the belief that images which made so many of us return with unanswered questions about their subtle subversiveness and disquieting beauty must have meanings that would be truly engaging to talk about and document.

The symposium which this publication documents was organized by the Art Gallery of Ontario's Senior Curator of Prints and Drawings, Katharine Lochnan, with the support of her colleagues Brenda Rix, David Wistow and Tracey Henriksson. Invited were a new generation of art historians who challenged the stricture of the canon, a theatre historian and a costume historian new to Tissot studies. Collectively their work was positioned to expand common understandings of Tissot's production as an artist of style and achievement, while raising important questions about our evolving understanding of the times in which he lived. We wanted, in short, to suggest certain things that were new, even if they were provisionally understood, and contentious in their declarations.

In the question period which followed the presentation of papers, areas for future investigation were raised, including the relationship of Tissot's dramas to the Victorian novel, and the development of his late work seen in the context of Symbolist orthodoxies. These have been addressed in this volume by four new contributors. The participants in the symposium whose works are included here are Caroline Arscott, Tamar Garb, Katharine Lochnan, Edward Maeder, Nancy Marshall and Ann Saddlemeyer. To these have been added Margaret Flanders Darby, Serena Keshavjee, Elizabeth Prelinger and Carole Silver. We acknowledge their contributions with pleasure and gratitude.

We are extremely grateful to Brian Allen and the Paul Mellon Centre for Studies in British Art for publishing these papers, and to Patrick McCaughey, director of the Yale Centre for British Art, for suggesting this possibility. Katharine Lochnan and her staff undertook the project with enthusiasm, commitment and a true spirit of curiosity that made all the difference in looking beneath the surface of appearances.

This initiative could not have been undertaken without the generosity of Alan and Sandra Gotlieb, whose single gift of nine-tenths of their collection transformed an already remarkable collection of nineteenth-century prints and drawings in our care, and to the late Arthur Gelber, an unstinting patron of the Gallery and its ambitions, whose gift of the balance through the Marvin Gelber Fund made all the difference.

In closing I would like to thank the Master Print and Drawing Society of Ontario, the Marvin Gelber Fund, and The British Council for their support in mounting the symposium which has given rise to this publication.

Matthew Teitelbaum
Director, Art Gallery of Ontario, Toronto

Acknowledgements

There are many individuals who have been instrumental in bringing this work to fruition. It would never have happened without Allan Gotlieb's passion for Tissot, and for the great gift of his definitive collection to the Art Gallery of Ontario. It was this which occasioned the exhibition and symposium, and gave rise to this book of essays. I would like to thank Allan and Sondra Gotlieb and the Gelber family for ensuring that the Marvin Gelber Print and Drawing Study Centre at the Art Gallery of Ontario is now a centre for the study of Tissot's prints.

My Director, Matthew Teitelbaum, challenged and inspired me to look at Tissot in new ways and to examine the role of prints in a broader context. I have been assisted at various stages in the evolution of the Tissot project by a superb team at the Art Gallery of Ontario: by interns Odilia Bonebakker and Tracey Henriksson, by staff Millie Minas and Brenda Rix, and by colleagues Michael Parke-Taylor, Maia Sutnik and David Wistow. I would like to thank all of them for their support and encouragement.

This publication is the result of the willing collaboration of a group of outstanding and extremely busy scholars who nonetheless responded with alacrity to our invitation to contribute, embracing the complex challenge of addressing Tissot's work in new ways. It has been a pleasure and a privilege working with them. We have had a friend throughout in Francess G. Halpenny, Professor Emerita, University of Toronto, who attended the symposium, encouraged me to search for a publisher, read and edited the manuscript, and assisted in putting together a prospectus. She has been at my side throughout the process. As editor I needed critiquing and I would like thank my longtime friend and collaborator Carole Silver for taking on this role.

Bridging the gap between the symposium and the publication necessitated a leap of more than faith. It was thanks to Malcolm Warner at the Yale Center for British Art, and the enthusiastic support of his director, Patrick McCaughey, who arranged a meeting with Brian Allen of the Paul Mellon Centre for Studies in British Art, that this book took shape. It has been a great pleasure working with Brian Allen and the staff of the Paul Mellon Centre, especially our editor, Guilland Sutherland, who has patiently shepherded us through the production process.

We have been aided in this venture by many friends. I would like to acknowledge and thank Willard E. Misfeldt, Michael Wentworth, and Christopher

Wood, whose books on Tissot have been at our elbows, for their encouragement and their assistance in tracking down photographs and works in private collections.

In closing, I would especially like to thank my husband, George Yost, for his interest and support at every stage of this project.

Katharine Lochnan

Introduction

Katharine Lochnan

TISSOT is one of the most attractive and intriguing artists of the second half of the nineteenth century. Enormously successful in his own time, he was all but forgotten until interest in academic art revived during the 1960s. Today he is one of the most sought-after artists on the international art market and there is growing interest in his work among scholars in a wide range of disciplines.

Tissot's first biographer, the costume historian James Laver, saw the artist's works primarily as a goldmine for fashion historians, an evaluation which prevailed for decades. Yet far from being simple fashion plates, Tissot's ambiguous narratives provide rich insight into issues of class, gender, and taste and are laced with ironic subtexts. Superficially attractive and appearing to leave nothing to the imagination, they are ultimately troubling and impenetrable. It is this dichotomy which has enticed a new generation of scholars to revisit them using a variety of novel analytical approaches.

After decades of neglect, Tissot was 'rediscovered' by a pioneering team, Henri Zerner, David Brooke, and Michael Wentworth, who were surveying the boundaries between the avant-garde and academic traditions. They collaborated on the catalogue of the landmark exhibition *James Jacques Joseph Tissot, 1836–1902: A Retrospective Exhibition* which took place in 1968 at the Rhode Island School of Design and at the Art Gallery of Ontario. The catalogue preface, co-authored by the respective museum directors, Daniel Robbins and William J. Withrow, provides a synopsis of the issues which framed the debate over the relative merits of Tissot in the 'age of formalism':

> Since the late 1950s there has been a gradual reassessment of academic nineteenth century painting, in part dictated by the shortage of major Impressionist and post-Impressionist work and also influenced by the developments in the art of our own time. There have been exhibitions and books to demonstrate that Victorian art was not so bad, and a taste has developed which is no longer confined to the intellectual or artistic community, a taste that only a few years ago would have been called camp. No amount of reevaluation will make a really good painter out of Bouguereau, nor a great painter even out of J. J. Tissot.

This flutter of interest stimulated scholarly investigation and paved the way for a series of significant publications and exhibitions in the 1970s and 1980s. Michael Wentworth's indispensible *James Tissot: Catalogue Raisonné of the Prints* (Minneapolis Institute of Arts, 1978), and his brilliant monograph *James Tissot* (Oxford: Clarendon Press) of 1984, constitute the bedrock of Tissot research. Nonetheless this reassessment of Tissot was conditioned by the taste of the times which ranked artists by their proximity to the avant-garde: Tissot inevitably emerged as 'second rate' because he did not fit the modernist mould.

Wentworth charted the territory and suggested new avenues for exploration. It is here that our authors begin. A complex artist, Tissot is best surveyed from multiple vantage points: rich insights have been contributed, and new questions raised, by our interdisciplinary group of art, literary, theatre, and costume historians who have looked at Tissot from the perspective of their own disciplines, concentrating particularly on questions of gender and class.

Almost all of the scholarly writing on Tissot until now has been by men. Since Baudelaire's 'world of women' was Tissot's central theme, a female perspective is not only appropriate but also, as these essays demonstrate, capable of yielding fresh insights. Thus nine out of the ten contributors to this volume are women. They have explored topics—among them voyeurism, exhibitionism, fetishism, kitsch, and spiritualism—which would have been considered tasteless, even unthinkable, fifteen years ago.

It is the revelation of gender and class conflict through psychodrama that lifts Tissot's 'social conversation pieces' of the 1870s and 1880s out of the realm of mere costume drama. The role of women and the relationship between the sexes lie at the heart of his modern-life dramas. Inhabiting 'separate spheres', as Marshall has indicated, gender roles are prescribed: she is passive while he is active, her realm is suburban and domestic while his is urban and commercial. The status of women is conditioned by their ability to attract and hold members of the opposite sex. Darby sees the fashionable conservatory as a metaphor for domestic enclosure, quoting John Stuart Mill who maintained that the hothouse cultivation of women was carried on 'for the benefit and pleasure of their masters'. She points out that Tissot set out 'to show ominous underlying realities: depths of feminine unease beneath frivolity, anxieties of entrapment beneath ennui' and that 'where nature is also artifice, nurture is also control'.

Tissot's female subjects are not what they appear to be. In order to penetrate the narrative subtexts we must learn how to decode dress and gesture. As Garb has pointed out, dress is no indication of status or class: Tissot's beautifully attired females are largely drawn from the *demi-monde* and would have been viewed as sexually available. She explores the eroticized pleasure of looking and consuming and discusses the 'sham elegance' of the self-created, commodified *parisienne*, who existed only to be looked at. Despite the fact that Tissot portrays women as commodified status symbols and the projection of male fantasies, we detect in their faces the first stirrings of independence. It is in part because he depicted women at this critical moment in history that his works are so fascinating today.

And what of men? Although they are less visible in Tissot's dramas, we are made acutely aware that women function within a patriarchal culture in which the ground rules have been established by and for men. When men are incorporated into the drama, they invariably play the role of voyeur, judge, or master. Even when they are ostensibly absent, their presence is frequently signalled by top hats, canes, and other paraphernalia. We detect, however, a challenge to the status quo in the confrontational stares of the women and the quarrelling or estranged couples.

If the role of women and the relationship between the sexes is central to the narrative, it is encapsulated by the much larger class drama in which increasing numbers of *parvenus* invade territory formerly monopolized by the aristocracy. At this time, the new equation of wealth with work and status collided with the old equation of wealth with leisure and class. Silver notes the analogy of Tissot to Trollope whose writings constitute an 'indictment of the vulgarity, commercialism, and moral and financial corruption of the *nouveau riche*, of a rising middle-class turned social-climbers, and of a fading gentry and aristocracy'. Upward mobility was discussed obsessively on both sides of the Channel, and class barriers were challenged and breached as never before. The embattled upper class concocted increasingly complex rules and subtle forms of etiquette to cover every aspect of dress and social behaviour, creating a minefield for the aspiring. Pretty girls, all gussied up, give away their origins by an awkward gesture, an inappropriate dress, or an unforgivable *faux-pas* such as arriving too early at a party. Social climbing is a game of Snakes and Ladders: as Garb notes in her analysis of the aristocrat on the trapeze, this works in both directions. Tissot's works, like those of his literary contemporaries, also had a moral dimension.

Upward mobility required close observation. In Tissot's works the *dramatis personae*—artist, viewer, and critic—are engaged in a complex web of looking and seeing. Arscott points out how class consciousness is revealed by individuals covertly observing each other's dress and behaviour. Simply by looking at Tissot's works the viewer is drawn into what Garb calls 'the complex world of exhibitionism and voyeurism'. We are invited to participate through our involuntary response to facial expressions, gestures, or, as Maeder points out, the private semaphore of fan and umbrella language. This gives Tissot's work a theatrical quality which Saddlemyer relates to naturalist and realist developments in the theatre. She notes that Tissot employed the concept of the 'fourth wall', which incorporates the audience into the drama, a decade before it makes its first appearance in the theatre.

Silver calls Tissot's works 'visual invitations to narrative', and points out that their interpretation assumes a familiarity with the conventions of the Victorian comic and tragic novel. Attempts to decode them are irresistible and the artist tempts us by embedding clues. Yet his narratives are deliberately ambiguous and ultimately mysterious. Instead of illustrating fictions, they mirror real-life situations, and the viewer is only permitted to glimpse part of a much larger story.

Everything in Tissot's works has a symbolic function, whether overt or covert. By decoding the costumes, architectural settings, and narrative elements we gain admission to the private world of the protagonists. The panes of glass and web of rigging in *A Passing Storm* suggest psychological barriers and tensions, while the lewd griffin carved on the counter in *The Shop Girl* reinforces the voyeuristic theme of window shopping. Prelinger, pushing this discussion beyond the limits of iconographic interpretation, sees Tissot 'infusing "ordinary objects" with an inner life that often exceeds that of his human figures'. She notes that the 'hyperrealism' of his style, in combination with 'hothouse settings' crammed with bric-a-brac, create a 'world of displaced desire' and 'a complex of fetishisms' which links them to symbolism and 'the prevailing ethos of decadence'.

There is much repetition, at times verging on the cinematic, within Tissot's visual narratives. Individuals, costumes, props and sets may appear more than once in the same work, or move from picture to picture. While Prelinger sees this 'strategy of repetition' as a means of creating 'mesmerizing internal cross-references', Silver points out that it is through this device that Tissot creates internal narrative, a structure of self-allusion, which can be seen once again as a visual analogue to Trollope whose characters reappear from novel to novel.

We have yet to grapple with that most difficult phenomenon for the modern viewer: Tissot's devotion to Spiritualism and the Catholic revival. Keshavjee points out that, along with other 'neo-Romantics', Tissot was drawn to alternative philosophies which sought to legitimize religion through science, and

xiv

maintains that 'the pan-Western critique of Enlightenment positivism in which Tissot was involved was fundamental to emergent modernity', In his earnest attempts to render the invisible visible, Tissot appropriated the imagery of spirit photography to replicate the appearance of ectoplasm in mezzotint. His religious meditations gave birth to biblical illustrations of hallucinogenic proportions.

Lochnan argues that John Ruskin was unintentionally prescient when he described Tissot's paintings as 'mere coloured photographs of vulgar society'. Tissot appropriated the subject matter, imagery and palette found in a wide range of popular print sources including hand-coloured fashion plates, photographs, chromolithographs, even oleographs. His paintings and prints, encoded with the look and taste of the 'vulgar society' which he was depicting, became both aesthetically and socially subversive. Tissot depicted the dilemmas and predilections of the *nouveau riche* by holding a mirror up to nature. That 'vulgar society' loved to see itself reflected in his mirror was the ultimate irony. Framed and glazed, his paintings take their place among the luxury consumer goods they slyly immortalise.

Responding to Baudelaire's call for a new art which would find its subjects in modern life, Tissot focussed on 'la comédie humaine', creating an archaeological site for modern scholars. What makes his works so appealing to a growing circle of specialists is the fact that they are windows through which we may look into Tissot's world. This illusion was deliberately manufactured by the artist using every trick in his impressive technical arsenal. Instead of participating in the avant-garde stylistic discourse which gave rise to what we call modern art, Tissot strove to create paintings of such verisimilitude that we feel as if we can step through the picture frame into an earlier moment in time.

In this collection of essays Tissot emerges as an artist acutely aware of the paradoxes of his age, an artist who set out to explore the relationship between external and internal reality, and left us with an indelible series of images. They not only constitute a rich source of documentary information: their seductive surfaces are only skin deep. Tissot's works depict the elegant social veneer which conceals disturbing underlying dramas: they are layered with ironic subtexts alluding to the undercurrents of a highly materialistic, class-conscious age in which gender roles and the relationship between the sexes were shifting dramatically. Encouraged to play the role of voyeurs, we are seduced by their superficial attractiveness and apparent transparency only to discover that they are not 'pretty pictures' at all, that closer inspection renders them more opaque. It is ultimately this attraction–rejection phenomenon which fascinates, even mesmerizes, viewers and scholars. These essays raise as many questions as they answer, not only about Tissot and his age but about how to look at art in a dramatically shifting theoretical environment. They should be seen as experimental forays pointing in new directions. By wiping bits of the mirror clean we hope to contribute to the reassessment of Tissot as a major nineteenth-century artist.

I   Tissot, *Too Early*, 1873, oil on canvas, 71.1 x 101.6 cm. Guildhall Art Gallery, Corporation of London/ Bridgeman Art Library, London/New York

II   François-Claudins Comte Calix, Fashion Plate no. 1433 for *Les Modes Parisiennes,* August 1870, etching transferred to lithographic stone and hand-coloured, 27.3 x 20 cm. (sheet). Gift of Mr. R. P. Dennistoun, Royal Ontario Museum Library, Toronto

III *Gathering Shellfish*, Japanese hand-coloured photograph from the Schilling Collection, in *Souvenirs from Japan* (Ukiyo-e Books, Leiden)

IV William Dyce, *Pegwell Bay, Kent — A Recollection of October 5,* 1858, oil on canvas, 63.5 x 88.9 cm. © Tate Gallery, London, 1998

V Tissot, *The Captain's Daughter*, 1873, oil on canvas, 72.3 x 104.7 cm. Southampton Art Gallery/ Bridgeman Art Library, London/New York

VI Tissot, *A Passing Storm*, 1876, oil on canvas, 76.8 x 99.7 cm. Gift of the Sir James Dunn Foundation, The Beaverbrook Art Gallery, Fredericton, New Brunswick

VII   Tissot, *In the Conservatory (The Rivals)*, c.1875-8, oil on canvas, 42.5 x 53.9 cm. Photograph courtesy of The Richard Green Gallery, London

VIII   T. Baines, 'Group of Bamboos' from *Nature and Art* (London, 1866), vol. 1, chromolithograph, 22.4 x 14.9 cm. Robertson Davies Library, Massey College, Toronto

IX Tissot, *The Bunch of Lilacs*, c.1875, oil on canvas, 50.8 x 35.5 cm. Christie's Images, London/ Bridgeman Art Library, London/New York

X Tissot, *The Gallery of H.M.S. Calcutta (Portsmouth)*, c.1877, oil on canvas, 68.5 x 92 cm.
©Tate Gallery, London, 1998

XI Tissot, *Portsmouth Dockyard (How Happy I Could Be With Either)*, 1877, oil on canvas,
38.1 x 54.6 cm. ©Tate Gallery, London, 1998

XII Tissot, *The Ball on Shipboard*, c.1874, oil on canvas, 84 x 130 cm. ©Tate Gallery, London, 1998

XIII Tissot, *Hush!*, c.1875, oil on canvas, 73.6 x 112.2 cm. ©Manchester City Art Galleries

XIV Tissot, *Young Woman in a Boat*, c.1870, oil on canvas, 50.1 x 64.7 cm. Private Collection/ Bridgeman Art Library, London/New York

XV Tissot, *The Circle of the Rue Royale,* 1868, oil on canvas, 215.9 x 330.2 cm. Private Collection, London, UK / Bridgeman Art Library, London/New York

XVI Tissot, *A Convalescent*, c.1876, oil on canvas, 74.9 x 97.7 cm. Sheffield Galleries and Museums Trust, UK/Bridgeman Art Library, London/New York

XVII Tissot, *The Letter*, c.1876-8, oil on canvas, 71.7 x 107.3 cm. National Gallery of Canada, Ottawa

XVIII Tissot, *London Visitors*, c.1874, oil on canvas, 160 x 114.3 cm. Toledo Museum of Art, Toledo, Ohio; purchased with funds from the Libbey Endowment, gift of Edward Drummond Libbey

XIX Tissot, *Portrait of Mlle L. L. . . .* , 1864, oil on canvas, 124 x 100 cm. Musée d'Orsay, Paris/
Bridgeman Art Library, London/New York

XX Tissot, *October*, 1878,
oil on canvas, 216 x 108.7 cm.
Private Collection/ Agnew's,
London/ Bridgeman Art
Library, London/ New York

XXI Tissot, *The Shop Girl*, 1883-5, oil on canvas, 146.1 x 101.6 cm. Art Gallery of Ontario, Toronto, gift from Corporations' Subscription Fund 1968

XXII Tissot, *The Political Lady*, 1883-5, oil on canvas, 142.2 x 101.6 cm. Albright-Knox Art Gallery, Buffalo, New York

XXIII Tissot, *The Sporting Ladies*, 1883-5, oil on canvas, 147 x 102 cm. Courtesy Museum of Fine Arts, Boston, Juliana Cheney Edwards Collection

XXIV Tissot, *Mediumistic Apparition*,
1885, mezzotint in green ink on *chine
appliqué*, 60.3 x 44.5 cm. Art Gallery of
Ontario, Gift of Allan and Sondra
Gotlieb 1994

XXV Tissot, *William Eglinton*, 1885,
etching printed in sanguine on cream laid
paper (unique proof), 15.6 x 10.1 cm.
Art Gallery of Ontario, Gift of Allan and
Sondra Gotlieb 1994

The Medium and the Message: Popular Prints and the Work of James Tissot

Katharine Lochnan

THAT GREAT VICTORIAN judge of art John Ruskin delivered his verdict in a review of the Grosvenor Gallery exhibition of 1877 when he dismissed Tissot's paintings with the remark: 'most of them are, unhappily, mere coloured photographs of vulgar society'.[1] These words followed Tissot back to Paris, and continue to dog his reputation to the present day.[2] Although pompous, Ruskin's statement provides us with a clue to understanding Tissot's artistic programme. Not only did the paintings look like coloured photographs, they did indeed depict 'vulgar' society.

While Paris suffered an economic depression following the Franco-Prussian War, London went through a decade of unprecedented prosperity and social change. The new British middle class, its wealth based on industry, trade, and commerce, had more disposable income than ever before, and was eager to acquire the attributes of culture and gentility.[3] This fuelled the contemporary British art market and turned popular artists into wealthy and respected members of society. Tissot, who had made a fortune during the Second Empire, fled from Paris after the suppression of the Commune in June 1871 and arrived in London with a few hundred francs in his pocket. Forced to start again, he at first produced attractive costume-dramas. Once established, he began to make the modern conversation-pieces that were ultimately to give rise to Ruskin's critical attack.[4]

At the time, French and British middle- and upper-class society believed that appearances must be maintained at all costs. Looked at closely, society was not what it seemed to be: in a period when romantic love and marital fidelity were promulgated as ideals, a double standard for men was tacitly accepted which placed women in complex emotional situations. Fearing the incursions of the *nouveau riche*, the aristocracy devised increasingly complex and subtle codes of dress and etiquette so that the upwardly mobile were confronted by a social minefield. They lived in terror of committing an unforgettable *faux pas* by revealing their origins through an unladylike gesture, as in *Boarding the Yacht*, 1873 (fig. 20 on p. 54), arriving too early at a party, as in *Too Early*, 1873 (pl. I), or wearing an inappropriate dress, as in *The Political Lady*, 1883–5 (pl. XXII). The seductively beautiful painted surfaces of Tissot's social conversation-pieces are

1. Tissot, *Mrs. Newton Asleep in an Armchair*, c.1878–9, oil on canvas, 52 x 44.5 cm. From the Collection of Albert E. Cummings

only a veneer, a metaphor for contemporary society. Their beauty is skin deep: their content reveals the underlying tensions which characterized his age.

It is this contradiction between appearance and reality that makes Tissot's work compelling and provides us with an invaluable record of the class and gender dramas of his age. The women of London and Paris who are featured in his work, however handsomely got up, are not what they appear. Comfort and finery guarantee neither respectability nor happiness. Although their identity may remain the subject of conjecture, Tissot was drawn to the women of the *demi-monde* whose lives were focussed on attracting and pleasing the opposite sex. His passive English women betray feelings of boredom, melancholy, or hostility, while his French women appear unapologetically scheming, coquettish, or brazen. All of Tissot's women have one thing in common: however awkward their social dilemmas, however tortuous their dramas with men, on the surface everything appears to be smooth and beautiful.

Tissot has long been considered the foremost recorder of fashion of his day. However, he was not taken seriously as an artist before the rediscovery of his work in the late 1960s, when he escaped oblivion only to be assigned second-class status. He has been perceived as an artistic hybrid, suspended between the French and English schools and their respective avant-garde and academic movements. Analysis of his art from such traditional vantage points as the evolution of national schools and the modern movement has led to his being seen as an artist who does not 'fit in', and therefore incapable of making either the imaginative or technical leap to Impressionism. His social and financial success has given rise to deep suspicions that he combined academic with avant-garde tendencies for purely mercenary reasons. Yet even his most damning critics agree that Tissot could work in any style with such success that he earned an unenviable reputation for plagiarism. An oil sketch such as *Mrs. Newton Asleep in an Armchair*, c. 1878–9 (fig. 1) reveals his ability to capture a moment from life using a broken brush stroke which would have qualified him as 'Impressionist' by any definition of the term.

It is only by suspending judgement, and looking both at and beneath the surfaces of his paintings and prints to see what they tell us about the artist's intention, that we can fully appreciate his highly original contribution. Instead of trying to fit him into the French or English school, or focussing on what he did not do, we will look at what he *did* do, and see whether his message or messages are significant, and whether they were conveyed effectively.

The Realist Movement

After his conversion to realism around 1863, Tissot adhered to the Realist agenda throughout his life. There was no one way to paint a Realist picture: Realism was more ideologically than stylistically based. Along with the friends of his Paris student days, Whistler, Degas, Manet and George du Maurier, Tissot paid close attention to the writings of Charles Baudelaire. In his review-essay 'The Salon of 1859', Baudelaire divided the 'Realists' into two camps: 'positivists' and 'imaginatives'. Rejecting the empirical approach of the former, Baudelaire embraced the subjective approach of the latter, and maintained that the true artist should 'only paint in accordance with what he sees and what he feels'.[5] The Impressionists, who began in the Realist camp, saw Tissot at the outset as one of themselves. In 1873 Degas urged Tissot with no success to exhibit in the first Impressionist exhibition, writing: 'The Realist movement no longer needs to fight with the others, it already is, it exists, it must show itself as *something distinct*, there must be a *salon of realists*'.[6]

Tissot turned away from Leysian 'style troubadour' narratives[7] such as *Way of Flowers, Way of Tears*, 1860 (fig. 63 on p. 157) and found his true direction in

1863 when Baudelaire's essay 'The Painter of Modern Life' appeared in *Le Figaro*. In this immensely influential piece the critic exhorted artists to take their subjects from modern life. In place of a non-existent classical ideal of female beauty, he urged them to record the temporal aspects peculiar to each era, country, profession and social class. He recommended the world of modern women as an appropriate subject, maintaining that the beauty of the age was epitomized in her costume, gesture, bearing, gait, manners, and morals. It may have been Baudelaire's lines, 'in that vast picture-gallery which is life in London or Paris, we shall meet with all the various types of fallen womanhood — of women in revolt against society — at all levels'[8] which inspired Tissot to explore, on both sides of the Channel and on a personal and professional level, the world of women.

Tissot's paintings are literally and figuratively a Realist window on his world. He set out to create the illusion that nothing really separates us from his *dramatis personae* so that, by a simple act of the imagination, we can step into the world behind the picture frame. While he leaves nothing to the imagination when it comes to physical description, he leaves everything to the imagination when it comes to decoding his ambiguous narratives. The *doubles entendres* embedded in his dramas of the 1870s and 1880s invite a subjective response from the viewer. Although it was later seen in Paris as an English affectation, Tissot covered his canvases with glass, a substance used symbolically in many of his works, for example *A Passing Storm*, 1876 (pl. VI), to represent a barrier which is simultaneously real and illusory. Communicating through facial expressions or gestures, his characters draw us into the *mise en scène*: depending on our gender we may be made to feel like a voyeur or confidante by *The Political Lady* (pl. XXII), and propositioned or invited to walk through an open door by *The Shop Girl* (pl. XXI).[9]

Tissot has been much criticized for his lack of aerial perspective,[10] but far from seeking those atmospheric effects which are inextricably linked with our understanding of 'Impressionism', he abjured both aerial perspective and broken brushwork in the interest of verisimilitude, and headed in the opposite direction. As the dramas become more intense, the impression of airlessness increases: in *The Political Lady* (pl. XXII) the air seems to have been pumped out, leaving us gasping and identifying viscerally with the leading character.

Modern-Life Subjects and Caricature

An interest in popular imagery was part of Realist ideology and played a key role in the transformation of late nineteenth-century art. Precedents for modern urban subjects were not to be found at the Paris Salon but in popular prints and photographs. Baudelaire held caricature in high regard since it was one of the few artistic genres that looked for its subject matter to modern life.[11] Tissot's portrayal of British society was all the more incisive because, admitted into the best circles, he was able to observe it carefully, understand its dynamic, and see it with the objectivity of a foreigner who stood outside the class system. From 1869 to 1877 he created mildly satirical lithographic portraits for *Vanity Fair* such as that of Frederic, Lord Leighton entitled *A Sacrifice to the Graces* (fig. 29 on p. 71).

In 1874 British critics began to suspect that Tissot's modern-life paintings also had a subtle satirical undertow, and that this was linked in some way to his choice and application of colour, which was not what one expected of a Paris-trained artist. In 1874, *The Ball on Shipboard* (pl. XII) was called 'garish and almost repellent' by the critic of the *Illustrated London News*. He thought that it was 'strange to find a foreigner painting in a still brighter key than the highest "exhibition pitch" of our native artists'[12] and observed that the picture was conceived in black and white and, 'however gay the superadded tinting', could 'hardly be regarded as "colour" in the higher artistic sense'. The critic had put his finger on Tissot's artistic programme: the satirical element and *naiveté* of his colouring were both intentional and inseparable.

Modern-Life Subjects and the Fashion Plate

Baudelaire began 'The Painter of Modern Life' by extolling the charms of fashion plates, and recommending them for study.[13] At their most sophisticated and beautiful in Paris during the 1860s, they were printed in black and white and selectively hand-coloured using watercolour or gouache according to conventions common to popular prints of the era. Details of costume were picked out in strong local colours, and set off against backgrounds which were subtly washed with colour. This method had the effect of flattening the costume, and causing it to jump out of the background. The hand-coloured fashion plates of the 1860s and 1870s reveal the popular taste for the bright, often garish, colours made possible by the new aniline dyes. Described as 'conversation pieces', they depicted fashionably dressed women in elaborate interior or exterior settings, and provided artists with inspiration for modern-life subjects.

Tissot, whose father was a linen-draper and mother a milliner, would have been exposed to fashion plates from childhood. Baudelaire's remarks may well have kindled his professional interest as they first make their presence felt in his work in 1863.[14] The woman sweeping out of *The Confessional*, 1866 (fig. 2) recalls

2. Tissot, *The Confessional*, 1865, oil on canvas, 115.4 x 69.2 cm. Southampton Art Gallery

Baudelaire's description of the *parisienne* whose 'skilfully composed toilette . . . is inseparable from the beauty of her to whom it belonged'[15] and can be compared with a plate from *Le Bon Ton, Journal des Modes*, c.1860 (fig. 3). Her pose reflects the conventions of fashion plates which ensured that the costume was not only the most prominent feature in the work but that it was arranged in a way that would display it to maximum advantage.[16] By 1868 such idealized genre scenes had become so popular in France that Emile Zola wrote sarcastically in 'Mon Salon': 'If your painting is as flat as a coloured engraving in the Magasin des demoiselles, and if your figures look like cardboard dummies dressed by Worth, your success will know no bounds'.[17]

LE BON TON
Journal des Modes

3. Anonymous 19th-century
French Fashion Plate, no. 234 in
Le Bon Ton, Journal des Modes,
c.1860, etching transferred to
lithographic stone and hand-
coloured, 28 x 28 cm. (sheet).
Costume and Textile Section,
Royal Ontario Museum,
Toronto, Gift of Mr R.P.
Dennistoun

Because Paris was the centre of the fashion industry, French plates were published simultaneously in London.[18] The dapper Tissot would have had easy
access to French fashion plates following his move to London and would have
examined them closely, since the post-war period marked a turning-point in the
history of fashion[19] inaugurating 'the era of ribbons, frills, and flounces'[20] featured in his paintings of the 1870s. *Too Early*, 1873 (pl. I) echoes the fashions, gestures, and gaudy combination of pink and red featured in contemporary fashion
plates found in journals such as *Les Modes Parisiennes* in 1873 (pl. II), and the
colours jump out naively in much the same way.

Realism and Colour Photography

Tissot's interest in fashion plates helps to explain the selective use of local
colour over a black and white base which is found in the artist's early works.
However, it was not fashion plates that came to mind when Ruskin saw Tissot's
British conversation pieces at the Grosvenor Gallery in 1877 but 'mere coloured

photographs'. These were fighting words at a time when the debate over art and photography was becoming increasingly polarized. Although Baudelaire and Ruskin initially embraced photography for its documentary value, they became vehement opponents when it began to encroach on the domain of the fine arts. In his 'Salon of 1859', Baudelaire maintained that Daguerre was sent as his 'Messiah' by 'a revengeful God' to a 'multitude' which believed that art was 'the exact reproduction of nature,' hence 'Photography and Art are the same thing'. In an attempt to expose the false logic of this syllogism, Baudelaire denounced the 'photographic industry as the refuge of every would-be painter, every painter too ill-endowed or too lazy to complete his studies', and concluded that 'by invading the territories of art, [Photography] has become art's most mortal enemy'.[21]

Ideologically drawn to new technologies as a facet of modern life, the Realists, including Courbet, Manet, Whistler, and Degas, used photography in their work. Given the tenor of the critical debate, they were understandably discreet. Photographs were not only useful for recording works of art, acting as aides-memoires in place of sketches, and transferring images from canvas to print-making matrices, they framed modern life in new and exciting ways and gave rise to novel compositional ideas. Tissot was an early advocate of photography, using it from the late 1850s to record his paintings and substituting photographs for preliminary sketches during the latter half of the 1870s and early 1880s.[22]

The recent publication by Heinz K. Henisch and Bridget A. Henisch, *The Painted Photograph: Origins, Techniques, Aspirations* makes it possible for us to contextualize the remark of Ruskin's with which I opened this essay. Following the invention of photography in 1839 photographers kept searching for ways of making colour photographs, but the technology did not exist in the nineteenth century. Instead, black or sepia and white photographs were selectively hand-coloured. The debate within the artistic community over photography and art was paralleled by a debate within the photographic community over the colouring of photographs. The proponents of artistic photography regarded hand-colouring as 'an illegitimate mixing of media, a "cover up".'[23] Although popular with the general public, especially when used in conjunction with daguerreotype portraits and stereoscopic views, it was frowned on in sophisticated circles: 'an educated eye was expected to appreciate the subtleties of monochrome, and not to crave the colours of the natural world'.[24] Those who supported the colouring of photographs argued on the basis of truth to nature.[25] Sir Henry Cole, director of the South Kensington Museum which opened in 1851 with an educational mission, saw photography, both black and white and hand-coloured, as having enormous value for documenting and disseminating information about works of art. Hand-coloured prints were commissioned, accessioned, and sold to the public at the new museum, and soon began to revolutionize the study of art.[26]

There were gradations in the quality of hand-colouring. Many photographs were crudely coloured, while others reveal considerable aesthetic sensitivity. Some of the finest were made in Japan during the 1860s and 1870s for the burgeoning *japoniste* market in Paris and London (pl. III).[27] These records of contemporary Japanese life, which provided Western artists with their first glimpse of Japanese costume and customs, continued many of the themes and conventions of representation found in Japanese woodcuts. *Ukiyo-e* were embraced by Baudelaire and the Realists as soon as they found their way onto the Paris market in the early 1860s.[28] As a pioneer *japoniste* who was famous for his 'Japanese studio', and as drawing-master to Prince Tokugawa Akitake in 1867–8, it is reasonable to assume that Tissot was familiar with Japanese hand-coloured photographs.[29]

The hand-colouring of photographs followed the same conventions of colouring found in fashion plates and other popular prints, with the same idiosyncratic results. Pale green, brown, and blue watercolour washes were selectively applied to the background, and a palette of gaudy colours, notably acid yellow, hot pink and strident red, was applied to costumes in the foreground.[30] This combination gives the hand-coloured photograph a naive charm and causes the brightly coloured forms in the foreground to jump out of the composition.

In 1873 Tissot began to make contemporary conversation-pieces which resemble coloured photographs: these include *The Captain's Daughter* (pl. V), *Too Early* (pl. I), and *Hush!* (pl. XIII). His monochromatic black or sepia and white base is washed in places with thin glazes of colour, while jarring yellows and discordant pinks and reds appear to jump out at the viewer. These works have long been criticized for being 'colourful rather than coloured', since 'local tints take precedence over any unifying tonal approach'.[31] It was works of this genre that were exhibited at the Grosvenor Gallery in 1877 — among them *The Gallery of H.M.S. Calcutta (Portsmouth)* (pl. X), and *Portsmouth Dockyard (How Happy I Could be with Either)*, (pl. XI) — giving rise to Ruskin's remarks.

Tissot's appropriation of effects found in hand-coloured photographs for his paintings in oil on canvas, while a novelty, was not unprecedented. A search for antecedents leads to William Dyce's *Pegwell Bay, Kent – A Recollection of*

October 5, 1858, 1858 (pl. IV). This work imitates the physical characteristics of hand-coloured photographs and draws on popular souvenir photographs of sea-side resorts. The artist applied pale blues and greens selectively over a mono-chrome base, reserving strong local colour for the bright red shawl which simul-taneously flattens its wearer and leaps naively out of the composition.[32] From the title it is clear that this was a scene remembered rather than a glimpse of nature. The Henisches point out that 'a variety of visual enigmas can be created by partial colouring, resulting in images in which the colour represents life and the monochrome evokes dream', and they note that nineteenth-century artists were aware of this.[33] It is possible that Tissot was interested in simulating these effects in order to create the sense that the psychological dramas he depicts lived on in the memory of the *dramatis personae* and the artist.

The seriousness of the threat posed by photography to reproductive engrav-ing paled in light of the implications of other technological advances made during the late 1860s and early 1870s. Oversize photographic images could be produced using a solar enlarger[34] and projected or printed on canvas so that a painter could simply go over the image with oil paint to create the final result.[35] Enlarged portrait photographs printed on canvas and overpainted with oils were enthusiastically embraced by the upwardly mobile who saw them as a relatively inexpensive substitute for the painted portraits which had been a coveted status symbol of the aristocracy for centuries. The Henisches observe that while 'the painted photograph was generally associated with the conservative lower class, such practices spread to the studios of respectable artists'.[36] We have at present no way of knowing whether Tissot's studio was among them but this possibility cannot be ruled out. These practices shed a new light on Ruskin's reference to 'hand-coloured photographs' and their association with 'vulgar society'.

Given Tissot's interest in photography and his use of it in place of prelimi-nary sketches in the late 1870s, he could not have been ignorant of the intense debate about the artistic merits of photography, coloured and uncoloured. We must assume that he deliberately gave these paintings the look of hand-coloured photographs in order to encode his subjects with the appearance and taste of the 'vulgar' society depicted. He must have been aware of the technology which made possible the transfer of photographs to canvas. Whether he employed it or not, the very fact that he made paintings which looked as if they were created in this way was as aesthetically subversive as his depiction of the upwardly mobile was socially subversive. The evocation of hand-coloured photographs in oil painting triggered both Ruskin's artistic and social prejudices.

Chromolithographs and Oleographs

Tissot's paintings not only make reference to hand-coloured fashion plates and photographs in their subject matter and technique, but some actually employ the same bright colours made with aniline dyes and the saccharine imagery to be found in commercial colour reproductions. As a contributor of colour lithographs to *Vanity Fair*, Tissot was familiar with the extraordinary technological advances made in colour printing during the 1860s and 1870s when chromolithography rendered hand-colouring obsolete, and in the 1890s he employed chromolithography in making his Bible illustrations.

The commercial application of chromolithography led to a flood of images which quickly made the process synonymous with vulgarity.[37] In response to popular taste, chromolithographs frequently employed garish colours whose superimposition gave the work a naive charm. Tissot's *In the Conservatory (The Rivals)*, c. 1875–8 (pl. VII) recalls the gauche palette and luxuriant foliage found in such relatively tasteful chromolithographs as *Group of Bamboos* from *Nature and Art*, vol. 1, 1866, (pl. VIII) published by Day and Sons, the leading British colour printers.[38]

When Tissot exhibited his series of paintings *La Femme à Paris* in Paris in 1885, their appearance defied categorization by medium. A critic wrote: 'On ne sait pas plus si c'est de l'huile que de l'aquarelle, du pastel que de l'oléographie'.[39] Oleographs were chromolithographic reproductions of paintings printed on canvas and covered with a layer of varnish. They became increasingly popular during the early 1870s as the quality improved and the price fell.[40] An oleograph in the British Museum's Prints and Drawings collection, Jules Scalabert's *'M'Aime-t-il?'*, 1882 (1885-7-11-232), can be compared in its subject and handling to Tissot's *Young Lady in a Boat* c.1870 (pl. XIV). Since the resemblance of his paintings to 'vulgar' colour reproductions was evident to Tissot's contemporaries, we are forced to conclude, yet again, that he did this in order to stamp his work with the look and taste of the 'vulgar society' to whom oleographs appealed.

Wood-Engraved Illustrations

Tissot was consistent. He invoked popular print sources in every medium including etching and mezzotint. Etching was the preferred printmaking technique of the Realists who were central players in the 'etching revival' of the 1860s. They drew in a deliberately naive, crude manner, flattening their compositions and creating a sense of recession through perspectival constructions

TERRIBLE RESULT OF THE HIGHER EDUCATION OF WOMEN!

4. George du Maurier, *Terrible Result of the Higher Education of Women!,* wood engraving, 17.1 x 22.3 cm., from *Punch* (24 January 1874), p. 38. Photograph courtesy The Edward P. Taylor Reference Library and Archives, Art Gallery of Ontario, Toronto

which were often ambiguous or steeply raked. In place of the delicate hatching considered intrinsic to the medium since Rembrandt, they attacked their copper plates with a heavy hand, producing strong, dark lines which stood out so boldly against the white of the paper that their critics compared them to gothic woodcuts.[41]

After creating a small group of unflattering Realist portraits in the manner of Courbet between 1860 and 1861, Tissot stopped etching until 1875 when the revival hit its stride and a strong collector market emerged.[42] As he was at this time living in London, he took his cues initially from the leaders of the British etching revival, the rival brothers-in-law James McNeill Whistler and Francis Seymour Haden.[43] Although Tissot was drawn into discussions about 'Art for Art's sake' over Whistler's dinner table[44] and flirted with Aestheticism, creating beautiful drypoint portraits and pulling unique proofs on vellum and oriental papers, he was not at heart an Aesthete.

5. Tissot, *The Political Woman*, 1885, etching and drypoint, 40 x 25.4 cm. Art Gallery of Ontario, Toronto, Gift of Allan and Sondra Gotlieb

He was a Realist whose strength was story-telling, and his most powerful etchings are of narrative subjects executed in a strong black line. This proclivity dovetailed nicely with Victorian taste. While the dark line and strong contrast can be traced to his French Realist beginnings,[45] both line and content recall the British wood-engraved periodical illustrations of the 1860s and 1870s which Wentworth has called the '*ukiyoe* of the English illustrated magazines'.[46] Numerous parallels can be found between Tissot's themes and stories and illustrations in *Punch,* the *Illustrated London News*, and *The Graphic,* which he must have read from the time of his arrival in England. Not surprisingly, his modern conversation-pieces echo the wood-engravings of George du Maurier, his old acquaintance from student days in Paris and leading contributor to *Punch*, whose *Terrible Result of the Higher Education of Women!*, 1874 (fig. 4) appears to anticipate Tissot's etching *The Political Woman* of 1885 (fig. 5).

6. Tissot, *Les Adieux*, 1871, oil on canvas, 100.3 x 62.6 cm. Bristol Museum and Art Gallery

7. John Everett Millais, *A Huguenot, on Saint Bartholomew's Day, Refusing to Shield Himself from Danger by Wearing the Roman Catholic Badge*, 1852, oil on canvas, 92.7 x 61.6 cm. The Makins Collection

Victorian Reproductive Engravings

The lucrative market for reproductive engravings after popular paintings in Britain during the 1870s made wealthy men of popular artists and their publishers, foremost among them John Everett Millais and William Holman Hunt. Tissot's first success at the Royal Academy in 1872, *Les Adieux*, 1871 (fig. 6), was closely modelled on Millais' popular painting of 1851–2 *A Huguenot, on St. Bartholomew's Day, Refusing to Shield Himself from Danger by Wearing the Roman Catholic Badge* (fig. 7); Tissot's design was subsequently engraved by John Ballin (fig. 8), and published by Pilgeram and Lefèvre, one of only six other commercial reproductive prints made after Tissot's paintings.[47]

8. John Ballin after Tissot, *Les Adieux*, 1873, mixed mezzotint, 73 x 47.5 cm. Art Gallery of Ontario, Toronto, Gift of Allan and Sondra Gotlieb

Like his friend Manet, Tissot began to use etching to reproduce his own paintings, no doubt for a variety of economic, aesthetic and ideological reasons.[48] In doing so, he was aligning himself with the painter-etcher movement spearheaded by Haden who urged painters to interpret their own work in etching and campaigned vigorously against professional reproductive engravers.[49] To make his work better known, and maximize his income, etching was his best alternative. His decision to give his etchings the highly finished appearance of Victorian reproductive engravings must have been intentional, his way of encoding this medium with the taste of 'vulgar society'.

Tissot's etchings based on paintings are not mere reproductions of works conceived in another medium. When the superficially attractive colours are stripped away, and the dramas graphically restated in black and white, Tissot's etchings are tougher than his paintings. In the etchings which were conceived as an integral part of the project *La Femme à Paris*, such as *The Political Woman*, the powerful black and white patterns, the flattening of the picture space and the use of violent perspective create claustrophobic images which are much more disturbing than their painted counterparts. Far from being regressive, these very detailed works can be seen as proto-symbolist, as is argued later in this volume by Prelinger.

Amateur Photography

Following the death of his mistress Kathleen Newton and his return to Paris, Tissot made four mezzotints which are among the most ambitious in the history of the medium. Falling into disuse after its heyday in the late eighteenth century, mezzotint enjoyed a short-lived revival led by Haden in the 1870s. It is so closely identified with the British school that it is known in France as 'la manière anglaise'. Tonal rather than linear, it was an ideal medium for the reproduction of paintings prior to the invention of photography. Well-suited to the evocation of atmospheric and lighting effects, it has been used creatively throughout its history to depict dreams, visions, psychological states, and supernatural phenomena.

Mezzotint was an appropriate choice, for these works are *memento mori* of Tissot's life in England. Made after paintings, like so many of his etchings, the psychological intensity of the image is much greater in half-tone than colour. Methods for transferring photographs to printmaking matrices were employed by a number of artists during the 1870s, including his friends Manet and Degas.[50] Whether Tissot employed these methods or not in making his mezzotints, they do closely imitate the appearance of photographs, which by the 1870s had joined the ranks of popular prints. Photography was the first printmaking technique that could capture actual moments in time. This was precisely the impression that Tissot wanted to give.

The mezzotints also have a strange, surreal quality not found in paintings of the same subjects. *The Garden Bench,* 1883 (fig. 79 on p. 192) appears at first glance to recall a happy moment prior to Kathleen's death. Looked at more closely it has a funereal aspect: Kathleen's ecstatic gaze seems frozen, her breath stopped, her eyes glazed, and her face a waxen mask of cloying sweetness. *The Little Nimrod,* 1886 (fig. 89 on p. 201) depicts the children playing in a nearby park while she lay dying. Here Tissot simultaneously evokes his lost past and the transience of youth. The children appear as brittle figments of the artist's imagination, no more substantial than origami figures or the autumn leaves which fall around them. In *Mediumistic Apparition,* 1885 (pl. XXIV), arguably the strangest print in the history of mezzotint, Tissot imitates the appearance of popular spirit photographs in depicting his dead mistress as Keshavjee points out.

Coda

In 1885, after his *La Femme à Paris* series was attacked by Paris critics, Tissot had a vision and devoted the rest of his career to illustrating the Bible. A Realist to the end, he wrote in the introduction to *The Life of our Saviour Jesus Christ*: 'For a long time the imagination of the Christian world has been led astray by the fancies of artists. . . . Is it not time in this exact century to restore to reality—I do not say to realism—the rights which have been filched from it?'[51] Published in France in 1896–7, and later in England and America, it became an international best-seller largely on account of its extraordinary chromolithographed illustrations (figs. 60 on p. 151 and 88 on p. 199). Their supposed archaeological accuracy was based on field trips to the Holy Land, and the sense of verisimilitude they projected was such that when the original gouache illustrations were exhibited in London and Paris 'men removed their hats and women knelt before them'.[52] Tissot's critics, of course, considered them vulgar and tasteless. Their cinematic quality finds its logical sequel in the great biblical film epics of the 1950s.

In the 1870s, painting was positioned at the top of a theoretical hierarchy of artistic media and printmaking at the bottom, where reproductive engraving and original etching vied for first and second place. Those print media which enjoyed wide popular appeal or commercial application were beyond the pale. Caricatures, fashion plates, photographs, chromolithographs, oleographs, wood-engraved illustrations and reproductive engravings were seen by the artistic establishment as at best instructive or amusing and at worst tasteless and a threat to the fine arts. Although he would have been well aware of this, Tissot deliberately chose to imitate the appearance of these 'vulgar' forms of printed imagery in his paintings and prints.

If the effective delivery of the message inherent in a work of art depends to a large extent on the choice of an appropriate medium and the way in which it is manipulated, in the eyes of his critics Tissot used the right media in the wrong way. By the incorporation of popular visual references and the deliberately naive application of colour, Tissot gave his work the ring of authenticity which underscored his theme. He indelibly stamped his work with the look and taste of the society which he was representing and created works which inadvertently appealed to the very people whose solecisms he was portraying. The ironic encoding within his paintings reveal Tissot as an artist of sophistication and integrity, and his work provided a commentary on both the art establishment and the class system. What Ruskin found most objectionable was the idea that oil painting, a medium reserved for the most serious subjects, would be used to dignify, through imitation, 'mere coloured photographs', a medium unworthy of a place on the lowest rung of the artistic hierarchy. This notion was as aesthetically subversive as the upward mobility of 'vulgar society' was socially and politically subversive. For this Tissot could neither be understood nor forgiven.

Tissot portrayed not only external reality: he delved beneath the surface and provided glimpses of the deeper psychological realities which characterized his age. No other artist enables us to step back in time and re-enter so completely the world of London in the 1870s or Paris in the 1880s. It is this invitation to step through the picture frame that fascinates the public today, and makes Tissot Baudelaire's quintessential 'painter of modern life'.

I would like to thank the former director of the Art Gallery of Ontario, Maxwell L. Anderson, and Michael Wentworth for encouraging me to give the paper on Tissot in the Toronto symposium which became the basis for this essay. I would like to thank my colleague Maia-Marie Sutnik for introducing me to the subject of hand-coloured photographs; Hugh Wyley and Jack Howard in the Far Eastern Department of the Royal Ontario Museum and Martin Barnes of the Print and Drawing Department of the Victoria and Albert Museum for showing me hand-coloured occidental and oriental photographs; Anthony Griffiths and Andrew Clary of the Department of Prints and Drawings at the British Museum for introducing me to oleographs; and Marie Corey of Massey College at the University of Toronto, for showing me chromolithographs.

1. John Ruskin, *Fors Clavigera: Letters to the Workmen and Labourers of Great Britain*, Letter LXXIX, 18 June 1877 (New York: John B. Alden, 1885), 3:61. Ruskin also launched his famous attack on Whistler in the same letter.

2. James Laver, *Vulgar Society: The Romantic Career of James Tissot 1836–1902* (London: Constable and Co., 1936), 54: 'to the eyes of cultivated French people, familiar with the paintings of Manet, the canvases of Tissot seemed like coloured photos'.

3. P. Mathias, *Retailing Revolution: A History of Multiple Retailing in the Food Trades based upon the Allied Suppliers Group of Companies* (London, 1967), 15.

4. Michael Wentworth, *James Tissot* (Oxford: Clarendon Press, 1984), 93.

5. Charles Baudelaire, 'The Salon of 1859', originally published in the *Revue française* between 10 June and 20 July 1859, repr. and trans. Jonathan Mayne, *Baudelaire: Art in Paris, 1845–1862* (London: Phaidon, 1965), 155.

6. *Degas Letters*, ed. Marcel Guérin, trans. Marguerite Kay (Oxford: Bruno Cassirer, 1948), 39, quoted in Wentworth, *Tissot*, 122.

7. For Leys, see Prelinger's essay in this volume.

8. Baudelaire, 'The Painter of Modern Life', repr. and trans. Jonathan Mayne, *Baudelaire: The Painter of Modern Life and Other Essays* (London: Phaidon, 1964), 37. This essay was written in 1859–60.

9. These ideas were developed in conversation with Tamar Garb, Caroline Arscott, Nancy Marshall and Edward Maeder, while looking at Tissot paintings on display at the Art Gallery of Ontario in 1996.

10. *Illustrated London News* (16 May 1874), 470, quoted in Wentworth, *Tissot*, 115.

11. Baudelaire's essays 'Some French Caricaturists' and 'Some Foreign Caricaturists' in Mayne, *The Painter of Modern Life*, 166–96.

12. 'Fine Arts Exhibition of the Royal Academy', *Illustrated London News* (16 May 1874), 470, quoted in Wentworth, *Tissot*, 115.

13. Mayne, *The Painter of Modern Life*, 1–3, n1.

14. The first work which demonstrates an interest in fashion plates appears to be *The Two Sisters*, 1863, which is executed in the manner of Gustave Courbet. C. Wood, *Tissot* (London: Orion Publishing Group, 1986), 32.

15. Mayne, *The Painter of Modern Life*, 30–1.

16. For conventions of representation appropriated from fashion plates by artists see Mark Roskill, 'Early Impressionism and the Fashion Print', *Burlington Magazine*, CXII, no. 807 (June 1870): 392.

17. Quoted in Marie Simon, *Fashion in Art: The Second Empire and Impressionism* (London: Zwemmer, 1995), 186.

18. During the Franco-Prussian War and the Siege of Paris from October 1870 to April 1871 it was impossible for the British to secure the latest plates from Paris. Simon, *Fashion in Art*, 170.

19. Vyvyan Holland, *Hand-Coloured Fashion Plates* (London: Batsford Ltd., 1955), 105–9.

20. Holland, *Hand-Coloured Fashion Plates*, 133.

21. Baudelaire, 'The Salon of 1859' in Mayne, *Baudelaire: Art in Paris*, 152, 153.

22. See Willard Misfeldt, *The Albums of James Tissot* (Bowling Green, Ohio: Bowling Green University Popular Press, 1982).

23. Heinz K. Henisch and Bridget A. Henisch, *The Painted Photograph, 1839–1914: Origins, Techniques, Aspirations* (Philadelphia: The Pennsylvania State University Press, 1996) quoting J.E. Buerger, *French Daguerreotypes* (Chicago: University of Chicago Press, 1989), 115.

24. Henisch, *The Painted Photograph*, 212.

25. Henisch, *The Painted Photograph*, 25. In 1857 H.H. Snelling wrote in *The Photographic Art Journal*, 10:346, 'the coloured photograph has an advantage over the best works of the best art masters – for the latter cannot rival the former in truthfulness to nature'.

26. Henisch, *The Painted Photograph*, 222–3.

27. See Margarita Winkel, *Souvenirs from Japan: Japanese Painting at the Turn of the Century* (London: Bamboo Publications, 1991), and Pierre Loti, *Once Upon a Time: Visions of Old Japan. Photographs by Felice Beato and Baron Raimund von Stillfried* (Paris: Les Editions Artaud, 1984).

28. Given the substantial literature on the influence of these popular prints on the work of Tissot and his contemporaries I will not revisit the subject here although his interest in *ukiyo-e* is yet another aspect of his involvement with popular prints. See Michael Wentworth, *James Tissot: A Catalogue Raisonné of His Prints* (Minneapolis: The Minneapolis Institute of Arts, 1978), 14–15, and Michael Wentworth, 'Tissot and Japonisme' in *Japonisme in Art: An International Symposium*, ed. Yamada Chisaburo (Tokyo: Committee for the Year 2001, 1980), 127–46.

29. Wentworth, 'Tissot and Japonisme', 133. Wentworth speculates that the etching *The Prodigal Son: In Foreign Climes*, 1882, and the painting (Musée de Nantes) were 'doubtless' based on an early photograph of Japan. Also in Ikegami Chuji, 'James Tissot, Drawing Instructor of Tokugawa Akitake' in *Japonisme in Art*, 151, notes that on 5 August 1868 Shibusawa Eiichi wrote in his diary: 'In the afternoon the painter appeared. Had photographs.' It is not possible to say what these were.

30. Aniline dyes used for the dyeing of textiles became available in the form of liquid colours for tinting albumen prints about 1860 (Henisch, *The Painted Photograph*, 65).

31. Wentworth, *Tissot*, 49.

32. H.K and B.A. Henisch note that 'in the decade from 1855–1865 landscape pictures in stereograph form became fashionable particularly in Britain and France and a number of tinted specimens survive, including one Scottish view made in 1857 by Roger Fenton' (*The Painted Photograph*, 170). They also cite an unsigned article on 'Photography', published in Dicken's *Household Words*, no. 156, 19 March 1853, 54–61, describing the activities of a fashionable London studio where two charming young assistants are at work in the 'colouring room' one dipping her brush into a pot labelled 'sky', and the other into a box labelled 'flesh'. The clients, photographed indoors, were to be set against a clear blue sky 'with particular attention paid to the gentleman's red coat: "When we don't paint coats bright enough, people complain. They tell us that we make them look as if they wore old clothes"' (*The Painted Photograph*, 214).

33. Henisch. *The Painted Photograph*, 16.

34. Henisch, *The Painted Photograph*, 103, quotes an article in *The Art Journal,* 34 (July 1863): 138, explaining how the image could be transferred to canvas using a solar enlarger, and either fixed by the artist by drawing over it, or simply painted over: 'thrown by the solar camera upon their own canvas, forming no permanent picture there and leaving no mark, but remaining as long as the artists' need for them to make their drawing in outline, or even finish the portrait on canvas without drawing a line . . . if they would test how they are progressing, and how their color acccords with nature, they have but to shut out the image of the camera in order to examine their picture by the admitted light of the day'.

35. For a detailed discussion of enlarging, projecting, and printing photographs on canvas see Henisch, *The Painted Photograph*, ch. 4 'Color on Hard Media', and ch. 5 'Photographs on Canvas', 101–53.

36. Henisch, *The Painted Photograph*, 163, quotes P. Gillett, *The Victorian Painter's World* (New Brunswick, New Jersey: Rutgers University Press, 1990), 51, who points out

that in 1893 Walter Sickert maintained that 'paintings done from photographs should be described as such in art catalogues' and 'William (Blake?) Richmond reported that he had heard of painters who were [actually] painting over photographs on their canvases'.

37. Douglas Druick and Peter Zegers, *La Pierre Parle: Lithography in France, 1848–1900*, exh. cat. (Ottawa: National Gallery of Canada, 1981), 76–7. 'Because of strict censorship of political caricature under the Second Empire, energy was channelled into satires on manners. The images predominating in these satires focused on the pursuit of pleasure. The iconography of entertainment found in these lithographs parallels that found in the paintings of Manet and of the Impressionists and in the images of the illustrated press. It also echoes the descriptions of such entertainments in the novels by Emile Zola and Guy de Maupassant'. After 1870 chromolithographed 'estampes' replaced the fashion for tinted lithographs coloured by hand. Sentimental and religious subjects became a staple of chromolithogaphy. 'By the late 1880s, firms produced daily thousands of technically commendable chromolithographs at low prices for a market seduced by their garish colour. In becoming so remarkably popular chromolithography had paid a price: the very word had become synonymous with commercial productions devoid of artistic value'.

38. Frederick Goulding, who was to become the printer of Tissot's etchings in 1875, worked for Day and Son, the leading lithographic printers in Britain.

39. '*La Femme à Paris*: Exposition Tissot', *La vie parisienne*, 23 (2 May 1885): 255, quoted in Wentworth, *Tissot*, 167.

40. Luis Nadeau, *Encyclopedia of Printing Photogaphic, and Photochemical Processes* (Fredericton, New Brunswick: Atelier Luis Nadeau, 1990), 2:59 b.

41. Philippe Burty, 'La Societé des Aquafortistes', *Gazette des beaux arts*, Ser.1, 14, No. 2 (1863): 190.

42. Perhaps he stopped etching in order to avoid the critical controversy that flared up in 1862 following the appearance of the first portfolio of the Société des Aquafortistes. Philippe Burty, the critic for the *Gazette des beaux arts*, attacked the work of Legros and Braquemond who he dubbed the 'pontifs of the new church which has been baptised realism', and who sought to give their etchings 'the firm, rather rough, appearance of 15th century German woodcuts forgetting that each process has its own completely different character', accusing them of 'careless drawing' and 'childish *naivete* in composition'. Sales were disappointing, and the publisher Cadart began to search for 'more finished and attractive plates'. Bracquemond, Manet, and Legros were furious, and Whistler, like Tissot, never submitted a plate. See Katharine A. Lochnan, *The Etchings of James McNeill Whistler* (London: Yale University Press, 1984), 137–40.

43. The title plate of his set *Ten Etchings by Tissot*, published in 1877, *The Three Crows Inn* (W. 29) made clear Tissot's debt to Whistler's Realist 'Thames Set' plate *Rotherhithe* (K. 66, 1860), published in 1872. *Le Chapeau de Rubens* (W. 8, 1875) recalls Haden's *La Belle Anglaise* (S. 90, 1864).

44. Alan Cole, 'Diary', 16 November 1875, Library of Congress, Pennell Collection.

45. Tissot's etchings can be compared to those of Félix Bracquemond and Edouard Manet to whom Bracquemond taught etching. Tissot's *Quarelling* (W. 18, 1876) may be compared to Braquemond's *La Terasse*, also of 1876.

46. Wentworth, 'Tissot and Japonisme', 138, and Wentworth, *Tissot*, 93.

47. Wentworth, *James Tissot: Catalogue Raisonné*, 349.

48. In this he would have been consistent with other leading etchers in his circle, notably Manet and Whistler. See Lochnan, 'The Gentle Art of Marketing Whistler Prints', *Print Quarterly*, 14, no. 1 (March 1997): 3–15.

49. This brought Haden into open conflict with the Royal Academy which exhibited reproductive engravings, but refused to recognize original etching which it deemed a medium fit only for *amateurs*. By espousing this position, Tissot would have found himself, along with Haden, in opposition to the Royal Academy. See Lochnan, *The Etchings of James McNeill Whistler*, 216–17.

50. Jay M. Fisher, *The Prints of Edouard Manet*, exh. cat. (Washington: International Exhibitions Foundation, 1985), 18, points out that by 1861–2 Manet was using photographs to transfer his design from paintings to copper plates, sometimes making them himself. He 'could reduce the scale of the composition to the size of the copper plate'. After the basic outlines were on the plate, Manet worked toward an interpretation of the original – not an exact reproduction'. Douglas Druick and Peter Zegers write in 'Degas and the Printed Image' *Edgar Degas: The Painter as Printmaker, 1856–1914*, ed. Susan Welsh Reed and Barbara Stern Shapiro, exh. cat. (Boston: Museum of Fine Arts, 1984), xxi–xxii, that 'by the 1870s it was common-place for painters to have their works photographed and Degas was not alone in using such photographs as the basis for tracings used in preparing prints and reproductions. His use of photographs became increasingly sophisticated, the results more independent of their sources' (xxxvi).

51. James Tissot, *The Life of our Saviour Jesus Christ* (The People's Edition, London: Sampson, Low, Marston, 1897) 1:9.

52. Laver, *Vulgar Society*, 60.

Image or Identity: Kathleen Newton and the London Pictures of James Tissot

Nancy Rose Marshall

Until the middle of the twentieth century art historians referred to Kathleen Newton, one of Tissot's models, as '*La Mysterieuse*'; like Shakespeare's 'dark lady of the sonnets' Newton existed only in the painter's depictions of her, the facts of her life shrouded in historical misrepresentations. In 1946, however, an article in an English newspaper identified her as the woman with whom Tissot had lived from 1876 until 1882, and other scholars have since discovered the basic outlines of her biography.[1] Rather than endowing her with an autonomous identity, these new facts only served to emphasize her existence as a reflection of Tissot the artist, and in many ways she remains as mysterious refracted through Tissot's genius as she was before biographical records were available. Given the paucity of information about the real woman named Kathleen Newton, paintings for which she posed have traditionally functioned as stand-ins for her actual being and are therefore frequently interpreted as revelations either of her character or of the nature of Tissot's relationship to her.[2] Yet these pictures are not, after all, actually 'Kathleen,' transparent representations through which we can discern her 'true' nature or personality, unfixed qualities irretrievably lost to us. In this paper I wish to interrogate the extent to which knowledge of Kathleen Newton's identity is necessary to make meaning out of images for which she modeled, investigating other interpretive strategies available to their first viewers, the Victorian urban bourgeoisie. Yet, after examining other ways in which these works can be read, I will return to the traditional biographical mode of interpretation with two paintings which resonate in a way I cannot avoid seeing as bound up with Tissot and Newton's relationship.

Born Kathleen Irene Ashburnam Kelly in 1854, the woman who eventually became *La Mysterieuse* traveled to India in January 1871 to marry Isaac Newton, a surgeon. The marriage ended abruptly when Kathleen professed her preference for a Captain Palliser whom she had apparently met on the journey to India. Probably pregnant with Palliser's child by March 1871, she was divorced by Newton in a case which began in May of that year. The child, Muriel Mary Violet Newton, was born in England in December. Five years later, in March of 1876, Kathleen gave birth to a son at her sister's home in St. John's Wood; shortly thereafter she moved around the corner into the house of James Tissot,

9. Tissot, *In the Sunlight*, 1881, etching and drypoint, 20 x 30 cm. Art Gallery of Ontario, Toronto, Gift of Allan and Sondra Gotlieb

suggesting that the painter was the father of the boy, somewhat absurdly christened Cecil George Newton.[3] From 1876 to her death of tuberculosis at age twenty-eight in November of 1882, Kathleen lived with Tissot in an unconventional relationship, becoming one of the primary models for his painting.

Newton and Tissot's life together is often read as a tragic romance—a star-crossed love pitifully frustrated first by the Catholic beliefs which prevented their marriage and then by her untimely death. Frequently images in which Kathleen appears, such as the 1881 etching *In the Sunlight* (fig. 9), are seen merely as records of the couple's idyllic period of happiness in St. John's Wood. Alternatively art historians look for signs of her wasting illness in pictures such as *Woman in an Armchair*, 1881–2 (fig. 10). Admittedly, it is compelling to read the paintings for which Kathleen Newton posed through the lens of biographical knowledge. Such interpretations strike a chord within all of us who love a good story, especially one structured around the universal themes of love and death.

But this type of interpretation can lapse all too easily into subjective assessment masquerading as objective analysis. The etching *Summer Evening* of 1881 (see fig. 80 on p. 192), for example, prompted the recent comment that 'it clearly shows that she did not have long to live,' yet, according to another writer, in the

10. Tissot, *Woman in an Armchair*, 1881–2, oil on canvas, 90.2 x 68.3 cm. Musée Baron Martin, Gray, France

same painting, 'there is no indication of the hovering shadow of illness that was to claim her life the following year'.[4] I note these discrepancies not to argue that one is more accurate than the other, but merely to point out how difficult — or at least biased — biographical speculation can be.

We must remember that Tissot did not create paintings of Kathleen Newton solely as a private record of his family life. Rather, he was intent on earning an income with these productions, and many of them went to exhibitions at art institutions or dealers. For example, *Quiet* (see fig. 91 on p. 206), modeled by Newton and her niece Lilian, appeared at the Royal Academy in 1881, the last year of Newton's life. If records of Newton were merely poignant mementos for Tissot, how could he bear to expose them to public scrutiny? Contemporary audiences were largely ignorant of the identity of the models for Tissot's paintings; rather they employed a range of other interpretive strategies upon their encounters with the works. To what extent, therefore, should we privilege the fact of Kathleen Newton's relationship to Tissot in order to understand the pictures in which she appears? Simply mapping the images onto her biography can be a reductive move which overlooks some of the complexities provided by the cultural context in which they appeared.

Some representations of Kathleen are, of course, straightforward portraits. Perhaps we can establish a continuum of sorts, in which images with the original title bearing her name represent Tissot's overt attempts to record her character and personality in paint. For example, an etching first shown at the Dudley Gallery exhibition in 1877 under the title 'Portrait of Mrs. N.' was intended as a depiction of Newton, fashionably dressed in a fur-trimmed shawl and wide brimmed feathered bonnet. Following the continuum, we come to the many paintings and etchings for which Kathleen, her son, her daughter, and her niece modeled, such as *The Garden Bench* of 1882 (for the mezzotint, see fig. 79 on p. 192). These works take on many aspects of portraiture, in their lack of overt narrative content and the frontal poses and outward gazes of several figures. But they were not exhibited under the sitters' names and so are more closely aligned with genre painting. Other pictures, such as *The Orphan,* 1879, situate Newton in a story seemingly unrelated to her own life, or like *October,* 1877 (pl. XX), use her form as a vehicle for allegory. The artist even incorporated images of Newton into a *cloisonné* enamel vase. Clearly the category 'images of Kathleen Newton' is a fluid one.

Rather than attempting to reconstruct the life of the model through these works, I wish to look elsewhere to develop possible interpretations for them. My contention is that the contemporary urban sites and the particular type of modern life painting in which Tissot situated Kathleen Newton meant more to contemporary audiences than did her individual identity. In this paper I will examine two depicted locations, the Louvre and Tissot's suburban garden, to explore alternatives to biographical readings of these works; I will then look at two pictures which actually appear to encourage such a biographical analysis.

The Museum and the Modernity of Perception

Around 1879, Tissot painted several scenes in the Louvre including two oil versions of *Visiting the Louvre,* c. 1879 (fig. 11). Newton seems to have modeled for this, appearing in an ulster and black bonnet, and it has been suggested that the images chronicled a trip taken by Tissot and Newton to Paris in October 1879.[5] Indeed, the pictures convey a documentary quality by including sculptures actually in the Roman collections of the Louvre; for example, silhouetted against the background of *Visiting the Louvre* is a statue of Marcus Aurelius. And the

11. Tissot, *Visiting the Louvre*, c.1879, oil on canvas, 36.9 x 26.6 cm. Photograph courtesy The Richard Green Gallery, London

locations in which the figures pose are identifiable, in this case the Petite Galerie. But these images are more than mere souvenirs of a vacation; rather, they can be read in light of a number of social issues, such as contemporary museum-going practices, the democratization of private art collections in the nineteenth century, or—the issue which concerns me here—the differences accorded to male and female perceptive powers by various discourses of the Victorian middle classes in the 1870s.

In all of the pictures in this series the male museum-goers are looking at guidebooks and gazing attentively up at the ceiling paintings, while the woman neglects the art entirely. In *Visiting the Louvre*, one older man frames an object with his fingers and spectacles while another man consults a catalogue, but the woman, although she holds a visual aid in the shape of a lorgnette, abandons it in favour of an unmediated gaze—at us, rather than at the artworks around her. In other, similar images of tourists by Tissot such as *London Visitors* of 1874 (pl. XVIII; for the etching, see fig. 47 on p. 129), men read manuals, educating themselves about their surroundings, while women look without knowledge of what they are seeing. This consistent differentiation of male and female sightseeing bears examination in the ways it at first appears to correspond to and reinforce the ways women were encouraged to look, both at the world in general and at art in particular.[6]

The nature and scope of middle-class female vision was defined in a range of nineteenth-century institutions and texts, including medical definitions, images of women looking at art, and etiquette manuals. In the eighteenth century, the founder of the influential pseudo-science of physiognomy, Johann Lavater, had categorized the feminine gaze as superficial, composing a list of gender traits which read in part, 'man surveys and observes—woman glances and feels'.[7] In characterizing the male gaze by its power of penetration, steadiness, and perceptiveness, and the woman's by its sensitive and wavering instability, Lavater formulated an enduring opposition: men 'surveyed,' with the word's connotations of measuring and controlling; women glimpsed life timidly and emotively.

This gendered split was sanctioned by the emergent field of opthalmology. Women's eyesight was found to be anatomically, as well as functionally, less sound. Physicians' manuals characterized female eyes as weaker and more prone to diseases such as glaucoma, a phenomenon occasionally attributed to the traditional feminine tasks of night watching or sewing. Moreover, the female reproductive system itself was a source of weakness: menstrual and uterine difficulties, pregnancy, and lactation were all cited as causes of ocular disturbance. Women's weak vision was therefore construed as biologically determined.[8]

Throughout the century, images and writings about the lady connoisseur also contributed to the notion that a female gaze was superficial.[9] Unless paintings engaged their domestic interests, women could not appreciate them, implied the writer of the satirical ode 'Academy Belles' in an 1867 edition of *London Society*:

> In pictures of children they revel—
> Call Hayllar a duck and a dear,
> And Millais (when down to their level)
> The pet of all painters this year. . . .
> Of harmony, colour, and keeping
> They're ignorant—joking apart;
> And a picture of Baby sleeping
> They think is the highest of art.[10]

12. Adelaide Claxton, *Academy Belles*, engraving in *London Society*, vol. 12 (July 1867)

The woman's gaze, which 'glanced and felt,' was appropriate to the absorption of the moral and spiritual, but not technical, qualities of art.[11] Tissot's woman in the museum space cannot therefore be expected to comprehend the glories of the artworks around her. The artist's choice of location, the classical sculpture galleries of the Louvre where he would have spent many hours as a student attempting to master the sanctioned poses of the academic tradition, underscores the weight of history and culture from which she is excluded.

Not only could they not look critically, but women in gallery spaces, as in Tissot's Louvre pictures, became aesthetic objects themselves. In the accompanying illustration to the ode 'Academy Belles,' by Adelaide Claxton (fig. 12), the female presence distracts the male art lovers from serious consideration of the paintings, and the poem comments:

On drawing and chiaroscuro
His mind for a moment scarce dwells
Ere it wanders to watch the demure row
Of Dainty Academy Belles.[12]

Likewise, the men in Tissot's museum series looked knowledgeably at art; the women, on the other hand, displayed themselves for the viewer. In *Visiting the Louvre*, the sinuous contrapposto pose of the woman with one leg shifted forward echoes the sculpture directly over her shoulder; her raincoat, the colour of the marble, falls into classical folds. And the triangular shape of her mantle endows her with a resemblance to the busts surrounding her. These formal analogies emphasise that the woman is another object for visual consumption in the museum. Clearly, however, the accompanying men do not realize this fact; only the viewer is privileged by this exciting—and possibly illicit—exchange of glances with the depicted woman. A ladylike mien, dictated by the proliferating etiquette books of the time, was a demurely downcast gaze, and a woman should avoid calling attention to herself by staring. The way girls 'looked' had to be regulated from youth in order to prevent unacceptable deployments of the gaze, for in the words of one social commentator, 'the audacious stare is odious, the sly, oblique, impenetrable look is unsatisfactory'.[13] A middle-class woman's need to protect herself in public, like the scientific and cultural assessments of female eyesight, prevented her from visually absorbing her environment in the manner to which a man was accustomed.

Clearly, however, the lady in the Louvre paintings does not cleave to the prescribed female gaze of self-effacement or absence. Rather, ignoring the dictates of etiquette, the woman returns our look directly in an exchange which goes unnoticed by her male protectors. Registering this look, we are compelled to reconsider the meaning of the picture; perhaps the woman in the museum is not excluded from its primary concerns after all. In *Visiting the Louvre*, the elderly man's opaque spectacles occlude his vision, humorously suggesting that misguided connoisseurs overlooked the beauty of modern femininity in their pretentious admiration of the ruined fragments of long dead cultures.[14] Their male companions lost in the past, the women were free to engage others in the distinctly modern interplay of the gaze between strangers. Moreover, the fact that the woman directly engages the viewer's eye seems to render the man impotently external to the painting's central narrative.

As historians of the nineteenth century frequently note, one of the subtle means by which women could convey their sexual availability during this period was through a look easily read by prospective partners, and therefore the direct gaze of a female in the street was potentially charged with covert invitation. Vision and sexuality were inextricably linked at this time, one medical text even citing sexual intercourse as a source of visual disturbances, explicitly linking vision and desire.[15] The ambiguity of these women's actual intentions was the operative aspect of this sort of charged encounter. In the way it evokes the possibility of the eroticized exchange of glances with a woman in a public space, *Visiting the Louvre* bears affinities to Tissot's paintings of the Parisienne discussed in Tamar Garb's article in this volume. Tissot implies that the woman's gaze represents the peculiarly modern visual exchange in the public space of the city, whereas the accompanying men are still encumbered by outmoded types of perception.[16]

Occupying the space in front of the canvas, Tissot positioned himself — and the implied viewer — as a very different type of man. The artist was a worldly man, or at least wanted to appear to be one; for example, posing as the Bohemian man-about-town, he encouraged his friend Edgar Degas in his love affairs in a letter of 1862: 'And Pauline? What about her? Where are you now with her? . . . I can't believe that by the time I'm back your virginity in relation to her will still be intact. You must tell me all about it'.[17] Such words suggest he was a modern gentleman alert to the game of trading private gazes in public. His museum series, rather than validating the relevance of ancient history and the wealth of cultural tradition, suggests instead that such pursuits are being replaced by an appreciation of contemporary life and its practices. These pictures enact Tissot's own abandonment of history painting, for which he had trained in the very spaces depicted, in favour of the gratifications of modern life subjects; Kathleen Newton was merely a model for the image upon which that transition was enacted.

City and Suburb in Tissot's Garden

In 1879 Tissot exhibited eight such modern-life pictures at the Grosvenor Gallery, London's alternative to the Royal Academy. Unusually for exhibition practices of the time, he included three strikingly similar works, now lost: *Under the Chestnut Tree (The Hammock),* 1879 (fig. 13, etching), *The Hammock,* 1879 (fig. 14) and *A Quiet Afternoon* (fig. 15). Wearing a fashionable black dress and swinging in a hammock in the artist's garden in the London suburb of St. John's

13. Tissot, *Under the Chestnut Tree (The Hammock)*, 1880, etching and drypoint, 27.8 x 18.4 cm. Art Gallery of Ontario, Toronto, Gift of Allan and Sondra Gotlieb

14. Tissot, *The Hammock*, 1879, oil on canvas, whereabouts unknown. Reproduced from the albums of photographs Tissot kept of his own work. Private Collection

15. Tissot, *A Quiet Afternoon*, 1879, oil on canvas, 58.4 x 83.8 cm. Whereabouts unknown

32   *Marshall*

Wood, Kathleen Newton posed for this series.[18] Visible behind her are the fishponds, colonnades, and garden ornaments of Tissot's own careful design, which he represented frequently. The critical reaction to this group of images illustrates the extent to which Victorian viewers participated in a type of meaning-making predicated not on identifying the models but rather on a range of connotations of the depicted urban sites, and centred on a new and unstable category of city space, the suburb. The initial interpretation of these pictures was also determined by the artist's detailed technique, for the apprehensive discussions of his work contained a curious slippage between style and subject matter.

Although no reviewers explicitly named Kathleen Newton, they indicated that they recognized the location of this idyll as suburban London. One writer commented that *A Quiet Afternoon* and its accompanying exhibits were, as he termed them, 'pictures of the "detached villa" kind'.[19] Literally, this charged phrase referred to one of the most common architectural types of the suburbs, the free-standing house, by which St. John's Wood had been the first neighbourhood to be distinguished. Taken in a more general sense the comment was meant to summon up a particular set of associations around a new architectural typology. Throughout the nineteenth century, London was re-designed according to the mutually reinforcing dictates of the emergent ideologies of industrial capitalism and the nuclear family, growing increasingly segregated and specialized as new train and omnibus lines aided the development of outlying residential neighbourhoods. The suburb—and St. John's Wood in particular, because of the high walls which uniformly characterized this area—came to be seen in the popular imagination as places of privacy and home life into which one could escape from the pressures of the city.

The space of *A Quiet Afternoon,* with its sense of snug, peaceful enclosure, its foliage-covered wall preventing our eye from moving into the distance, its conservatory and patch of flower garden, was easily read as suburbia. Another picture at the Grosvenor, *Going to Business* (fig. 16), reinforced this identification by depicting the site in relation to which the suburb was defined, London's financial district. The businessman in his cab rushes past St. Paul's Cathedral in an image which implicitly contrasted Britain's secular commercial power with its greatest national religious icon. Pointedly, the gentleman ignores the cathedral altogether in favour of a more secular gospel, the newspaper. *A Quiet Afternoon* and *Going to Business* therefore functioned as representations of the opposite ends of the by now well-established suburb–city continuum, and indeed were viewed as such, as we shall see.

In the Grosvenor paintings, Tissot heightened divisions between the two depicted worlds by creating a stark contrast between the verdant garden and the dirt and grime of the city. The oddly exaggerated vertical thrust of *Going to Business* is strikingly different from the easy horizontal spread of *A Quiet Afternoon*. A reviewer described the St. John's Wood paintings in terms of 'heavy colour' and 'intensely bright green grass,' while the other work is a study in monochrome so severe as to appear almost grisaille.[20] The monochrome served to emphasize the picture's theme, for the sharpest differentiation between black and white occurs in the old man's costume, making him the palette, so to speak, from which the picture was generated and therefore implying that the businessman was the source of the gray tonality and the grimy soot produced by modern industry.

These formal dissimilarities between the two pictures reinforced the differences between the spaces they depicted. The cab is heading toward the centre of the City, in which were located the major institutions of trade including the Bank of England and the Royal Exchange; this area was noted for its lack of women.[21] A clock hovers over the scene in the steeple in the upper left corner of the canvas, reminding the viewer of the new meaning of time under industrial capitalism in this part of London.[22] Time was now 'spent'; it had exchange value. In fact the hansom cab itself linked time and space in a new way, for it could be hired by either the time or the distance traversed, the latter calculable in terms of the

16. Tissot, *Going to Business*, 1879, oil on canvas, 43.8 x 25.4 cm. Suzanne McCormick Collection

former.[23] *Going to Business* therefore treated the male world of commerce and hurried commuting, of masculine labour and clock time; conversely, *A Quiet Afternoon* was a realm of feminine leisure and 'tea-' or social time.

The garden of the suburban detached villa, then, embodied the antithesis of the public world of male, paid employment, representing a private, domestic retreat not subject to the dictates of hourly wages. Although the hammock moves, it does so unproductively; rather than traveling through space from one point to another like the hansom cab, it sways back and forth merely for pleasurable sensations. Similarly, the villa garden on one level opposed the modernity of the city in its notional timelessness, its dependence on natural cycles, and its privileging of space over time. If, as David Harvey has posited, space became less important than time in the working world, as life was increasingly defined by haste and efficiency, then in the garden, the primacy of space was reasserted.[24] And indeed, *A Quiet Afternoon* orchestrates space for visual pleasure, dwelling on its depth of field, in contrast with the lack of recession in *Going to Business*.

The two pictures, then, clearly illustrated the divide articulated by nineteenth-century social and economic discourses between the space of work — production — and the space of the family — reproduction. As recent works on the sociology of gender have pointed out, middle-class men commuted easily between the two realms, alternating between the roles of businessman and suburbanite, in a new type of movement which altered the sense of the space of the city.[25] Middle-class women, on the other hand, did not have this new mobility. This familiar notion of 'separate spheres' was both geographically and ideologically real, becoming mapped onto the physical shape of the city and reinforced by pictures such as Tissot's.[26]

However, despite the fact that Tissot's exhibited works of 1879 clearly differentiated and categorized their subjects in a way which appeared to reflect the hegemonic doctrine of separate spheres, they nonetheless received a good deal of vituperative criticism. One writer complained that 'in the picture of "The Hammock"... the aberration or the willful perversity of the painter is as ludicrous as it is offensive' and another fumed, 'this year [Tissot] tries our patience somewhat hardly, for these ladies in hammocks, showing a very unnecessary amount of petticoat and stocking, and remarkable for little save luxurious indolence and insolence, are hardly fit subjects for such elaborate painting'.[27] In an attempt to determine why the pictures evoked such anxiety, we need to re-examine the meaning of the charged phrase 'pictures of the "detached villa" kind.'

I would argue that the presence of *Going to Business*, depicting the commerce of the City, initiated a desire to read the suburban pictures as a comfortable escape from this world and at the same time frustrated that desire. The most revealing critical account appeared in the humorous magazine *Punch,* which created a narrative around three of the pictures, entitling *A Quiet Afternoon*, 'The Naughty Old Man; or, I'll tell your Wife how you spend your afternoons in Fair Rosamond's Bower Villa, N. W.' The satire continued, discussing *Going to Business* and returning to *A Quiet Afternoon*:

> [The businessman] leaves Fair Rosamond in the bower, and is off to the City. Is it now that the Naughty Old Man, who has a clerical cut about him, takes advantage of his absence to pay his visit? It is quite a drama. . . . And the businessman, meanwhile, is in the Hansom, going East. . . . And the latter murmurs to himself, 'Drive on Cabby! Ah! Is she good, she of the Abbey Road, St. John's Wood?'[28]

It would seem that 'is she good?' was the question at the root of reviewers' anxieties about the suburban images. Regardless of whether *Punch* was insinuating inside knowledge of Tissot's personal life — he was, after all, at this time living with Kathleen Newton without benefit of matrimony — the way the magazine referred to St. John's Wood reminded the informed reader that, in addition to being a domain of domesticity, it was also an area famous for fashionable kept women. As the 1879 *Routledge's Guide to London* explicitly stated, ' "pretty horse-breakers" have taken up their abodes in large numbers in . . . St. John's Wood'[29] and another commentator darkly proclaimed that the female inhabitants of the area were composed of 'divorced wives, not married to anyone in particular, mysterious widows whose husbands have never been seen, married women whose better halves were engaged in the City'.[30]

Ironically, although Kathleen Newton was of course a real mistress, this fact was unnecessary in order for viewers to see her as one. Regardless of viewers' knowledge of her identity, then, the woman in black became a disturbing *femme fatale* once seen through the lens of this knowledge. Indeed, *Punch* went on to describe *The Hammock* as:

> Rosamond, in her web, waiting for the flies. This is called *The Hammock.* It ought to have been *The Web.*
>   'Will you walk into my Garden?'
>   Said the Spider to the Fly.

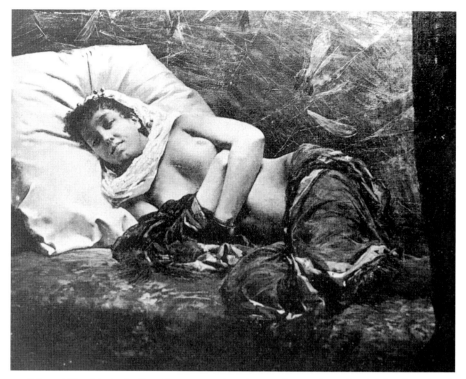

17. Edouard Zier, *l'Araignée*, 1889, oil on canvas, whereabouts unknown. Reproduced *Salon Illustré* (1889)

‘ ’Tis the prettiest little garden
That every you did spy.
The grass a sly dog plays on;
A hammock I have got;
Neat ancles you shall gaze on,
Talk — *à propos de bottes*’.[31]

The writer was expecting his audience to be familiar with French popular culture in ways beyond a mere comprehension of the language. The image of the
voracious female as a spider in a web was embedded in Parisian discourse about
prostitution and female sexuality, appearing in cartoons, drawings and oil paintings explicitly relating to the prostitute waiting for her prey. For example,
Édouard Zier's 1889 Salon painting, *l'Araignée* (fig. 17) was described by
Armande Silvestre as a '*marchande d'amour*'.[32] The drowsy old man can be seen
as her spent victim drained of, presumably, money and semen: male potency in

all its forms. This allusion to French tropes suggests that *Punch* construed the painting for a very specific audience, composed of bourgeois males entertained rather than shocked by the implication of sexual impropriety — the same sort of viewer addressed and constituted by the Louvre pictures, in fact.

Other critics, although more circumspect than the writer for *Punch,* revealed by their comments concerning the unseemly display of petticoats and stockings that they recognised — and condemned — the potentially disruptive nature of the depicted woman. One peculiar remark about the model's 'insanity of expression' becomes clear in light of the fact that prostitution was explicitly linked with mental illness in this period.[33] Perhaps more conservative Victorian viewers were disturbed by the way the pictures appeared to set up the comfortable and familiar dichotomies of suburb/city, family/business, private/public, only to expose them with a perverse twist; the woman is not a leisured wife but is herself also in business as both salesperson and commodity, a kept mistress. The order and efficiency of *Going to Business* is, on closer examination, formally echoed in *A Quiet Afternoon*, and the rigid geometry of the forms of St. Paul's and the cab find their equivalent in the taut horizontals and verticals of the grid-like trellis and flower beds in the background of the garden. The pictures thus seem to have drawn on, yet at the same time undermined, a host of comforting binary oppositions upon which the dominant culture rested. When read against one another in this way, the City and the suburban pictures implied that Britain's powerful empire was made possible and supported by the seedy underside of sexual commerce, an unsettling notion which perhaps provoked *Kensington* magazine's telling comment about the potential threat this situation posed: 'Ladies reclining in hammocks recur too often — one in black 'Under the Chestnut Tree' with a large Japanese parasol open beside her, and displaying rather more than ankles in black stockings, irresistibly reminds one of a Zulu with his shield.'[34] The papers at this time were full of images and reports of the Zulu War. The British defeat in January of the same year surprised and shocked the nation. The absurd comparison of Tissot's painted woman with a Zulu warrior indicated the extent to which she was seen as a threat to the health of the empire.

On one level, then, the figure in Tissot's Grosvenor paintings takes her place in the ever-growing catalogue of 'sexually deviant women in nineteenth-century painting'.[35] Yet it is not enough to uncover the economies of gender, money, and sex which linked the physical and ideological spaces of the city and feel that our interpretive task is done — that we have been able to 'expose' the truth 'behind' the images. After all, had Tissot overtly represented a prostitute and her clients, his painting would not have been sanctioned by an establishment institution such as the Grosvenor. Indeed, he seems to have taken some steps to prevent his model being mis-read in this way, including a prominently displayed wedding ring in both *A Quiet Afternoon* and *Under the Chestnut Tree,* a code of respectability which apparently did not resonate strongly enough in this particular instance.

Contemporary critics indicated that the depicted woman hovered ambiguously on the divide between respectability and deviance, an instability emphasized by the conflicting opinions concerning her location, the suburban garden of the detached villa. For many Victorians these new neighbourhoods were not peaceful havens of domesticity, but rather threateningly indecipherable products of the modern age. For instance, an article in the *Architect* of 1883 referred to the suburbs as a '*terra incognita*,' comparing them to the American prairie and their residents to pioneers in a 'perfect wilderness'.[36] This fear may have been due to the fact that the suburbs were products of rampant speculative building, representing capitalism at its most unrestrained in the way they voraciously consumed land at an uncontrolled pace.[37] Such speedy growth meant that it was difficult to define and comprehend suburb and city alike, given the confusion as to where one began and the other left off.[38] The blurring of the previously clear-cut categories 'city' and 'country' effected by the suburb also prevented the easy description of this novel landscape, in which the garden became a defining, deceptively attractive element. As another writer for the *Architect* warned in 1873:

> All is not gold that glitters; and all may not be Arcadian that looks green, especially in the neighbourhood of London . . . the inmates sigh for both the town and the country; for the town which they intended to leave behind but which has followed them in a form that is spoilt, and for the country which they expected to reach, but which is as far off as ever.[39]

In this way the ambiguity of the woman in Tissot's pictures, whose identity as a respectable bourgeois wife was open to question, was inflected by and in turn contributed to the ambiguity of her idyllic suburban garden surroundings.

Intriguingly, audiences interpreted not only the subject matter of the paintings but Tissot's art itself in terms of the meaning of certain city spaces; Tissot's own moral health was at stake. *The Daily Telegraph* compared Tissot to the gentleman in the hansom cab, urging him to drive 'eastward' like the old man:

The sooner [the artist] abandons Armida's garden full of hammocks, rock-ing-chairs, Japanese knick-knacks, bull-rushes, and slim sirens in black silk stockings and high-heeled shoes, the better it will be for his great and well-deserved, but at present sorely endangered, celebrity.[40]

The gardens of St. John's Wood in this case were seen as having a corrupting influence on his art and, by extension, on the artist himself. Although this may have been a specific reference to the artist's private life, it was more likely an indi-cation of distaste for his apparently trivial modern-life subject matter. Whiling away his time in an enchanted and perhaps emasculating garden, Tissot the man and artist was morally weakened in the eyes of the critics. Unlike the business-man, Tissot did not clearly differentiate between the spaces of his work and his domestic life. Like the potential prostitute, he earned his living in part in the domestic sphere, blurring the same carefully established borders.

Much as the review in *Punch* is useful in unpacking the layers of meaning in the exhibited works, the *Daily Telegraph* helps us grasp how Tissot's art-making itself was perceived. After terming the painter a 'manufacturer,' the critic for the paper continued in this vein, tellingly outlining his perceptions of Tissot's artis-tic method:

Mr. Tissot has seemingly come into possession of a hammock, several rock-ing chairs, and an assortment of Japanese fans and parasols as additions to his stock of artistic 'properties,' and with the help of these and one slim female model in the tightest-fitting of corsages, the most sweeping of trains, and who is not at all averse from a liberal display of her black silk hose and her high-heeled shoes, the painter 'fabricates'—that is really the only word to use—a number of compositions which only need some prettily executed flowers and some strong effects of sunshine on a verdant lawn in the middle distance to be, from Mr. Tissot's point of view, complete.[41]

To fabricate means 'to construct from diverse and usually standardized parts.' Tissot's exhibition of the three similar pictures posed by Kathleen Newton not only admitted but celebrated the fact that his images were created through a process of arranging and reproducing studio props, that they were— 'it is really the only word to use'—fabricated. Just as the possibility that the depicted woman could be a mistress pointed to the extent to which all relation-ships under capitalism were mediated by money, Tissot's style of art production might be seen as admitting that an artist was subject to the same laws as the assembly-line factory worker. His images, all surface and no substance, were interchangeable 'fabricated' commodities. This was indeed 'painting of the "detached villa" kind' in both subject matter and style, one reinforcing the other to underscore various anxieties about female—and male—sexuality, the meanings of urban spaces, the money economy, style and content, surface and subtext—anxieties, in short, about London's transition to modernity. Like the Louvre series, the Grosvenor paintings used Kathleen Newton's image to address particular modern concerns, including the destabilization of bourgeois gender roles and the potentially pleasurable ambiguity of female chastity.

But what about Kathleen Newton?

So far, this paper has declined to take into account that there was in fact a real woman who posed for the images in question, a woman with whom the artist had a close personal relationship, preferring instead to examine other avenues of historical and contextual interpretation. But perhaps one can throw the baby out with the traditional art-historical bath water by too doggedly ignoring this relationship, for some pictures invite and benefit from this sort of speculation. As if they were deliberately formulated in the autobiographical mode, certain works seem to resonate with personal meaning. Two other works for which Newton posed, *Richmond Bridge,* c. 1878 (fig. 18) and *Waiting for the Ferry* of 1878 (fig. 19), offer examples of this sort of image. The canvases work as pendants, both depicting couples along tourist sites of the Thames, with the man longingly contemplating the woman who turns away from him once again to look out at the viewer.

Like the Impressionists, who traveled to the Parisian suburbs along the Seine to find subject matter, Tissot explored the new tourist activities of the middle classes, becoming his own subject in the process. The two sites, Richmond to the west of London and Gravesend to its east, were popular destinations for short day trips from the city. Described by the *Illustrated London News* as a place of 'repose and recreation within an hour's railway ride of [London's] dusty, noisy streets and wearisome bustle of social vanity or commercial greed', Richmond was famous for its landscape scenery.[42] The well-known bridge in the background was especially admired for its graceful, classical proportions. In contrast, the figures in *Waiting for the Ferry* sit on the busy Tilbury dock in front of the Old Falcon Hotel in Gravesend.[43] After the railway was built in the 1850s, Gravesend was only an hour away from the centre of London and cheaply accessible, as tourists could take a train to Tilbury station and catch the ferry

18. Tissot, *Richmond Bridge*, c.1878, oil on canvas, 37 x 23.5 cm. Private Collection

steamer — for which Tissot's group waits — to the other side of the river.[44] There they could watch the shipping, enjoy the famous taverns, or stroll the teeming pier. By the 1870s, the town had lost its rural character, and Tissot's images of it offer a dramatic contrast to the lush green at Richmond, particularly in the facture of the water. In *Waiting for the Ferry,* the brushstrokes are clearly visible, coarsely indicating 'water' by an unmixed series of alternating brown and white horizontal dabs. In *Richmond Bridge,* however, the brushstrokes disappear in order to create the sense of a smooth, pure surface. In reality the Thames at Richmond was as dirty as it was at Gravesend, fouled in the summer months by sewage and silt. The debate about solutions to this problem raged throughout the 1870s, yet Tissot ignored reality in favour of depicting rural purity, creating two similar scenes with dramatically contrasting backgrounds.[45]

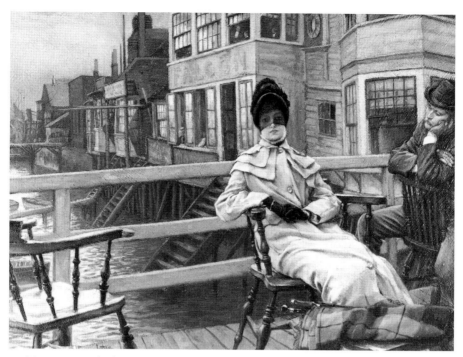

19. Tissot, *Waiting for the Ferry*, c.1878, oil on panel, 26.6 x 35.5 cm. Private Collection

These works, then, set up the elements of happy and successful courtship in their evocation of romantic daytrips down the Thames, only to be complicated by the ways they interfere with narrative convention. In *Richmond Bridge*, the woman appears self-absorbed, her back and shoulder turned to the man who slumps in depression or defeat; the arches in the background frame the two in such a way as to isolate them from one another. And, unlike the swans in a study for the picture (oil on panel, private collection), which swim in the same direction, the birds in the mid-ground of this painting are at right angles to one another, suggesting that all is not harmonious between the central figures. Similarly, the unity represented by the tiny couple on the glowing green bank in the background is both literally and figuratively distant from the troubled situation of the pair in the foreground.

Even more than *Richmond Bridge*, *Waiting for the Ferry* resonates with tension, producing a sense of psychological distance between the sexes. Although the man gazes intently at the woman, pressing his leg urgently against her chair as if to pull her within his sphere, she seems oblivious of his stare. The remote uncanniness of the woman's gaze in *Waiting for the Ferry* is amplified and complicated by her veil.[46] In the contexts in which Tissot painted it, the veil seems to have signified travel, its wearer dressed to present an image for the public sphere of mass transportation, attempting to protect herself both from the elements and the equally damaging stares of strangers. A veiled woman therefore signaled unattainability and distance, removed as she was from public scrutiny. Yet a transparent veil such as the one in *Waiting for the Ferry* did not just guard the public woman, it also drew attention to her, for the fact that her eyes were covered and difficult to see made them that much more enticing, as Mary Anne Doane has noted in her study of the veiled *femme fatale* in film.[47] The veil roused and sustained desire by hinting that there was something alluring underneath it—something to which the artist had special access through his unique powers of divination.[48]

Sketches of the sites suggest actual trips taken by Tissot to these locations.[49] Therefore the finished pictures survive not as exact records of those personal experiences but as incorporations of them, for doubtless Tissot enacted the very tourist itineraries discussed above in his romantic/artistic jaunts with Kathleen Newton. Although the final paintings appear to have been modeled by Newton's brother, Frederick Kelly, Tissot himself occupied the place later taken by Frederick in a photograph he used in constructing another version of *Waiting for the Ferry*, further enhancing the artist's personal connection with these images.[50] Under the chair which balances the composition of *Waiting for the Ferry* and competes with that of the seated man, Tissot signed his name, positioning himself as a rival. As in the Louvre works, then, Kathleen Newton looks not just at the viewer but at the painter himself, and the romantic tension set up by the composition takes on another dimension.

Yet the mood of *Waiting for the Ferry* is not celebratory and loving but sombre, emphasized by the muted tonalities, the pensive poses, and the fact that fully half the picture is empty of human figures, with the man cut off on one side and an empty chair occupying the other side, conveying a feeling absence or lack. The woman is oddly frozen, fixed in place by a rigidly symmetrical triangular composition comprised of the staircase behind her on one side and her body on the other. The veil contributes to the sense of melancholy in its funereal connotations and the way it renders the woman's features indistinct, as if she is fading from view. The blackness of her bonnet and veil composes the darkest part of the picture; in terms of artistic technique, the colour black was thought to be the 'most retiring of all colours,' and so this patch in the centre of the canvas pushes the woman's face beyond our reach.[51] And with his head in his hand, the man resembles the traditional emblem of melancholy. Travel itself could occasionally represent death, prompting associations of the ferry for which the woman is waiting with that of Charon's service across the river Lethe into the underworld. And of course Kathleen Newton herself was literally slipping away from Tissot, wasting away from tuberculosis during this period of their life together.

Recently several art historians have suggested that some of the compelling strangeness of Tissot's friend Édouard Manet's paintings derives from the left-over traces of the models themselves, of the unavoidable feeling that the works had been posed.[52] And as Michael Fried asserts, 'the forcefulness with which Manet's works of the first half of the 1860s asserted the reality of their models . . . is . . . clearly a function of the frequency with which a key figure in those paintings gazes directly out toward the viewer.' *Waiting for the Ferry* and a few other works in which the image of Kathleen Newton intently regards us seem to share this slippage, baring their technique of production. This 'reinstitution of identity' perhaps occurred because Tissot could not let the models become mere anonymous images in a figure painting. Rather, he wished to create images which spoke indisputably about his own life story, deploying an autobiographical mode of picture-making. Kathleen Newton was too emotionally charged a figure for Tissot to let her lapse comfortably into paint; rather, the memories of traveling to the tourist sites of Gravesend and Richmond with her were present to him as he was creating the canvases, making them resonate on an apparently personal level. Significantly, the paintings are both very small—smaller indeed than most of the works Tissot is known to have shown. This endows them with a less public, more intimate address than that of exhibited works and implies that they were intended for a different audience, one which was familiar with the relationships between the depicted figures and the artist himself.[53]

Perhaps on rare occasions the identity of the models and the lived experience of the painter can powerfully affect the final picture, making them images of personal significance in a way which may be discerned by later viewers. Marcia Pointon has proposed an interpretive approach which allows for what she terms 'intersubjectivity,' a process by which 'makers and consumers of art invest images with communicative identities and relevances that are particular as well as communal'.[54] In this way she negotiates the gap between artist's intention and viewer reception. Works such as *Waiting for the Ferry* are especially suited to this process of intersubjectivity, this investing of meaning by artist and viewer. Our desire to find a romance in this picture prompts a mode of reading in which we engage with the subjectivity of the artist in his relationship to the actual person who enabled him to generate this image.

The poignancy of *Waiting for the Ferry* may also represent Tissot's meditation on the inability of art to fulfill desire: in the end we must acknowledge that the woman is nothing but paint. Representational painting is always predicated on lack, for that which it represents so convincingly must necessarily be absent. Depicting a desired object, then, is always a doomed project, but one which Tissot found urgent; with *Waiting for the Ferry*, he seems to be enacting this project and its desperate nature.

After Newton's death, Tissot painted her spiritual materialization as she appeared to him in a séance with the medium William Eglinton in London in 1885, known from a mezzotint entitled *Mediumistic Apparition,* 1885 (pl. XXIV).[55] Despite the fact that he issued at least 350 prints of this work, indicating he saw its commercial potential as well, Tissot fetishized the original of this 'portrait' of Newton, keeping it with him in a room in which he performed certain personal spiritual rituals.[56] For Tissot to have resorted to spiritualism was not unusual or overly credulous in the period, when it was hardly the marginal activity it is now. But the fact that he did so suggests that he did have a strong emotional connection to the woman who triggered such a response. This effort to engage with Kathleen even after her death suggests the artist's attempt to control or manage his desire for her.[57]

We have now returned full circle to the question of the relevance of the 'real' Kathleen Newton to a work such as *Mediumistic Apparition*: is it a portrait, a touching tribute to lost love, or a pragmatic capitalizing on a fashionable parlour game? Perhaps it can be all three simultaneously.

James Tissot's paintings of Newton, then, are neither re-presentations of her authentic inner self nor simple transcriptions of her features. Neither wholly her identity nor merely her image, these pictures are ambivalent mediations between the two. They also embody Tissot's own attempts to organize his emotional and intellectual reactions to both the actual and the represented Kathleen Newton.

This paper is based on material drawn from my Ph.D. thesis, '"Transcripts of Modern Life": The London Pictures of James Tissot 1871–1882' (Yale University, 1997). I would like to thank Katharine Lochnan and Caroline Arscott for inviting me to present it, as well as Jules D. Prown, Esther Da Costa Meyer, Thomas Crow, Carol Armstrong, and John House for their critical commentaries on this topic.

1. Marita Ross, 'The Truth About Tissot,' *Everybody's Weekly* (15 June 1946): 6–7. See also David Brooke, 'James Tissot and the *"ravissante Irlandaise"*,' *Connoisseur* (May 1968): 55–9.

2. Tissot's love affair with and depictions of Kathleen Newton correspond with that of Dante Gabriel Rossetti and Elizabeth Siddall. See Griselda Pollock and Deborah Cherry, 'Woman as Sign in Pre-Raphaelite Literature: The Representation of Elizabeth Siddall,' in Griselda Pollock, *Vision and Difference: Femininity, Feminisms, and the History of Art* (London and New York: Routledge, 1988), 91–114.

3. For a discussion of Cecil's paternity, see Michael Wentworth, *Tissot* (Oxford: Clarendon Press, 1984), 126–7 and n.4.

4. Christopher Wood, *Tissot: The Life and Work of Jacques Joseph Tissot 1836–1902* (Boston and Toronto: Little, Brown, and Co., 1986), 113; 120; Willard Misfeldt, *J.J. Tissot, Prints from the Gotlieb Collection* (Alexandria, VA: Arts Services International, 1991), 126.

5. *James Tissot*, ed. Krystyna Matyjaszkiewicz (New York: Abbeville Press, 1985), 122.

6. Recent scholarship, such as Jonathan Crary's examination of the ways Victorian visual technologies ordered and defined vision, has neglected gender differences in the way people learned to see. See *Techniques of the Observer: On Vision and Modernity in the Nineteenth Century* (Cambridge and London: MIT Press, 1990).

7. *Essays on Physiognomy Designed to Promote the Knowledge and the Love of Mankind*, trans. Thomas Holcroft (London: B. Blake, 1840), 403.

8. W. Spencer Watson, *Eyeball-Tension: Its Effects on the Sight and its Treatment* (London: H. K. Lewis, 1879), notes that of his 46 glaucoma cases, 32 were female, a fact he attributed to the female pursuits of needlework and night watching, noting that a large proportion of these patients were depressed or nervous. He also believed that emotional excitement and cessation of menstruation caused glaucoma (2–3, 36). T. Wharton Jones, *Defects of Sight, Their Nature, Causes, Prevention, and General Management* (London: John Churchill, 1856), cited prolonged suckling of infants a source of visual stress for mothers(81). He noted that hysterics, pregnant women, postpartum women, and those with disturbed menstruation were subject to sudden blindness (105).

9. For example, a popular magazine described a young female viewer at the opening of the Royal Academy, 'scribbling her criticism on the margin of the catalogue, doubtless for the benefit of some aftercomer whom she wishes to impress with respect for her discriminating powers in Art.' 'First Day of the Royal Academy Exhibition,' *Sharpe's London Magazine* 9 (1856): 80. This character considers and judges the art work not for her own edification but in order to impress a potential husband with her ornamental knowledge.

10. *London Society* 12 (July 1867): 11–12.

11. Through its mode of address and the nature of the material presented, art criticism for a female readership also shaped its audience to a great extent. In her analysis of one art journal from the early nineteenth century, Ann Pullan determined that this writing functioned to construct 'the bourgeois female viewing "subject" as a "proper lady".' '"Conversations on the Arts": Writing a Space for Female Viewers in the *Repository of Arts* 1809–15,' *Oxford Art Journal* 15, no. 2 (1992): 15–26, quotation on 15.

   Indeed, reviews of art exhibitions in ladies' magazines were often lightweight and overly complimentary rather than thoroughly analytical. For the most part, they avoided discussions of artistic technique, as women required only the training which would allow them to recognize elevating subject matter; as one critic reminded his reader, her 'genial part is to generate and foster, in the society of which she forms a half, a sense of moral and intellectual beauty.' F. C., 'On the Appreciation of Truth in Art,' *The Ladies' Companion* (July 1850): 185–6. This critic explained: 'I do not propose to weary the amateur with technical disquisitions on the executive principles of Art. She requires to have her attention called to those higher and purely intellectual excellencies.'

12. *London Society*, 11–12.

13. An anonymous writer begins, 'the way of looking must be regulated in the young.' *Habits of Good Society* (London: Virtue and Co., 1875), 266. He or she added that a 'fast' lady was distinguished by her 'hard, *blasé* look' (267). Rather, 'a pleasing modest reserve, and retiring delicacy, that avoids the vulgar stare of the public eye, and blushing, withdraws from the gaze of admiration, is beyond all doubt one of the principle beauties of the female character,' declared another writer in *Etiquette for Ladies and Gentlemen* (London: Milner and Co., 1874), 69. Etiquette manuals were of course prescriptive rather than descriptive texts, and we cannot assume that they described behaviours which were always actually carried out, but these discourses speak of the way the dictating class wished to view itself.

14. As Caroline Arscott points out elsewhere in this volume, the male with compromised vision was a favourite trope with Tissot.

15. 'Excessive indulgence in venery, whether among married or unmarried, is sometimes a source of muscular fatigue, and consequently of congestion of the eyes.' *Woods' Household Practice of Medicine*, ed. Frederick A. Castle, MD (London: Sampson Low, 1881), vol. 2, 250–1. In France, the word '*voir*' even became slang for copulation. For more about the French use of the word 'to see' and significance of the woman looker, see Deborah Bershad, 'Looking, Power, and Sexuality: Degas' *Woman with a Lorgnette*,' in *Dealing with Degas: Representations of Women and the Politics of Vision*, ed. Richard Kendall and Griselda Pollock (New York: Universe, 1991), 95–105, 99.

16. Fashionable ladies, such as the woman in *Visiting the Louvre*, further weakened their ability to take in their surroundings visually, according to contemporary medical theories about eye defects caused by tight clothing such as corsets and, particularly, women's boots. In 1870, *The Period* quoted the *Medical Press* about the new fashion, which found that, 'high-heeled boots . . . are sure to bring on opthalmic afflictions. . . . "since the new-fashioned boot made for and worn by ladies has come into use, we have been consulted in various instances for a weakening of vision and a stiffness

about the ocular apparatus."' 'Apropos de Bottes,' 27 August, 175. This belief that women wearing boots risked their visual health represented a displacement of anxiety about women's increasing mobility and access to the city.

17. *Degas*, ed. Jean Sutherland Boggs (New York: Metropolitan Museum of Art, 1988), 54.

18. All three images are unlocated and known only through black and white photographs. *Under the Chestnut Tree* exists only in etching form.

19. 'The Grosvenor Gallery, Second Notice,' *Daily Telegraph* (10 May 1879): 3.

20. 'Notes at the Grosvenor Gallery, *Kensington* (June 1879): 383–6, 385. The *Daily Telegraph* described them as 'some strong effects of sunshine on a verdant lawn in the middle distance.' 'The Grosvenor Gallery, Second Notice' (10 May 1879): 3.

21. P. Villars, *London and its Environs*, trans. Henry Frith (London: George Routledge and Sons, 1888), 7–8.

22. Nigel Thrift, 'The Creation of Capitalist Time Consciousness,' in *The Sociology of Time*, ed. John Hassard (London: Macmillan, 1990), 115. He notes that clocks in workplaces and schools were intended to create a new sense of time in order to create a workers' consciousness.

23. 'A good average idea of distance may be obtained by consulting one's watch, allowing 7½ minutes for every mile,' advised Jay Ess in *Ess's American Guide to London and its Suburbs* (London and New York: Wyman and Sons, 1872), 13.

24. *Consciousness and Urban Experience: Studies in the History and Theory of Capitalist Urbanization* (Baltimore: Johns Hopkins Press, 1985), 15.

25. *Consciousness and Urban Experience*, 9.

26. Nancy Cott, 'On Men's History and Women's History,' *Meanings for Manhood: Constructions of Masculinity in Victorian America*, eds. Mark Carnes and Clyde Griffin (Chicago: University of Chicago Press, 1990), 206–7.

27. 'The Grosvenor Gallery, Second Notice,' *Daily Telegraph* (10 May 1879): 3; 'The Grosvenor Gallery, Second Notice,' *The Spectator* (31 May 1879): 691.

28. 'Grosvenor Gallery Guide', *Punch* (21 June 1879): 286.

29. London: George Routledge and Sons, 1879, 27. J. Ewing Ritchie's 1880 *Days and Nights in London* (London: Tinsley Bros.) described the types of women frequenting the by-then closed Argyll Rooms in central London as 'painted and bedizened females, most of them "born in a garret, in a kitchen bred," driving up in broughams from St. John's Wood or Chelsea or Belgravia, with their gallants, or "protectors"'(26).

30. Author of 'Ethelwynn's Secret,' 'A Brave Girl,' Chapter 45, *The London Journal* (September 1876): 166–7, 166.

31. 'Grosvenor Gallery Guide', *Punch* (21 June 1879): 286.

32. *Le Nu au Salon* (Paris: E. Bernard, 1889), np. *'Dans un coin cependant, l'araignée silencieuse guette et attend. Et, pour attirer les sots seulement, elle a écrit sur sa toile ces mots qui sont un blasphème: Marchande d'Amour.'*

33. Anthea Callen, *The Spectacular Body: Science, Method and Meaning in the Work of Degas* (New Haven and London: Yale University Press, 1995), 50–62, discusses the links between the two conditions made in France at the same time.

34. 'Notes at the Grosvenor Gallery,' *Kensington* (June 1879): 385.

35. I would argue that the prostitute makes a good subject, both for the artist and the critic (and the art historian) because the discovery of such a figure in a representation of a woman enables the creation of a dense narrative woven by the interlinked economies of gender, money, and sex. As we see in the *Punch* story and indeed in this paper as well, the morally questionable female propels story; she is never understood to represent merely herself, but rather draws the viewer/reader into a notional network of sequential events—attraction, sex act, payment.

36. 'Househunting,' *The Architect* (22 September 1883): 169–70, 169. Quoted in Donald J. Olsen, *Growth of Victorian London* (New York and Harmondsworth: Penguin Books, 1976), 207.

37. One writer called the speculative builder 'a creation or organism unknown to science or art.' 'Suburban Building,' *The Architect* (6 January 1877): 12.

38. 'The Suburbs of London and their Improvement', *The Builder* (2 September 1879): 1044–5. The author compared the current indefinite boundaries to the days of the walled fortified London, writing of 'the poverty and chill aspect of the suburbs of [London] and the main approaches to it' (1044). There was a call for regulation of suburban building; for instance, *The Builder* of 10 October 1879 reported that the findings of the 'Social Science Congress' dictated the need for such controls (423).

39. 'London Suburban Villas,' *The Architect* (11 October 1873): 181. Likewise, *The Architect* of 1876 said 'a modern suburb is a place which is neither one thing nor the other; it has neither the advantage of the town nor the open freedom of the country, but manages to combine in nice equality of proportion the disadvantages of both.' Quoted in F.M.L. Thompson, 'Introduction: The Rise of Suburbia,' in *The Rise of Suburbia* (Leicester: Leicester University Press, 1982), 3.

40. 'The Grosvenor Gallery, Second Notice,' *Daily Telegraph* (10 May 1879): 3.

41. *Ibid.*

42. 'Holiday at Richmond' (30 May 1874): 511.

43. Tissot had painted an earlier work in this exact location, *Waiting for the Ferry* of 1873. The hotel was a relic of the Middle Ages, having been built in 1370.

44. Anon., *The Pictorial Guide to Gravesend and its Rural Vicinity* (London: William S. Orr and Co., 1845), 13, 8.

45. The *Saturday Review* discussed the 'black and offensive slime' observed in the Thames by the visitors to Kew and Richmond. 'The Thames at Richmond' (13 September 1873): 344.

46. Tissot represented this same model wearing a veil and ulster in *Crossing the Channel* (exhibited at the 1879 Grosvenor Gallery) and in *The Ferry* (1879), as well as in a pair of compositions about travel at his 1882 one-man exhibition at the Dudley Gallery, *By Water (Waiting at Dockside)* and *By Land (Victoria Station)*.

47. She notes that the see-through veil 'simultaneously conceals and reveals, provoking the gaze.' *Femmes Fatales: Feminism, Film Theory, Psychoanalysis* (New York and London: Routledge, 1991), 49. For a discussion of the use of the veil in French culture and painting, see Marni Kessler, 'Sheer Material Presence, or the Veil in Late

Nineteenth-Century French Avant-garde Painting' (Ph.D. diss., Yale University, 1996). She has found that this sort of demi-veil depicted here was used practically for traveling, to protect the face from wind and dust.

48. Tissot himself may have been aware of the elusively attractive qualities of the veil, as an amusing anecdote relates. Declared one of Tissot's neighbours, 'we never took a stroll together and passed a pretty woman but he commented on it. Once he said, "There goes a *jolie demoiselle*." I turned and saw the lady wore a thick veil. "Nonsense," I said, "how can you tell? She is wearing a veil." "*"Qu'importe?!"*' cried Tissot, "I can divine that her features are beautiful."' Alan Montgomery Eyre, *St. John's Wood: Its History, Its Houses, Its Haunts, and Its Celebrities* (London: Chapman and Hall, 1913), 254.

49. Sketch of the Falcon Tavern reproduced in Matyjaskiewicz, *Tissot*, cat. 112; sketch of *Richmond Bridge* in sale catalogue, Sotheby's London, 19 June 1989.

50. Art historians have sometimes assumed that it was a self-portrait of Tissot in these paintings. See Wood, *Tissot*, 92 or Wentworth, *Tissot*, 131. Matyjaszkiewicz tentatively identifies the man in the paintings as Frederick Kelly (*Tissot*, 130–2).

51. George Field, *A Grammar of Colouring* (London: Lockwood and Co., 1875), 103. Kathleen Newton's birth certificate states that she died of phthisis, or tuberculosis, in 1882, but whether she had the signs of wasting illness at this stage is unknown.

52. Carol Armstrong first advanced this idea in 'To Paint, To Point, To Pose: Manet's *Déjeuner sur l'herbe*,' a paper delivered at the meeting of the College Art Association, 19 February 1994, now published in *Manet's Déjeuner sur l'herbe* (Cambridge: Cambridge University Press, 1998). Michael Fried built on this notion by suggesting that Manet's work entailed a 'complex relationship involving the painting and the model, both of which were before his gaze.' Due to Manet's involvement in this mutual dynamic, Fried posits, the beholder of the painting feels 'supererogatory to a situation that ostensibly demanded [their] presence, as if [their] place before the painting were already occupied by virtue of the extreme measures that had been taken to stake it out.' 'Among factors producing this impression is treatment of the model, who the viewer is made to feel is present before the painter — the painter-beholder — and *by virtue of that fact* is not present to him', *Manet's Modernism, or, The Face of Painting in the 1860s* (Chicago: University of Chicago, 1996), 345, 344. With Tissot, although we get the sense that Kathleen was indubitably present to the painter, she is *also* present to us.

53. *Waiting for the Ferry* with the children is 12 x 14 inches, the version without the children is 10½ x 14 inches, the sketch for *Richmond Bridge* is 11½ x 7¾ inches, and *Richmond Bridge* itself is 14½ x 9¼ inches. Willard Misfeldt asserts that Tissot's *carnet*, the log book in which he recorded many of his sales transactions, contains a record of the sale of *Richmond Bridge* to McLean's, where presumably it was exhibited. Private communication, 26 June 1996.

54. *Naked Authority: The Body in Western Painting 1830–1908* (Cambridge and New York: Cambridge University Press, 1990), 1.

55. In an eyewitness account of this event, two figures 'gradually became more and more plainly visible, until those nearest could distinguish every feature . . . M. Tissot, looking into her face, immediately recognized [his companion] and, much overcome, asked her to kiss him. This she did several times, the lips being observed to move. . . . After staying with him for some minutes, she again kissed him, shook hands, and vanished.' John S. Farmer in *Twixt Two Worlds: A Narrative of the Life and Work of William Eglinton* (London: Psychological Press, 1886), 187. Jacques-Émile Blanche in *Portraits of a Lifetime* (London: J. M. Dent and Sons, Ltd., 1937), 65–6, recorded a séance for Tissot in which the 'spirit' turned out to be the painter Albert Besnard's model and the medium was jailed for fraud. In Wentworth, *Tissot*, 177.

56. Edmond de Goncourt described the following visit to Tissot's house in Paris in the 1890s: 'Et dans le crépuscule, se refusant à chercher des allumettes, avec une voix qui se fait tout à fait mystérieuse et des yeux vagues, il nous montre une boule de cristal de roche et un plateau d'émail, qui servent à des évocations, où l'on entend, assure-t-il, des voix qui se disputant. Il tire d'une commode des cahiers, où il nous montre des pages entières, contenantes l'historique de ces évocations, et nous montre enfin un tableau représentant une femme aux mains lumineuses, qu'il dit être venue l'embrasser et dont il a senti sa joue ses lèvres, de lèvres pareilles à des lèvres de feu.' *Journal* 3, 1118, quoted in Wentworth, *Tissot*, 178.

57. The language of spiritualism 'specialized in the metaphoric performance and the actualization of desire.' Diane Basham, *The Trial of Woman: Feminism and the Occult Sciences in Victorian Literature and Society* (Hampshire and London: Macmillan, 1992), 108.

The Invisible and the Blind in Tissot's Social Recitals

Caroline Arscott

I N THIS ARTICLE I will be discussing a series of watching figures in Tissot's work. In Tissot's pictures figures are very often subject to libidinous looks and/or the steady watching of surveillance. There is nothing unusual about this. We can find any number of French or British paintings or novels of the period where there is a preoccupation with the exercise of sight as the channel of desire and communication, as well as a resource for defensive vigilance. Voyeurism, roguish or coquettish glances, a forbidding glare—these are the stock-in-trade of the adventurers, sweethearts and chaperones of art and fiction. Moreover a substantial body of theoretical work has argued that the modernity of the nineteenth century is characterised, particularly, by a revised visual regime, underpinned by an increasing investment of power in vision.[1] The exercise of vision has been identified as a crucial aspect of modern state authority and, in a different intellectual framework, as a functional component of psychic subjectivity, beleaguered or ideologically bolstered in modern industrial conditions.[2]

Vision was a functional component of modernity and was, one might argue, redefined as it was put to new purposes. There was a revision of the importance of sight and the value of looking. Sight was upgraded in many ways and became a primary mode of acccess to the world. There was a reshuffling of relationships between different faculties and authorities and we can discern a shift in the relationship of sight to sound, of icon to word, and of the evidence of the eyes to the authority of inherited tradition or established text. Commodity display and advertising could thrive in the deafening environment of the modern city street. Empirical investigation took over some of the territory of Scripture. Benjamin has argued that desire and perception alike were recast in the rhythms of factory production.[3] It is in this context of heightened visual attention, in response to the demands of industrial society, that the coded display of class identity should be understood. Visual scrutiny was an essential part of bourgeois life, as minute shades of social distinction were assigned or claimed by means of small variations in dress or bearing.[4] Courtship made use, as it always had done, of the exchange of lovers' glances and of wordless signs of interest or invitation. At the same time members of the middle classes were impelled to read the array of visual signals as indicators of social legitimacy. Lovers looked for signs of passion, but members of a social group also looked out for illegitimate intruders.

20. Tissot, *Boarding the Yacht,*
1873, oil on canvas, 71 x 53.4 cm.
Private Collection,
photograph courtesy Crane
Kalman Gallery Ltd., London

Tissot's protagonists were conceived of as inhabiting a world where the endurance or enjoyment of various kinds of regard was a crucial part of social existence. Tissot's work is cognate to those bourgeois narratives where morality is invested in the undemonstrative, but romance is linked to display and the frisson of an incautious look, sent or detected. The officer's fingers frame the roving eye in *Boarding the Yacht,* 1873 (fig. 20), and focus the drama for all three characters. In *The Captain's Daughter,* 1873 (pl. V) the telescope, with a full key for deciphering signals, lies useless on the table because the young woman is not concerned to exchange signals with the lovestruck youth. My contention is that the watching is often extended in Tissot's pictures beyond the standard *dramatis personae* of such bourgeois dramas. There are additional witnesses who may not be noticed. Those who are apparently blind, distracted or presumed uninvolved are subtly drawn in to the standard stories, thus destabilising the narratives of social signals sent, received or intercepted. We need to take into account the presence of footmen and sailors assisting in scenes of bourgeois leisure. Sometimes even

21. Tissot, *Young Ladies Looking at Japanese Objects*, oil on canvas, 55.8 x 39 cm. Private Collection, London

the furniture and ornaments provide the opportunity for covert observation. What else are we to make of the complacent stance of the portly Japanese figurine in *Young Ladies Looking at Japanese Objects* , 1869 (fig. 21)?[5] Ultimately the holes in flower pots, the centres of nasturtium leaves, the crystal orbs of chandeliers and even the buttons of a button-surfaced sofa may be said to offer so many eyes.

In *The Organ Grinder*, 1878 (fig. 22) a street entertainer stands facing into the picture space. We don't see his eyes but, from the tilt of his head, we know that his face is turned to the balconied first storey of the smart upper-middle-class terrace. In the clear expanse of the driveway, on the bottom left of the picture, his trained monkey is squatting, but, in a stance analogous to its master, it lifts its upper body and faces towards the house, its arms spread, ready to bring the cymbals together with a crash. We are shown the silk covering of the mechanical organ, light in colour and traced across with squiggly lines to indicate the exotic decoration. This partially covers the works, but holes are left for thick leather

22. Tissot, *The Organ Grinder*, 1878, etching, 26.2 x 16.4 cm. Art Gallery of Ontario, Toronto, Gift of Allan and Sondra Gotlieb

straps at the top, for carrying handles at the side, and at the back a gap allows the man to grasp the crank with his left hand as he grinds out a tune. The decorative cover hangs down at the right of the man's legs, showing that the organ extends right across his body, acting as a substantial apron.

This is a rough working man whose coarse jacket forms one of the blackest regions of the print. The dirt of the city street is metaphorically concentrated in this blackness, and constitutes an alien presence in the white, high-toned atmosphere of the Regent's Park terrace. The cloth of the coat has no drape and we can imagine it to be stiff with dirt, or just from the clumsiness of the stuff. Tissot has drawn attention to similarities between the man's own clothes and the gaudy cloth over the instrument. At first glance we are apt to confuse the pointed corners of the coat and those of the organ-cover.[6]

TALENT APPRECIATED.

Jemima Cook. " OH, MARY ! HOW *WELL HE* PLAYS ! "
Mary Parlourmaid. " DOESN'T *HE* !! SUCH *EXPRESSION* !!! "

23. George du Maurier, *Talent
Appreciated*, wood engraving, 17.1
x 11.1 cm., from *Punch* (27 April
1869), p. 168. Photograph courtesy The Edward P. Taylor
Reference Library and Archives,
Art Gallery of Ontario, Toronto

It strikes one as paradoxical that the signifier of the exotic, the arabesque patterning and presumably carnival colour of the cover of the organ is being made
continuous with the drab and filthy habiliment of the player. But this is an elaboration on a paradox already signalled first by the monkey and, secondly, by the
organ itself. The monkey is a brute dressed up in a bright, braid trimmed, but-
toned soldier jacket. Equally the dark box of the organ is rigged out in its bright
cover.

How should we react to this street entertainer? It is helpful to refer to the
accounts of organ grinders and other street musicians in the pages of Henry
Mayhew's *London Labour and the London Poor*, issued in a four-volume edition
in 1861–2 and widely circulated in England. I do not wish to suggest that Tissot
used this as a source but it gives us some clue to the complex response elicited by

such figures. Mayhew illustrates a blind female hurdy-gurdy player and depicts a male player of a street organ in the plate of stilt walkers.[7] He also interviews a number of organ grinders. The exasperated householder plagued by noisy buskers was a well-worn comic scenario, dating back to Hogarth,[8] but Mayhew moves beyond noting this comic frame of reference to consider graver matters. In the work of nineteenth-century commentators the denizens of the street, including itinerant street vendors and street entertainers, figured as walking sources of physical and moral disease, too idle to settle at a respectable occupation. As Nancy Marshall has pointed out organ grinders were very often Italian and a fearful response to their presence on the street was connected with a chauvinistic attitude to foreigners.[9]

We can see how even a comic presentation of organ grinders mobilised frightening associations when we consider the drawing *Talent Appreciated* made by George Du Maurier for *Punch* in 1869 (fig. 23).[10] At street-level the organ grinder plays to the householder, and is quite possibly ignored, but below-stairs a bare-armed cook and a finely dressed parlourmaid observe his performance covertly. Here the organ grinder is presented with a dark beard and his features fit a Jewish rather than Italian stereotype. The anti-semitic presentation of the villain, Svengali, of Du Maurier's *Trilby* comes to mind. The caption, 'Talent Appreciated' is a comment on the susceptibility of the lower-class auditors, who absurdly attribute expressivity to the automated process of grinding the organ. There is a touch of scandal about these women who take the opportunity to stare in fascination at the strange man at the door. We are made aware that they are musically undiscriminating and allowed to consider the possibility that they are sexually promiscuous. When the women indoors are servants this scenario is amusing and mildly scandalous. Were we to substitute bourgeois women for the servants, as Tissot's organ grinder etching with its open upstairs window suggests that we might, then the comedy would ebb away and only scandal remain.

A general fear of disease and immorality associated with foreign street entertainers was also sharpened into a suspicion of burglary where trained monkeys were concerned.[11] A short story in a collection of detective tales by James Maclevy from 1861 features a burglar who decides to set up as an organ grinder. The fine scarlet cloth that he steals to make the monkey's jacket, and a fine silk cravat for himself are the clues that lead to his arrest, so, in this example, larceny is linked to the very costume of the business. The monkey is also connected with lasciviousness.[12] Mayhew's metaphorical notion of the city streets as a system subject to blockage like the sewers below the streets, or the arteries and passages of the human body, has been pointed out.[13] His street folk may have been presented sympathetically, in many cases, as individuals but he conceived of their role in the system as malignant. Tissot's selection of the figure of an organ grinder keys into a range of associations and invites us to consider a network of issues concerning art, labour, morality and modernity.

Mayhew's description of one Italian performer who has a dancing monkey induces a *frisson* of revulsion in the reader and helps establish the distaste that a bourgeois observer would anticipate when brought close up to an unkempt street character.

> He was dressed in a brown, ragged, cloth jacket, which was buttoned over a long, loose, dirty, drab waistcoat, and his trowsers were of broad-ribbed corduroy, discoloured with long wearing. Round his neck was a plaid handkerchief, and his shoes were of the extreme 'strong-men's' kind, and grey with dust and want of blacking. He wore the Savoy and broad-brimmed felt hat, and with it on his head had a very picturesque appearance, and the shadow of the brim falling on the upper part of his brown face gave him an almost Murillo-like look. There was, however, an odour about him, — half monkey, half dirt, — that was far from agreeable, and which pervaded the apartment in which he sat.[14]

I include the whole paragraph because it contains a move from the evocation of filth to an aesthetic frame of reference, where the man's Italianness summons up Murillo's southern European picturesque, and then a return to the sense of revulsion. This offers an interesting parallel to the dual identity of Tissot's organ grinder: filthy slave to the machine and the source of artistic flourishes.

Picturesque depictions of shabby entertainers are common in Victorian painting.[15] In an image such as Thomas Graham's *A Young Bohemian*, 1864, (fig. 24) the delicacy of the girl accordionist contrasts with her rough circus surroundings. We are not given the stage front, glimpsed in top left-hand corner, but the back-scene or the side of a stage where we see, close up, the coarseness of planks and ropes, roughly hammered-in nails, and the giant crude stencilled letters of a sign. The girl and her accordion contrast with all this. Her gauzy dancing dress in spangled muslin is decorated with delicate pink artificial roses, her knotted paisley shawl sends swirls of pattern round her waist and shoulders, topped by a rosette of deeper pink. The accordion, with its pleats and inlaid decoration, is analogous to her figure. Yet with the prettiness there is considerable pathos because the costume is grubby for all its pleasing colour and her face and

24. Thomas Graham, *A Young Bohemian*, 1864, oil on canvas, 90.2 x 63.8 cm. National Gallery of Scotland

arms are striking in their pallor, hinting at deprivation. The sentimental picturesque consists in precisely this affective squeeze, release and squeeze of the grim and the gay. We sigh with the depressed instrument, tuned to the poignant and the libidinal notes by the pressure of her little fingers.

Tissot seems to assign artistry to his organ grinder rather than pinning him down as a picturesque or sentimental subject. The quality of the curling decorative lines on the organ cover give us a clue as to Tissot's theme here. These are the delicate, mobile, hand-made marks of the etcher. The same lines snake into the white area of the plate: most spectacularly in the case of the monkey's lead and the branches of the tree on the right. These are contrasted with the mechanical operation of the organ itself, where the turning of the crank is more akin to alienated labour than to imaginative art. The etching is based on an untraced oil painting, exhibited in Liverpool in 1879, and we should recognise that in the print the specifics of the medium come into play and amplify the allusions of the image. Etching itself can be contrasted to more mechanical reproductive print processes. Tissot participated in the etching revival of the 1860s and 1870s which involved artists such as Legros, Braquemond, Whistler and Seymour Haden.[16] The emphasis was on etching as an autograph, creative procedure in contradistinction to steel engraving or mezzotint. The motif of the barrel organ suggests forcefully that the issue of low, mechanical labour versus more elevated art is a salient one. Steve Edwards has shown that barrel organs were a frequent topos for the discussion of this kind of issue and were often invoked in contemporary discussions of photography.[17] In Tissot's image of the organ grinder there seems to be a simultaneous statement of base mechanism and virtuoso skill which makes this a troubling and resilient image. If we look at Mayhew's categories we find the following statement: 'The street musicians are of two kinds, the skilful and the blind'.[18] He goes on to explain that blind performers depended on pathos to attract contributions and so did not need to provide pleasing music. We cannot, however, slot Tissot's organ grinder into one of these categories. He is essentially unskilled since he only needs to turn the handle. On the other hand the figure appears physically repellent and is simply too close to the viewer for the comfort of a charitable response and a aestheticising appreciation of the picturesque. Another way to think about it, though, would be to assert that he encompasses both categories; he is a heterogeneous figure who, impossibly, is both skilful and blind. We would have to attribute to him an automatic virtuosity and a seeing blindness.

If the monkey's fantastic coat were removed or the chintzy cover of the organ taken away, we would be left with the mindless brute or the pre-programmed machine. The organ grinder's shabby coat, however, seems to hide the art fabric of his being. Despite many parallels with the monkey, not least the suggestion of a pale muzzle in his darkened face, he does in this respect reverse the monkey. It is important that this disparity is maintained. It provides some distance for the organ grinder both from the monkey as a traditional figure for the artist who does nothing but imitate and from the stereotype of the lascivious monkey. The opening of his coat emphasises the element of physical threat. We can imagine a bourgeois female left alone (with servants) in the house during the day, whose secure domestic space is being invaded by this gross man jangling the machine and almost flashing at her. The lower windows of the house are blind but we are given clear indications of an open upper window: there may be an individual affected by the sound and even looking down, though we do not see a pitying, horrified or fascinated onlooker. The bay frontage is a little like the organist's square instrument and one has the sense of the house front held in front of the inhabitant/s. The creeper growing up the front echoes the patterning on the organ cover, though the short rigid marks indicate a creeping dirt rather than a corresponding twisting flair and pleasure. These marks are more like the monkey's fur or the man's coat than the snaking lead or the sinuous motif. Where the entertainer's coat is open at the front we see a few lines standing for the cravat at his neck. These are branching and twisting lines, akin to the free floating branches or the lines of embroidery. This entertainer, then, is in a kind of motley, which conjoins the drab proletarian with a verso of glitter and flamboyant pattern.

For the picture's viewer, from a position behind the organ grinder's shoulder, the alarming street-identity is the recto, the art-identity the verso, and the initial triggering of bourgeois fear and repulsion on the part of the spectator, followed by the gradual realisation of a mitigating aesthetic aspect, leads us to attribute that sequence of response to the supposed lady of the house. However for the viewer, if there is one, behind the balcony, the resplendent aspect of the entertainer is to the front and the street dirt is a concealed verso. The colourful and ingenious entertainer turns out to be a mere animal or mechanic behind his apron. In this allegory of truth and creativity, is this a rendering of the delusion of audiences taken in by flashy academic art which is after all worthless mechanical mirroring? And is this to place the organ grinder as the kind of artist Tissot was criticised for being: lewdly crowd-pleasing and a manufacturer of photographic transcripts? These issues are surely alluded to, but, in the contest between the vantage point of the balcony and that of the driveway, the picture viewer's perspective wins out, as the double-sided organ grinder flips back, like a printing plate turned over to make a print. From our point of view, seeing the dirty back first, we can take the front to be the hidden truth. We are privy to the truth of the musician as a glittering creative artist, at core, who happens to be cloaked in a disguise of mere mechanism. Finally one needs to keep to the fore the palpable fear attaching to the image. The immediacy of this revulsion instructs us about how to order apprehension, perception and aesthetic pleasure in relation to the picture. It is this that allows one to read the figure of the organ grinder metaphorically as a kind of self-portrait.

I have been considering a picture that is unusual in nineteenth-century art for its large-scale and unglamourised depiction of a member of the lower orders, particularly given the markedly bourgeois setting. Moreover it is exceptional in Tissot's oeuvre, but I want to go on to consider analogous figures in other pictures by Tissot and suggest that it is less eccentric than it may at first appear.

Tissot regularly subverted conventional expectations by investing disproportionately in attendant figures.

Tissot showed *Too Early*, 1873 (pl. I) in London, at the Royal Academy, in 1873. Here the wide expanse of the parquet floor in a grand reception room is the stage for a social drama as the first guests of the party stand uncomfortably, waiting for more company to arrive. Tissot has given us an array of reactions to this situation and I want to establish the shades of differentiation in stance and attitude with some care. Under the crystal illumination of the social occasion minute differences in deportment are magnified, just as the single note of the bassist tuning his instrument resonates in the near empty room. At the centre of the picture a white-haired man lifts a gloved finger towards his chin in what might be an anxious, or bemused, gesture and turns his eyes towards the lofty heights of the room.[19] On either side, in a near-symmetrical arrangement, his two unmarried daughters stand stock still. The one on the left evinces some composure and is not entirely a figure of fun: there is a graceful turn to her body, and yet the horizontal placement of fan, sash and the neckline of her gown which tally perfectly with the moulding on the wall behind render her immobile. The one on the right with a red ribbon at her neck is caught frontally by the picture's composition and has placed her large gold fan symmetrically across her upper body. She seems fixed in place by her flanking position and then by the coincidence of her head with the whorl of the neoclassical plasterwork behind her. She gives the lie to this stillness, however, by the sideways sliding of her eyes. In front of them a third lady, possibly the mother or an elder sister, gives the impression of pacing about, leaning into the stride, her expression somewhat peevish as she drops her eyes, pulls in her chin and lifts her tightly closed fan towards her face. This large figure in pink seems to take up a disproportionate space, emphasising the small stature of the father. If we follow the lines in the parquet floor we see that she is liable to sweep down the others if she advances. Her skirts spread into the depths of the room for four large parquet squares, but there is only one (or one-and-a-half) squares' clearance in front of the two figures to her right. In the stillness of the room she represents a source of turbulence and we read the crosscutting swathes of her dress as rhythmic disturbance. By contrast the two figures leaning in the doorway betray neither the over-stiffness nor the over-excitement of the central figures. Relaxation verging on boredom alleviates the symmetry of their arrangement. The feet of the gentleman negligently cross over the swathe of the lady's gown. The formality of the crossing curves of the nearby neoclassical stool is achieved at the same time as a nonchalant intimacy that could be flirtation but chooses not to be. They are aware of one another but not bothering to interact. They have picked places where they blend into the doorway, where they are decorative adjuncts to the architecture rather than pinioned victims.[20] The relationship of these two figures to the architectural space and their manner of dealing with the occasion is quite the opposite of the gauche self-consciousness and the combination of rigidity and frenzy manifested by three out of four of the centrally placed figures. In this awkward social situation they have the class instinct to make themselves invisible. If they are cognisant of the comic cluster at the centre of the room, with its embarrassing excess of unpartnered young women, they show no sign of being observers. This is the trick of social survival for the truly cultivated. Elegant people know the way to signal and observe without ever manifesting complicity or concern. Tissot's satire is directed at the lack of breeding of the central group. They are shown as being precariously positioned in the urban bourgeoisie: rich enough to participate in an upper-middle-class soirée, but not of the class. Too humble in origin, or provincial in their experience, they are painfully conspicuous.

There are, of course, other observers. Two maids peep round the door. Their presence is not really authorised but, effectively concealed, they giggle and give the picture's viewer the cue as to the vulgar comedy available. They offer one instance of the way Tissot co-opts unexpected watchers quite outside the cast of bourgeois characters, but their presence, in fact, serves to distract us from another kind of surreptitious watching to be discerned in the group of musicians. The leader is humbly attending to the instructions of the lady of the house: there is a comic parallel between the way she towers over him and the way that the diminutive and unsettled paterfamilias in the centre of the room is borne down upon by the lady in pink. On either side of the leader, the musicians are absorbed in their business but the trumpet player on the left and the fiddle player on the right stare forward impassively. These two are licensed to inhabit the ballroom and yet it is shocking to discover that they stare out into the area where the bourgeois rituals take place. The younger whiskered musician is doubled—in this picture of so many instances of flanking symmetry—by the older violinist whose pince-nez reflects the light and gives him the appearance of having two blind, white eyes. As the viewer of the picture we are pinned by these two gazes and so they make explicit the kind of viewing that the spectator of the picture engages in. These are the witnesses to embarrassment. They are the missing male admirers of the naked display of the young women in the ballroom. Their gaze is one of knowledge and potentially of desire and yet, as a pair, they are seeing and blind. This is where I see a parallel with that extraordinary figure of the organ grinder, whom I described as embodying a kind of seeing blindness. So much more discreet than that large and threatening artist-proletarian, these players-on-command also invade the precincts of the bourgeois home and are the more all-seeing for being practically invisible.

A question arises. Could the young seeing musician be blinded, as so often happens in myth, in punishment for viewing the forbidden? Is that what we are shown in the figure of the older musician? And yet the older man continues to watch despite his blindness. Indeed his watching is the more penetrating for the fact that we do not see his eyes. This would point to the further mythic trajectory of the witness punished with blindness who goes on to a fuller experience of sight. The blind seer is a powerful cultural icon.

Derrida explores a store of mythological and Biblical instances of visionary blindmen in his book *Memoirs of the Blind* (1990). The stories of Tiresias, Tobit, Isaac, Samson, Polyphemus and others are invoked in support of his argument which seeks to identify representations of these figures as representations, or kinds of disguised self-portraits in every case, of the artist. It is a paradoxical position, as he readily acknowledges, but nevertheless he argues that drawing itself is closely linked with blindness. In his opinion it is, precisely, a seeing blindness and he describes the venture of the artist's pencil across the picture surface as the probing exploration of a blind person's stick. In logical terms he sees the artist being forced to look away from the world in order to make the image and so blind at the moment of making the drawing and, moreover, making a drawing from one-dimensional lines which divide the two-dimensional space but have no presence themselves and hence are invisible. This cluster of paradoxes is explored most fully in relation to self-portraiture. He writes about the fixity of focus on the two eyes in a self-portrait, or very often on a single eye. Looking fixedly at the eye of the self, he argues, is quite unlike looking at another's eye that looks elsewhere. The fixed examination effectively stops the eye seeing; it blinds it.

> For this cyclops eye sees nothing, nothing but an eye that it thus prevents from seeing anything at all. Seeing the seeing and not the visible, it sees nothing. This seeing eye sees itself blind.[21]

The twists and turns of Derrida's argument lead him to the notion that the spectator, who stands in the place of the self-portraitist's mirror, is complicit in this blinding and is then obliged to stand in for the gouged-out eyes: 'we rub out

25. Tissot, *Self-Portrait*, c.1865, oil on panel, 49.8 x 30.1 cm. The California Palace of the Legion of Honor, San Francisco, Mildred Anna Williams Collection

his eyes in order instantly to replace them: we are the double of his eyes. A bottomless debt, a terrifying prosthesis.'[22] He suggests that glasses worn by artists in their self-portraits, since they are prosthetic devices, can allude to this chain of events: seeing, blinding, drawing in the spectator to act as the substitute eyes. He also discusses cases where the shading hand or fingers of the sitter can effectively occlude an eye, or else act as a viewing device.[23] The curled finger cutting across the eye in Tissot's own *Self-Portrait*, c.1865 (fig. 25) could be considered in these terms. Additionally the spread fingers across the forehead presents a V-shaped viewing chink similar to that through which we see the captain's eye in *Boarding the Yacht*, 1873 (see fig. 20 on p. 54).

Derrida's ingenious comments alert us to the high stakes involved in being a spectator in a visual regime where knowledge and guilt are closely entwined.[24]

26. Tissot, *The Gardener*, c.1879, oil painting, location unknown, reproduced in James Laver, *Vulgar Society: The Romantic Career of James Tissot* (London, 1936), pl. XXII

The marginal figure of the servant in Tissot's painting of 1876–8 *The Letter* (pl. XVII) can be ignored, as the servant is by the foregrounded bourgeois figure. This young woman — magnificently dressed in mourning: widow or heiress perhaps — shreds a lover's letter in the solitude of the garden. As soon as we notice the servant however, and acknowledge that he could be watching her, we are obliged to compare our act of scrutiny with his sidelong regard. In a nineteenth-century context the picture was primarily addressed to a bourgeois audience. The class displacement heightens a sense of guilt and scandal — can the viewer be admitting to a low varlet's curiosity or desire in relation to this woman? At the same time the cloak of invisibility provided by class difference renders a consideration of this kind just on the borderline of the thinkable or the perceptible. The theme is much more explicit in the untraced painting *The Gardener*, 1879 (fig. 26), where

27. Tissot, *Croquet*, c.1878, oil on
canvas, 89.8 x 50.8 cm. Art Gallery
of Hamilton, Hamilton, Ontario,
Toronto, Gift of Dr and Mrs Basil
Bowman in memory of their
daughter Suzanne, 1965

the advancing woman with her daughter is once again placed in the security of a
domestic environment. Here, however, the foreground placement of the gardener gives him a physical presence that is hard to ignore: he takes on the scale of
the organ grinder. Moreover the garden sculpture of a goat's head artfully echoes
his bearded appearance and makes the suggestion of goatish lust inescapable.
This carries over to the signs of manual labour that replace the figure of the gardener in related works, such as the nested flower pots in *Croquet*, c.1878 (fig. 27).
The manual labour of the gardener might be thought of as relating to art in the
same way as the action of the organ grinder. All these devices make problematic
the act of depicting or viewing the upper-class beauty and, in a linked manner,

28. Tissot, *Room Overlooking the Harbour*, c.1876–8, oil on canvas, 25.4 x 33 cm. Private Collection

make problematic the act of picture-making itself. It would seem that Tissot is seeking to distance his art from the mechanical or commercialised replication of life around him. Following Derrida, one might argue that this leads him to stress the abyss between reality and representation and therefore to take the artist's step of undergoing blinding for the sake of a costly, exceptional vision.

The light reflects off one lens of the glasses of the attendant woman in *A Convalescent*, 1876 (pl. XVI). Elderly relation or chaperone, she is the blind/invisible witness to the tragic amours of the sickly reclining woman and the man whose presence is signalled by the stick and hat on the seat. Similarly the young lady in *Room Overlooking the Harbour*, 1876–8 (fig. 28) has a white-haired father or guardian who appears engrossed in his paper and is marked as blind by his monocle. He disturbs our sense of her reverie, acting as an inscription of knowledge. This latter witness is not removed in social station but his age removes him from the romantic arena and lends him that complicit detachment of experience.

The trumpeter in *Too Early* (pl. I) resembles Tissot himself a little, encouraging us to claim him as an artist in disguise. If, as I have suggested, these staring musicians are introduced as a trope and stand as a metaphor for the kind of observation carried out by the artist then we might ask whether Tissot is drawing on the notion that the artist is socially alienated and somehow déclassé. I think not, because the artist, who sees without being seen, who is invisible and yet present, is actually conforming to the behaviour of the most socially accomplished of the members of this social group. Low social standing keeps servants below the threshold of visibility in these bourgeois gatherings but the dandy who displays disdain for the mechanical interaction of vulgar society achieves a kind of invisibility by his *blasé* unconcern. Domna Stanton, in her composite study of the dandy, draws attention to 'l'air anglais' admired by commentators such as Balzac, Chapus, Barbey and Baudelaire. A certain phlegmatic apathy was recommended and a quasi-aristocratic unconcern could be manifested in an immobile rigidity of stance or in utter relaxation, both to be distinguished from the staccato, mechanical movements of the professional man. The powerful eye was frequently invoked as an attribute of the dandy who might dally with a poetic persona or take on a fearsome, demonic identity. Stanton brings together a number of examples to illustrate the potential violence of the dandy's eye, said to petrify its victim like a medusa's gaze or to mesmerise the subject with magnetic flashes.[25] Among the bystanders in the composition of *Too Early,* the languid gentleman in the doorway can be picked out as a figure who closely conforms to the dandy type. Many viewers would have recognised that the elegant figure was closely based on the caricature *A Sacrifice to the Graces* that Tissot published in *Vanity Fair* in 1872 of the artist Leighton (fig. 29).[26] *Too Early* therefore offers a depiction of musicians who indirectly refer to the artist's vision of the painter but also includes direct reference to a literal artist among the guests. The artist's vision that Tissot describes is an insider vision as much as it is the scandalised spying or leering of a social outsider.

In *Hush!* of 1875 (pl. XIII), another glittering scene where the relative insignificance of sound is played off against vital social activity of posing and observing, there is a similarly bespectacled musician at the piano. We just make out the spectacle frames and the blinding reflection on the lenses above the music stand. The huge mirror at the centre of the wall keys us in to the problematic of art's unseeing reflexivity and the potential for vision. Once again in this picture there are supplementary insider figures to align with the blinded musician.[27] In the doorway a bourgeois man stands partly hidden. All we see of him is the whited-out monocle. Just as significant is the grey-bearded man in the foreground who offers the languid detachment of the Leighton figure derived from *A Sacrifice to the Graces* in *Too Early*. He leans easily into the space of the animated young woman with a fan but does not turn to meet her eye. The one

29. Tissot, *A Sacrifice to the Graces* in *Vanity Fair*, 29 June 1872

eye that we can see is drooping and shows no pupil. Here again is the cultivated *habitué* of the upper-middle-class world who has moved beyond vain watching and reflexive signalling to the more sophisticated vision characteristic of the effaced mirror.

The scandal of the organ grinder is not, then, that he is alien but that he bears all the marks of a social insider. His deformities bear comparison with minatory goggle eyes of the victims of female wiles and social intrigue in the later series *La Femme à Paris* (1883–5). In *The Sporting Ladies* (pl. XXIII) optical prostheses and winking figures multiply alarmingly, all under the presiding presence of the pop-eyed aristocrat-acrobat. The fearful knowledge shared by artist and social initiates has marked the entire company. In *The Political Lady* (pl. XXII) the one-eyed men and women all mill around beneath a sculpture, perhaps a

30. Tissot, *The Provincial Ladies,* 1883–5, oil painting, whereabouts unknown. Reproduced from the albums of photographs Tissot kept of his own work. Private Collection

Judith and Holofernes, where the punitive slaying has been augmented by another disfigurement: the severed head has a spear through its eye.

Tissot reworked *Too Early* (pl. I) for *La Femme à Paris* series, calling the picture *The Provincial Ladies* (fig. 30). The central group is recognisable from the earlier picture, though the bearing of the young ladies is somewhat different: the young woman on the right is clearly putting on airs as she tilts her head back and the one on the left, still the most self-possessed, now directs her gaze straight out of the picture. The group of musicians has been shifted to the right-hand side of the painting. Despite the poor quality of the reproductions available we can see that the spectacled musician remains. Now he is skeletal among a decrepit ensemble, his cello bow a white blind man's stick. It is not hard to see this bow as a painter's brush or etcher's needle or, alternatively, a spear directed at the eye of his fallen colleague who has tumbled off the platform. Rather than being a piece of comic byplay this marginal incident offers us a key to the sinister workings of social rituals as they appear in this series. By this date Tissot had moved on to an exaggerated, manneristic depiction of *haut-bourgeois* echelons. The easeful visored watcher is no longer differentiated from agitated, vulgar participants because everybody participates in the augmented watching and winking, deploying their metal and glass eyepieces frantically, a cybernetic company where life and death are conjoined. The artist figure no longer stands aside, cloaked in invisibility, offering a sidelong critique. He can leap to his feet and wield the cello bow, making it a dart directed by a figure of death. The exceptional graceful figure among those awkward and over-emphatic provincials in *The Provincial Ladies* smiles, invitingly, straight at the viewer; but we realize, with a chill, that the festoons above her head resolve into the shape of a eyeless skull, grinning just as she does. We have to conclude that the enigmatic pools of her eyes promise knowledge and blindness in equal measure as we are pulled into the contagion of modernity to the tune of the blind artist musician.

I have traced a development in Tissot's work. In the earlier pieces I commented on a frisson of social unease that is conveyed to the viewer through the presence of libidinised witness figures. Figures appear on the margins who are tangential to the action and often subordinate in status. The recurrent motif of the whited-out eyes gives us a contradictory message about these figures, so that we consider them both blind and seeing. They seem to reveal an undercurrent of scandal in the otherwise polished and refined environments set out in the pictures. Their voyeuristic excitement destabilises the romantic world of love and restraint that appears in centre-stage. The circle that had seemed safe and closed harbours at least one contaminating intruder. The raw presence of such figures allows us to impute baser thoughts to the central protagonists. In his later *La Femme à Paris* series it appears that the hinted malaise has developed into a social plague. Scandal is no longer a well-hidden secret, it is flagrantly acknowledged by all the participants in the scenes. The special witness is now seen to be in open collusion with the social initiates. Social recognition, sexual pleasure and death are being dealt to all and sundry. Drawing on Derrida's account of the traditional association of the artist with a blind seer I have made a case for the identification of the 'special witness' figures with the artist himself. The strange and eccentric work from 1878, *The Organ Grinder,* works through some of these themes in a most explicit manner. For once in Tissot's work the socially marginal figure is allowed to stand in the foreground and the paradoxes of academic virtuosity and intrusive seduction on the part of the artist are explored. Tissot does not allow this to be a comfortable self-presentation. The gross and filthy physical presence of the organ grinder is inescapable. This essay has tried to show that his presence haunts much of Tissot's pictorial output.

My thanks to Katharine Lochnan of the Art Gallery of Ontario for inviting me to deliver a version of this paper in October 1996 at the symposium 'Unmasking Tissot'. I am very grateful to Gail Day for making valuable suggestions at the draft stage of this essay.

1. Michel Foucault, *Discipline and Punish: The Birth of the Prison* (1975), trans. Alan Sheridan (Harmondsworth: Peregrine, 1979). See also discussions in Hal Foster, ed., *Vision and Visuality* (Seattle: Dia Art Foundation, Bay Press, 1988); Martin Jay, *Downcast Eyes* (Berkeley and Los Angeles: University of California Press, 1993); and D.M. Levin, ed., *Modernity and the Hegemony of Vision* (Berkeley and Los Angeles: University of California Press, 1993).

2. For example, drawing on Lacan and Althusser, Jaqueline Rose, *Sexuality in the Field of Vision* (London: New Left Books, 1986); or the anti-Foucauldian argument of Joan Copjec, *Read My Desire: Lacan Against the Historicists* (Cambridge, MA: MIT Press, 1994).

3. W. Benjamin, *Charles Baudelaire: A Lyric Poet in the Era of High Capitalism* (1935–9) trans. H. Zohn (London: Verso/New Left Books, 1973).

4. See R. Sennett, *The Fall of Public Man* (London: Faber & Faber / New York: Knopf, 1986).

5. Wentworth cites Champfleury's joking inclusion of the figurines in the romantic dramas to be woven between Tissot's pictures in 1868: 'Ce petit drame amoreux m'intéresse. Il y a sans doute un jaloux dans la chambre à côté. La jaloux est un mandragore japonaise en bronze qui fait vis-à-vis à des fleurs japonaises. Il ne doit point avoir connaissance du billet,' Champfleury, *La vie parisienne* (1868), quoted M. Wentworth, *James Tissot* (Oxford: Clarendon Press, 1984), 72.

6. The jacket has a V-shaped back panel descending from the yoke, and side panels that form the skirt, opening in a vent to the small of his back: one sharp point emphasised, the other more tentatively sketched in, where it crosses the garden railings. The left hand side of the jacket has fallen quite open. We see the edge of the lapel at the top of the organ, and the bottom corner of his coat against the darker wood of the organ back. But the bottom of the coat, in particular, seems to function as a continuation of the barrel-organ cover.

7. H. Mayhew, *London Labour and the London Poor* (1861–2, repr. New York: Dover, 1968), 3:150–1.

8. Mayhew alludes to Hogarth: 'The well-known engraving by Hogarth, of "the enraged musician," is an illustration of the persecutions inflicted in olden times by this class of street performers; and in the illustrations by modern caricaturists we have

had numerous proofs, that up to the present time the nuisance has not abated.', *London Labour*, 159. Lewis Carroll wrote comic verses on the hurdy-gurdy player, C.L. Dodgson, 'Those Horrid Hurdy-Gurdies!', *College Rhymes*, 1860–1.

9. Nancy Marshall, '"Transcripts of Modern Life": The London Pictures of James Tissot 1871–1882', Ph.D. thesis, Yale University, Department of History of Art, 1997.

10. 'Talent Appreciated', *Punch*, 27 April 1869, 168. The caption reads: *'Jemima Cook.* OH MARY! HOW *WELL* HE PLAYS!" *Mary Parlourmaid.* "*DOESN'T* HE!! SUCH *EXPRESSION!!!?*" I would like to thank Kathy Lochnan for bringing this image to my attention and pointing out that Tissot and Du Maurier kept up their association from student days in Paris. See also the related cartoon *Punch*, 16 January 1869, 12, where the maid, Susan, is on the area steps but still behind the railings, touching hands with an amorous bread delivery man.

11. The man interviewed by Mayhew, 'Italian with Monkey', seems to be responding to an assertion made by Mayhew when he says: 'I don't know dat de monkey was train to go down de area and steal a de silver spoons out of de kitchen. Dey would be great fool to tell dat', *London Labour*, 179.

12. 'The Monkey-Jacket' in James M'Levy [MacLevy] (Edinburgh Police detective Staff), *The Sliding Scale of Life or Thirty Years' Observations of Falling Men and Women In Edinburgh* (Edinburgh: Nimmo, 1861). The monkey is lodged with a house of prostitutes and a parallel is drawn between their gaudy silks and satins and magenta ribbons and the fine scarlet coat and silk sash of the monkey. The prostitutes are referred to as 'Mrs. Gibbs' "female chimpanzees"' completing the chain of association between theft, organ grinding and lasciviousness.

13. David Trotter, *Circulation: Defoe, Dickens and the Economies of the Novel* (Basingstoke: Macmillan, 1988); Catherine Gallagher, 'The body versus the social body in the works of Thomas Malthus and Henry Mayhew' in Catherine Gallagher and Thomas Laqueur, eds., *The Making of the Modern Social Body* (Berkeley, Los Angeles, London: University of California Press, 1987).

14. Mayhew, *London Labour*, 179–80.

15. For example, Frederick Yeates Hurlstone, *A Young Savoyard*, n.d., Birmingham City Art Gallery; J.C. Horsley, *The Italian Hurdygurdy Boy*, n.d., Phillips' sale, 4–5 December 1996 (thanks to Liz Prettejohn for locating these works). Alexander Mosses, *The Savoyard*, c.1832, Walker Art Gallery Liverpool, makes a comic comparison between the hurdy-gurdy boy and his monkey.

16. Wentworth, *James Tissot: Catalogue Raisonné of His Prints* (Minneapolis: Minneapolis Institute of Arts, 1978); Katherine A. Lochnan, *The Etchings of James McNeill Whistler* (New Haven and London: Yale University Press, 1984); W. Misfeldt, *J.J. Tissot: Prints from the Gotlieb Collection* (Memphis: Dixon Gallery and Gardens, 1991).

17. Stephen Edwards, 'Factories of Meaning: the Industries of Photography in Britain 1835–1880', Ph.D. Thesis, University of Leeds, Department of Fine Art, 1996, passim. I appreciate Steve Edwards's ongoing advice concerning hurdy-gurdies and other matters.

18. Mayhew, *London Labour*, 159.

19. The *Art-Journal* critic described the 'somewhat vacant expressions' of the fashionably dressed ladies and gentlemen (*Art-Journal*, 1873, 238); the *Athenaeum* critic alludes to the father's expression: 'one face shows the wonder and amusement of the owner at being there at all' (*Athenaeum*, 10 May 1873, 605).

20. There was a comment on the social premium attaching to the door-post position (*Athenaeum*, 10 May 1873, 605).

21. J. Derrida, *Memoirs of the Blind: the self-portrait and other ruins*, (1990), trans. Pascale-Anne Brault and Michael Naas (Chicago: Chicago University Press, 1993), 57.

22. *Memoirs of the Blind*, 63.

23. He goes on to make a connection with Hoffmann's tale of automata and blinding, *The Sandman* and Freud's essay of 1919 'The Uncanny' considering the fear of castration and the linked fear deriving from the penalties of the *lex talionis*, which decrees punishment by blinding when the eyes are the source of guilt, *Memoirs of the Blind*, 62–3, 63 n.59.

24. It is interesting to compare the argument developed by Mieke Bal in *Reading Rembrandt: Beyond the Word–Image Opposition* (Cambridge: Cambridge University Press, 1991), ch. 8, 'Blindness as Insight: The Powers of Horror'. I am grateful to Joanna Woodall for pointing out the parallel.

25. Domna Stanton, *The Aristocrat As Art* (New York: Columbia University Press, 1980), 150–4, 165. 'The signs of the dandy's enormous power are invariably localised in his eyes, the mirror of his soul. In *Les Diaboliques* [by Barbey] the eyes of the Vicomte de Brassard "didn't bother to scrutinise, they penetrated". This phallic eye, which goes far beyond the *honnête homme*'s effortless penetration cuts through the receiver's surface like "a drawn sword" rapes him/her.' I am grateful to Katie Scott for drawing my attention to this book which compares French nineteenth-century constructions of the dandy with the *honnête homme* of the seventeenth century.

26. *Vanity Fair*, 29 June 1872, 'A Sacrifice to the Graces'.

27. There has been some debate over whether the picture contains a number of portraits. The musicians in this case may be intended to be read as members of the social circle rather than hired entertainers. It was suggested in *The Times* (29 May 1875, 6) that the violinist was based on Wilhemine Neruda (Lady Hallé). Other suggested identifications include the pianist, Sir Julius Benedict, and artists Guiseppe de Nittis and Ferdinand Heilbuth in the doorway. See Wentworth, *James Tissot*, 117–8; Christopher Wood, *Tissot* (London: Weidenfeld & Nicolson, 1986), 69; Russell Ash, *James Tissot* (London: Pavilion, 1992), plate 22.

Decent Exposure: Status, Excess,
the World of Haute Couture, and Tissot

Edward Maeder

IN THE MID-1930s, when the young James Laver was charged with writing about
Tissot, he was hard pressed to produce 20,000 words and much of his information was garnered from the artist's friends: his researches resulted in *Vulgar Society,
The Romantic Career of James Tissot 1836–1902*, published in London in 1936. Longtime Keeper of the Print Collection at the Victoria and Albert Museum, Laver is
considered today the father of costume studies. It is hardly surprising, given the
dearth of information available at the time about Tissot's private life, that Laver
approached the artist's work largely from the perspective of his own specialty:

> With woman, with the fashionable woman, Tissot was always preoccupied,
> at least until he abandoned mundane painting altogether. He excelled in
> depicting the *minutiae* of her toilet, the set of a hat, the fall of a flounce, even
> the material of which her clothes were made. No painter ever took more
> pains in the dressmaking of his figures than Tissot, and this not only provides
> the chief interest of his work today, but enables his canvases to be dated with
> an exactitude impossible in the case of painters greater, or less exact.[1]

While his book was a milestone in Tissot studies, the emphasis which Laver
placed on costume in Tissot's work led a generation of art historians to dismiss his
works as mere fashion plates. Now, ironically, just as Tissot is being reinstated as
an artist worthy of serious consideration, the costume subtext, essential to the
decoding of his ambiguous narratives, is becoming increasingly difficult for
modern eyes to interpret. We know that Tissot's seductive surfaces conceal
hidden meanings, and that his costumes and attractive surfaces are a veneer. To
understand his narratives, we need to learn how to decode both dress and gesture.

There are a number of important factors that influence fashion. In Tissot's day,
economics, industrial production, trade agreements, scientific developments in
the textile industries, the rise of *haute couture* in Paris, and the Aesthetic Movement in England all conspired to shape the world in which he lived and worked.

Born into a family supported by a linen-draper father and a mother who had
been a successful milliner, Jacques-Joseph Tissot was surrounded by a world of
textiles, and was closely attuned to the physical characteristics of fabrics and the
design of hats.[2] The city of Nantes, where he grew up, had been an important

textile centre as early as the sixteenth century, and large amounts of capital were invested in reviving that industry in the eighteenth century. Of special importance was the production of printed cottons and linens which were often blatant copies of Indian and English goods. The city was a rival of Jouey-en-Josas, birthplace of the highly successful and fashionable 'toile de Jouey'.

It is sometimes difficult for twentieth-century historians to comprehend the continued and important impact of the textile industry on the economy of Europe and, in particular, of France. Jean-Baptiste Colbert (1619–83), who brought skilled lace makers to France from Italy,[3] and who established the Gobelins Tapestry Works, understood the connection between fashion and finance in the seventeenth century. It was during the reign of Louis XIV that the patterns of taste established by the court led to French supremacy in this field,[4] a state which France has maintained almost unbroken to the present day. Louis XV kept his courtiers in check, and financially stretched, by requiring elaborate, expensive, and constantly changing dress at court. This kept them under his watchful eye and prevented the plotting which might have occurred had they been permitted to return to their *chateaux*.

The importance of coal and iron to the industrial development of Europe, and the comparative lack of such raw materials in France, was a major factor in the development of luxury industries there. Following the Napoleonic Era, industrial competition with England, Germany and the United States became more and more difficult. In France, coal was scarce and of poor quality.[5] The only way to protect the slowly growing industry was through high tariffs and, in most cases, a total prohibition on imports, until the Cobden treaty between Britain and France of 1860 which marked the beginnings of free trade between the two countries. The terms of the agreement sacrificed French heavy industrial production in favour of luxury goods, particularly wine and silk. The production of French silk, and the marketing of French fashion, became a national industry.

The best way to market French silks was by displaying them on the female form. Since the Middle Ages a man's wealth had been gauged by the dress of his wife. Throughout much of the eighteenth century elaborately woven, embroidered, painted and printed silks were broadly displayed on the extremely wide skirts created by the *panniers* or side hoops worn by the fashionable. This unnatural fashion, which extended the width of the lower part of the body to as much as two metres, continued in formal court wear as late as 1800 but the general trend towards the end of the eighteenth and the beginning of the nineteenth century was to a more slender style. In the first decades of Queen Victoria's reign

31. Tissot, *The Foursome*, c.1870, oil on canvas, 114.3 x 142.2 cm. Whereabouts unknown, photograph courtesy Christopher Wood, London

there was a revival of broadly expanding skirts and this ubiquitous shape proceeded to invade every corner of refined and even unrefined society. The fashion-conscious Tissot accurately recorded contemporary dress, including the fashionable hoop skirt seen in the delightful *A Luncheon*, c.1868,[6] although by the mid-1860s the influence of the British Pre-Raphaelites, who were opposed to the artificiality of the hoop, was being felt in both artistic and fashionable circles.

In the years preceding the invention of the cage crinoline in 1856, the 'eight layers of refinement'[7] which separated the well-brought-up young woman from the outside world included a chemise, corset, corset-cover, crescent-shaped pad worn at the back of the waist, and at least four or five petticoats. Only the outermost petticoat should have been trimmed with lace as it might be seen while walking or getting into or out of a carriage. Lace or embroidery on inner layers was considered inappropriate as it implied that they might be seen. This 'naughty' method of revealing undergarments continued to be considered a form of *risqué* behaviour. In *The Foursome*, 1870 (fig. 31), not only is a sizeable

32. Tissot, *Still on Top*, c.1874, oil on canvas, 87.6 x 53.3 cm. Auckland Art Gallery Toi o Tamaki, Auckland, New Zealand, Gift of Viscount Leverhulme, 1921

portion of the bosom visible but the delicately edged outer petticoat is also in view.

During the late 1860s silk petticoats became a new source of pride. Some women of the lower classes pinned newspaper over their linen petticoats so that, when walking, the sound of the rustling paper under their dresses could be mistaken for that of a silk petticoat. High style was not only visually aesthetic, it created its own music: the rustle of spring became the rustle of silk. The successful rendering of crisp silks such as those seen in *Still on Top*, c.1874 (fig. 32) enabled contemporary viewers to imagine the soft sounds they produced.

The predominance of France in the production of luxury goods was greater in the nineteenth than in any previous century.[8] Paris had long been the centre of international fashion. New styles were recorded in fashion plates which were imitated all over the world as quickly as the originals appeared on the streets of Paris. With the revival of interest in the French rococo led by the brothers Goncourt, a fascination with all things *dix-huitième siècle* piqued the interest of the newly rich, upwardly mobile, industrial class, affecting fashion as well as social etiquette.

Graceful physical movement, and the apparent ease with which it was accomplished, was one of the leading social graces developed in the Age of Enlightenment. As the merchant class became wealthier, it aspired to the superficial luxuries of the nobility, forcing the latter to adopt new methods of keeping newcomers at bay. Dancing masters employed by the aristocracy developed new and complex forms of movement, epitomized in dance, which required years of training to accomplish. Despite wars and revolutions, this bulwark of sophistication continued throughout the nineteenth century. The rococo revival gave it new impetus and power.

When Tissot registered at the Louvre as a student in 1858, he stepped directly into a Paris flooded with shops and women obsessed with the pursuit of elegance. In that year the former seller of fine fabrics in London, Charles Frederick Worth, together with his partner Otto Boberg, moved to Paris and opened Worth & Boberg at 7, rue de la Paix, with a staff of twenty seamstresses.[9] The glittering court of Napoleon III, presided over by the beautiful Empress Eugénie, supported French luxury goods, among them high fashion. Worth revolutionized the snug, cozy world of the French *modiste*. He realized that the only way to succeed was through royal patronage. In 1860 he dispatched his wife, Marie, with an album of design sketches to Princess Pauline von Metternich. Well known for her taste and influence, she soon fell under the spell of M. Worth and became the first courtier to wear a Worth gown. It was through this connection that the Empress Eugénie herself became a devoted patron of Worth.

In the 1860s the empress, who much preferred light and airy tulle, wore heavy brocaded silk to promote the French silk industry which was vital to the country's financial stability.[10] She referred to these as her 'political dresses'[11] and wore them until, like Tissot, she fled to England at the end of the Franco-Prussian war. Tissot's most prestigious portrait commission, *The Empress Eugénie and the Prince Impérial in the Grounds of Camden Place, Chislehurst*, c.1874 (fig. 33), depicts the widowed empress, dressed in mourning, standing beside her son and living in reduced circumstances with the shadowy remnants of her court.

33. Tissot, *The Empress Eugénie and the Prince Impérial in the Grounds of Camden Place, Chislehurst*, c.1874, oil on canvas, 106.6 x 152.4 cm. Château de Compiègne, photograph courtesy RMN – Daniel Arnaudet

Neither war, upheaval, nor the increased industrial power of foreign competitors could keep the French for long from their preoccupation with luxury. Worth created dazzling dresses in the spirit of the rococo, reflecting the luxury and frivolity of the *ancien régime*. Worth did not 'make dresses', he 'composed toilettes'. He used this term so much in the 1860s that it entered the vernacular and summarized his superior approach to dress design.[12] He adjusted his dresses on their wearers, changing this, changing that: in short the last tweak from the master and creator was indispensable.[13] Diana deMarly in her book on Worth states that 'shirred tulle, pleated tulle, draped tulle, puffed tulle, and layers of silk tulle upon silk tulle, were all employed as Worth conjured up these *nuages fragiles*. And what a gift to the portrait painter such gowns were. No need to labor for days on end painstakingly recording every leaf in a patterned brocade, or the *minutiae* of embroidery, but let the brush swoop across the canvas in great sweeps of translucent cloud, for they allowed for a much freer style'.[14] Dresses of the kind that Worth made famous can be found in numerous paintings by Tissot, the most spectacular example being the pink confection worn by *The Political Lady*, 1883–5 (pl. XXII).

Tissot depicted dress with such accuracy that these fashion details can often be used to date the works, as in the case of *Portrait of Mlle L.L. . .* , 1864 (pl. XIX) which was exhibited in the Paris Salon of 1864. The sitter wears a white blouse with a 'mannish' collar, highlighted with a jet brooch containing a cross and, perhaps, amber ear drops. The rather casual and uncontrolled hair indicates that she is unmarried. The plain black silk taffeta dress was then the height of fashion. The slight flattening at the front of the skirt with pleats continuing on both sides of the high waist sounded the death knell of the fully rounded crinoline. His sitter has, in fact, removed her crinoline 'cage' in order to drape her ample skirts over the book-laden table. According to Mme. Carette, lady-in-waiting to the Empress Eugénie, 'when in 1864 I arrived at the court, scarcely any hoops were worn, whilst the round and narrow skirts permitted one to go out without causing obstruction in the streets and catastrophes in the apartments.'[15]

Short jackets or 'vests' of the type see in *Portrait of Mlle L.L. . .* became popular in the late 1850s and were based on the 'Zouave' jacket, which was often red and sometimes boasted elaborate black braid trim. The jacket had military sleeves which were cut in two pieces and shaped in a curve to the arm, and the trim, or *passementerie*, consisted of a heavy woven braid with attached pompoms. Today it would be referred to as 'ball fringe' and associated with curtains, not without reason, for it can be seen in the background decorating the curtains and valance. In the spring of 1868, *Harper's Bazaar* announced 'the death of the crinoline.'[16] This newly established fashion magazine, which appeared simultaneously throughout Europe and the Americas, made changing modes in dress truly international.

Tissot not only depicted contemporary fashion, he also recorded antiquarian trends. *By the Fireside*, c.1870–1 (fig. 34) reflects Tissot's interest in the rococo revival. Tissot appears to have acquired 'old clothes' as studio props and to have used them in combination with modern elements to create an historical ambiance. Such items were easily purchased at the Marché au Puce and other venues in Paris. The rich brown and grey overdress is an original French Directoire period costume made during the 1790s. The black straw hat and the lace-edged *fichu*, wrapped over the upper arm and trailing down behind, also appear to be original eighteenth-century accessories.[17] The hairstyle is taken from fashion plates of the 1770s. The original dress consisted of two pieces: a type of coat known as a 'carrico', and a striped under-dress. The fullness of the fabric which falls from the back of the shoulders of the 'carrico' is gathered into pleats and held in place with a broad ribbon around the waist. The closely fitted

34. Tissot, *By the Fireside*,
c.1870–1, oil on canvas, 114.3 x
142.2 cm. Whereabouts
unknown, photograph courtesy
The Edward P. Taylor Reference
Library and Archives, Art
Gallery of Ontario, Toronto

sleeve with stripes on the straight of the grain, and the cuff of carefully pleated
and stitched self-fabric, are typical of eighteenth-century tailoring. The fabric
was woven using printed threads, in a technique called *chiné à la branche*.[18] From
the eleventh century, the irridescent fabric used in the overdress was created by
using a warp of one colour and a weft of another. The warp used here is in stripes
of dark gray and very light brown while the weft is gray. Over the centuries silks
woven using this technique enjoyed many revivals: one of the most important
took place at the end of the eighteenth century. Popular in the 1780s for both
dress and interior fabrics, the result resembles shadows. In the 1860s and 1870s
this technique enjoyed a revival in the weaving of ribbons.

The Foursome (see fig. 31 on p. 79), exhibited in the Salon of 1870, features
this dress once again. Virtually all the costume items and accessories appear to be
authentically eighteenth-century. The man on the right wears an embroidered

waistcoat of cream silk: in Paris during the 1780s a stylish gentleman might have had at least three hundred of these in his wardrobe. They were pre-embroidered on lengths of silk and sent to tailors to be custom made. The waistcoat seen here dates from the 1780s and was probably of the pre-embroidered type.

After moving to London in 1871, Tissot reflected both contemporary and archaising fashion trends. *The Farewell* of 1871 (see fig. 6 on p. 14) is a British 'period' piece incorporating some original costumes. The slender silhouette of the lady and the high wrapped stock collar and broad waistcoat lapels of the gentleman evoke the Regency period. Ladies' black-netted mitts were popular during the 1840s: however thin, they give the appearance of propriety, although the fine black thread lace is merely a symbolic barrier. Designed to set off the paleness of genteel hands, their web-like construction contributes to the illusion that the wearer was delicate (although they were in fact quite sturdy). The wearing of such accessories would have suggested to a contemporary audience that they were made by the lady, or her mother, indicating that she either comes from or has aspirations to the middle or upper class, since skill with the needle was one of the most important refinements of the nineteenth-century gentlewoman. However, the sleeve has been pushed up from the wrist to expose uncovered flesh: such exposure during in daytime suggests that she may be a woman of questionable character. The man is holding his gloves in his left hand; this permits the intimate contact of flesh-on-flesh with his right hand, which would have been thought shocking in the most rigid social circles.

One of the more puzzling tendencies to be found in Tissot's works is the re-use of costume, not only in different works but even in the same work. The mitts, hat and the ruffled silk wrap found in *The Farewell* are identical to those worn in *An Interesting Story* of 1872 and *Bad News (The Parting)* of 1872.[19] In *Too Early*, 1873 (pl. I) the three gowns inspired by Worth — the yellow on the left, the white at right of centre and the white worn by the woman on the right leaning against the doorway — are basically the same dress. These rococo inspirations, with their shirred lower skirts and clusters of vertical knife pleating, are as soft and delicate as their wearers would like to be perceived. The black or red velvet ribbons worn about the neck refer to the period *après la déluge,* when parties were given by 'survivors' of the French Revolution who frequently wore red or black silk ribbons around their necks to symbolize the guillotine from which they had been spared.

The dress found in *A Luncheon* (1868) is found again in *The Foursome* (c.1870), and there is a similar parallel in the dresses in *The Return from the*

35. Tissot, *Girl in an Armchair: The Convalescent*, oil on wood, 37.5 x 45.7 cm. Art Gallery of Ontario, Toronto, Gift of R.B.F. Barr, Esq., Q.C

Boating Trip (1873) and *Still on Top*, c.1874 (see fig. 32 on p. 80).[20] The black bonnet with striped ribbon found in *A Luncheon* reappears in a number of paintings including *Young Lady with a Fan*, c.1870–1, and *On the River*, 1871, and *Young Lady in a Boat*, 1870 (pl. XIV).[21] All three paintings feature a cashmere shawl that appears frequently in other works. This constant repetition may indicate that costume was, in fact, of lesser rather than greater importance to Tissot. Repetition may have increased the artist's facility in rendering a particular garment thereby simplifying the creation of the painting as a 'commercial' product. It may also have allowed him to focus both his own attention and that of his viewers on the complex, ambiguous narratives which are the focus of his work.

Dress may contribute to the ambiguous nature of the narrative. *Girl in an Armchair*, 1870–2 (fig. 35) features an attractive young woman reclining outside a conservatory, a place associated in the contemporary imagination with scenes of seduction (see Darby's essay in this collection). Her loose hair and semirecumbent pose bring to mind the temptresses depicted by the Pre-Raphaelite artists Dante Gabriel Rossetti and Edward Burne-Jones. The black *soutache* braiding and black seams of her dress, which stand out against the sparkling white ground, find their origins in central European folk embroidery and were frequently illustrated in fashion journals of the day. Such a dress can be read either as a fashion statement or as the last stage of mourning. Correct mourning dress, and all the complicated rules which governed it, was strictly adhered to in England, particularly following the death of the Prince Consort in 1861. While the black jet cross suspended from a black ribbon around her neck would be appropriate as mourning jewelry, it frequently appears in other paintings by Tissot.

The model does not appear to be wearing a corset: this may be a reflection of the tenets of the British dress-reform movement, which advocated freedom of movement and pioneered the removal of supporting undergarments. Dress reform had been an undercurrent in Britain since the late 1830s, but it was not until the 1870s that woman began to organize societies dedicated to this end. Doctors and scientists joined the groups for and against the reform and by the time the International Health exhibition took place in London in 1884, the lines were firmly drawn.[22] The Pre-Raphaelite artists, chief among them Rossetti and Burne-Jones, designed loose dresses based on medieval prototypes for their models and mistresses.

The socially ambitious women who populated the paintings of Tissot show-cased the 'acceptable' styles promoted in the fashion journals of the day. However, by the middle of the 1870s aesthetic and artistic dress was embraced by Worth himself, allowing him 'full expression of his artistic principles[;] . . . once Worth gave the innovation his blessing, this was a directive that it was safe for women to wear it'.[23] The dress allowance of an upper-middle-class woman was commensurate with her husband's income. In 1871 M. Worth's gowns ranged from £40 to as much as £5,000 each, while at the same period a professional man earned about £500 a year.[24] Lesser versions of Worth gowns, however, were available for a fraction of the cost of an original, and even Worth admitted that a woman could dress fashionably in Paris for £60 a year.

Tissot's women were not adherents of dress reform and the movement does not appear to have crossed the Channel; French women aspired to being as elegant and alluring as possible, and viewed the styles espoused by the dress-reform movement as ugly. For almost four hundred years corsets were considered indispensable to shape the female form into the aesthetic ideal of any given period. As the nineteenth century progressed, corsets became more and more complex; the industry employed tens of thousands of workers and by the end of the century Paris was producing five million corsets annually. The wasp waists of the corseted models in *The Artist's Ladies*, 1883–5 (fig. 38 on p. 102) indicate that, unlike the wives of many English painters, the French artists' ladies were wearing the most restrictive and fashionable corset of the day.

The complex underpinnings not only included the corset but other 'beauty aids' such as the wire bustle cage which produced the necessary shape for the popular bustle dress in the early 1870s and again in the mid- to late 1880s. We find it difficult to imagine how ladies were able to manoeuvre in these complicated and difficult dresses. The ability to wear fashionable dress properly could elevate them to a higher social plane, while the inability to do so quickly gave away the *parvenue*. True ladies were supposed to appear in these outlandish and difficult dresses as if they were perfectly natural forms of attire. The bustle dress is found in Tissot's painting *The Gallery of HMS Calcutta (Portsmouth)*, c.1877 (pl. X). The gowns depicted here make this one of Tissot's most sensuous creations; the fabrics are extremely sheer and, as was often the case, lined with pale pink silk taffeta to give the illusion of flesh. The appearance of the plunging back was probably created by inserting a panel of silk into the back of the dress. The form-fitting, 'princess dress' pushed all extravagance and decoration to the back, where it cascaded in a train which resembled a peacock's tail, and dragged along the ground. Contemporary ladies' manuals recommended that upon entering a home for the first time one should carefully observe the floor lest an unseen nail or other object should catch the train and thus cause embarrassment.[25]

Ease and assurance of movement had long been an important barometer of breeding and sophistication. Lord Chesterfield, when writing to his son in 1751, stressed the importance of his 'air and address'. He placed special emphasis on movement: 'Take particular care that the motions of your hands and arms be easy and graceful; for the genteelness of a man consists more in them than in any thing else, especially in his dancing.'[26] Elaborate costumes have always made movement difficult. In *Boarding the Yacht*, 1873 (fig. 20 on p. 54) the artist has chosen difficult physical feats for the ladies which they perform with a degree of awkwardness that reveals their inexperience. Negotiating narrow stairs on a ship is difficult at the best of times, but when trussed and bundled in acres of silk ruffles, skirts, overskirts, shawls and hats, mountaineering techniques are called for. At a time when it was considered vulgar to display any part of the leg, the very act of walking up or down such staircases increased the risk of such exposure.

And there is indeed a *risqué* element which underlies this precarious exercise which is as much about social as physical mobility.

While costume and body language hint at economic and social status, costume accessories provide clues to interpreting the narrative. Although the works themselves are mute, signals may be given, received, or missed by the *dramatis personae*. Flirtatious messages were sent in Tissot's day using flowers, fans, parasols, handkerchiefs and gloves. This was commonplace in court life in eighteenth-century France. The codes probably changed from hour to hour and from day to day so that only those of the innermost social circle were privy to the latest gestures and their meaning. Flowers have a long history in the rites of courtship. In the fifteenth century the 'maiden' was often depicted holding a rose or a carnation. According to tradition, after the flower-carrying betrothed met his *fiancée* for the first time, she was allowed to place the flower somewhere on her person. Her choice of position would indicate her response to the previously unseen marriage partner. If she hid it in an intimate place, it was the duty of the gentleman to find it, and a carefully placed flower on or about the lady's bosom had a long and gallant history! The 'lady' on the far left in Tissot's *The Foursome* (fig. 31 on p. 79) has added a large pink flower to her *décolleté*.

The rococo revival brought with it an obsession with fans.[27] In 1877 Daniel R. Shafer of Baltimore published a manual *Secrets of Life Unveiled*, which included a wide variety of information about etiquette and social graces. He suggested ways of sending messages using 'handkerchief flirtations', 'glove flirtations', 'parasol flirtations' and 'fan flirtations'.[28] For example, the codes for fan flirtation was as follows:

Carrying in right hand / You are too willing
Carrying in right hand in front of face / Follow me
Carrying in left hand / Desirous of an acquaintance
Closing it / I wish to speak to you
Drawing it across the forehead / We are watched
Drawing across the cheek / I love you
Drawing across the eyes / I am sorry
Drawing through the hand / I hate you
Dropping / We will be friends
Fanning fast / I am engaged
Fanning slow / I am married
Letting it rest on right cheek / Yes

Letting it rest on left cheek / No
Open and shut / You are cruel
Open wide / Wait for me
Shut / I have changed
Placing it on the right ear / You have changed
Twirling in left hand / I love another
With handle to lips / Kiss me!

And for parasol flirtations:

Carrying it elevated in the left hand / Desiring acquaintance
Carrying it elevated in right hand / You are too willing
Carrying it closed in left hand / Meet on the first crossing
Carrying it closed in right hand but the side / Follow me
Carrying it over the right shoulder / You can speak to me
Carrying it over the left shoulder / You are too cruel
Closing up / I wish to speak to you
Dropping it / I love you
End of tips to lips / Do you love me?
Folding it up / Get rid of your company
Letting it rest on the right cheek / Yes
Letting it rest on the left cheek / No
Striking it on the hand / I am very displeased
Swinging it to and fro by he handle on left side / I am engaged
Swinging it to and fro by the handle on the right side / I am married
Tapping the chin gently / I am in love with another
Twirling it around / Be careful; we are watched
Using it as a fan / Introduce me to your company
With handle to lips / Kiss me

Tissot frequently employed fans and parasols as props in such a way as to draw attention to them. Using the above key to parasol flirtations one might speculate that the lady on the left side in *Portsmouth Dockyard (How Happy I Could be with Either)*, 1877 (pl. XI) holding a closed parasol in her right hand, is signaling 'follow me' to the smartly dressed officer, while the woman on the right who sits back, annoyed, signals to her friend by holding an open parasol held in her right hand 'you are too willing'. Tissot would have been well aware, as would his audience, of the existence of such silent dialogues.

As Tissot left London for Paris in 1882, there occurred a milestone in the history of dress: the world began flocking to the newly established Jaegers in London. Dr. Gustave Jaeger had come from Stuttgart, Germany, the previous year to establish his 'Sanitary Natural Woollen System' in England.[29] He expounded the virtues of pure, undyed wool and its beneficial effects. There was a great deal of interest in this new health craze and two of its earliest proponents were Oscar Wilde and George Bernard Shaw. Wool shoes, wool corsets and even woollen lace on wool dresses were advocated by the renowned doctor. When first introduced the clothing was expensive but the impact it had on future generations, and the profound belief in the efficacy of wool against the skin, lives on today in many northern countries.

Fashion remained a powerful engine during the second half of the nineteenth century and the use of filmy and stylish fabrics was not abandoned for reasons of health, art or reason. The newly established class of wealthy American industrialists insisted that their wives be dressed by Worth and other Paris designers. France continued to lead the world in fashion and design excellence. The small French ribbon and silk shop of the type depicted in *The Shop Girl*, 1883–5 (pl. XXI) continued to thrive as it had done for at least two hundred years, and the women of Paris, be they wives or mistresses, continued to set the standard, however defined.

We are what we wear. We always have been and we always will be. It is in unspoken messages that we communicate much about who we are. We think our clothes cover us when, in fact, they reveal our true selves. As the costume historian, Stella Mary Newton, observed: 'our clothing provides a deadly means of communication as, silently, we inspect one another.'[30] We continue that inspection as we search the works of artists such as Tissot, for clues to unlock some of the hidden meanings implicit in his female forms encased in that second skin we call fashion.

1. J. Laver, *Vulgar Society: The Romantic Career of James Tissot, 1836–1902* (London: Constable and Co. Ltd., 1936), 10–11.

2. Krystyna Matyjaszkiewicz, 'Costume in Tissot's Pictures', in *James Tissot*, exh. cat. (London: Phaidon Press and Barbican Art Gallery, 1984), 64.

3. S. M. Levy, *Lace, A History* (London: Victoria and Albert Museum and W.S. Maney & Son Ltd., 1983), 36, and 41, n.29. Italian law was so severe that it imprisoned relatives of defectors and even sentenced to death lace makers who offered their services and expertise to a foreign government.

4. M. Von Boehm, *Modes and Manners in the Eighteenth Century* (Philadelphia: J.B. Lippincott Co., 1937), 34.

5. D.W. Brogan, *The Development of Modern France [1870–1939]* (London: Hamish Hamilton, 1967), 404.

6. *The Luncheon* is reproduced in Christopher Wood, *Tissot: The Life and Work of Jacques Joseph Tissot 1836–1902* (London: Weidenfeld and Nicolson, 1986), pl. 36.

7. C.W. Cunnington, *The Perfect Lady* (London: Max Parrish & Co. Ltd., 1948), 27.

8. Brogan, *Development of Modern France*, 411.

9. D. de Marly, *Worth, Father of Haute Couture* (London: Elm Tree Books, 1980), 31. Otto Boberg, born in Sweden in 1821 had studied art and worked in the clothing trades. He had more experience than Worth and had the ability to draw and sketch on paper.

10. For her journey to Egypt for the opening of the Suez canal in 1869, the empress took 250 gowns, the most important of which were certainly those of Worth. O. Fischel and M. von Boehn, *Modes and Manners of the Nineteenth Century, as Represented in the Pictures and Engravings of the Time*, trans. M. Edwards, 3 vols. (London: Dent, 1909), 3:97.

11. Mme. Carette, *My Mistress, the Empress Eugénie; or, Court Life at the Tuileries* (London: Deal and Sons, 1899), 178. The Empress often wore thick material of Lyons manufacture in order to encourage commerce in silks, Passementeries and lace.

12. Carette, *My Mistress*, 109.

13. deMarly, *Worth*, 108.

14. deMarly, *Worth*, 113.

15. Carette, *My Mistress*, 175.

16. *Harper's Bazaar* (1868), 384. A cartoon appeared on 11 April containing a tombstone and announcing the 'Rise and Fall of Crinoline'.

17. Edward Maeder, *An Elegant Art: Fashion and Fantasy in the Eighteenth Century* (New York: Harry N. Abrams. Inc. and the Los Angeles County Museum of Art, 1983), 148, no. 28, pl. 51.

18. P. Fayard, 'Elaboration et fabrication des tissus chinés à la branche' *Bulletin de Laison du CIETA*, (1983, nos. 57–58), 61–76.

19. Wood, *Tissot*, pl. 53, p. 58; and pl. 54, p. 59.

20. For *The Luncheon* see Wood, *Tissot*, pl. 36; for *The Return from the Boating Trip* see Wood, *Tissot*, pl. 70.

21. Wood, *Tissot*, 48–49, pls. 39, 40 and 41.

22. S.M. Newton, *Health, Art & Reason: Dress Reformers of the 19th Century* (London: John Murray, 1974), 90–7.

23. deMarly, *Worth,* 116.

24. deMarly, *Worth,* 100.

25. C. Walkley and V. Foster, *Crinolines and Crimping Irons: Victorian Clothes, How They Were Cleaned and Cared For* (London: Peter Owen Ltd., 1978), 31.

26. Mrs. Eugenia Stanhope, *Letters Written by the Late Right Honourable Philip Dormer Stanhope, Earl of Chesterfield to his Son, Philip Stanhope, Esq. Late Envoy Extraordinary at the Court of Dresden* (London: J. Dodson, 1774), 3:172.

27. E.S. Turner, *A History of Courting* (New York: E.P. Dutton & Co. Inc., 1955), 84. He states: 'It had an infinity of employments . . . it was something to hold. It was also something to drop, when it became necessary to drop something. . . . As a Frenchman said: "It prohibits what it permits, and intercepts its own message". Its main purpose, perhaps, was to tease, to tantalize. There are many so-called codes of fan language. . . . A woman with a fan could make her meaning clear enough without having to memorize a deaf-and-dumb language.'

28. Quoted in E. Aldrich, *From the Ballroom to Hell, Grace and Folly in Nineteenth Century Dance* (Evanston, Ill.: Northwestern University Press, 1991), 104.

29. E.T. Renbourn, *Materials and Clothing in Health and Disease: History, Physiology and Hygiene* (London: H.K. Lewis & Co. Ltd., 1972), 44–6.

30. Stella Mary Newton, 'Fashion in Fashion History', *Times Literary Supplement* (21 March 1975), 305.

Painting the 'Parisienne': James Tissot and the Making of the Modern Woman

Tamar Garb

What does a man look like beside his wife? He, black, plain, dull, smelling of cigars. She, pink, elegant, sparkling, her rice powder wafting all around her the perfume of ambergris? Does he not look like his own cook in his Sunday best?[1]

MEN AND WOMEN, wrote Nestor Roqueplan in 1869, appeared ineluctably different from one another. Seeing them together made this absolutely clear. Exuding a characteristically manly smell in their sombre suits, gentlemen were much more likely to resemble their own male domestic servants than were their made-up wives, perfumed, pink and showy in their resplendent *toilettes*.

James Tissot's *The Political Lady* (pl. XXII) represents just the sort of couple of which Roqueplan wrote. One of a series of fifteen paintings on the theme of *La Femme à Paris* exhibited in Paris at the Galerie Sedelmeyer in 1885, it shows a fashionable woman in a crowded public space, attended by her distinguished, wealthy male partner. The woman provides a flood of warm colour, a rosy presence alongside her austere companion. Elegant and youthful, her elaborate costume begs to be stroked while her haughty escort seems remote and untouchable, framing his female companion rather than inviting the viewer to dwell on his own auspicious presence. Representative of the type of the 'Parisienne', the ultimate counterpart to the bourgeois male, replete in the austerity of his columnar, egalitarian black and white costume — the uniform of character and purpose, thrift and self-control — this woman represents the glamour and superficial excesses that money and modernity could buy. If luxury was a necessity for a flourishing market economy, then women, adorned and ornamented, came to represent that luxury to itself.

In *The Political Woman*, the gentleman's face is altogether concealed. All we need to see is his slightly stooped posture, grey hair and customary costume to be assured of his position. It is his companion about whom men whisper behind their raised hands. It is she who must absorb their stares and delight their eyes at the same time as reflect back to them a belief in their own omnipotence and power. Woman's youth and beauty is her capital, that of her companion is money, position, status and, indeed, the woman he could muster at his side.

Shrouded in an abundance, even an excess, of lace, fur and cloth, Woman is the object of scrutiny, the admired, cherished jewel of which fantasies are made.[2]

When James Tissot set out to represent that mythic figure the 'Parisienne' in his series of paintings and etchings, he stepped into a highly contested field. Tissot bravely, some thought presumptuously, aimed at mounting an exhibition of a group of large, almost life-size, paintings chronicling the diversity of appearance, character and role of contemporary Parisian women. As a Frenchman recently returned from a long sojourn in London and now wishing to re-enter the Paris artworld, he would cast the eye of the partial outsider upon his countrywomen and subject them to close scrutiny.[3] He would show them at work and at leisure, at home and in society, indoors and outdoors, respectable and of ill-repute. In addition to the painted series, Tissot planned an edition of etchings, expected to appear in three series of five, to be published at six-monthly intervals between December 1885 and December 1886.[4] Each of the prints was to be accompanied by a short story centring on the principal figures of the paintings and etchings. As such the paintings would function as pictorial caesuras in a narrative outpouring which would be nothing short of encyclopedic. For the figure of the 'Parisienne' was herself so suggestive a spur to narrative and so much the product of narrative structures that her figure alone could function as a distilled story. One had only to say the word 'Parisienne' to provoke a series of well rehearsed narrative associations, expectations and assumptions. For Tissot, the entire endeavour would, ideally, constitute a taxonomy of contemporary femininity, combining image, icon and anecdote in what was supposed to be simultaneously a viable modern artistic project and a lucrative commercial venture.

In the event it was recognized as neither. While Tissot did indeed show his paintings at the Galerie Sedelmeyer in Paris in 1885 and at the Arthur Tooth Gallery in London in 1886, the reception of these was, at worst, highly critical, at best, lukewarm.[5] The experts were out to judge them not only as paintings but as adequate representations of the French fantasy of femininity for which the 'Parisienne' stood. The series of etchings was aborted after the first five were produced and Tissot never issued the three editions of five hundred prints which he had planned. Few of the stories were ever written and of those that were, most are difficult to trace and identify. But this does not mean that the works and the responses they stimulated are without interest. For this failed endeavour generated extensive copy and prompted much speculation on the idea of a national style and on the state of contemporary French womanhood. Most critics found Tissot's approach too 'English' and saw his wooden array of dressed-up mannequins as an insult to French femininity mounted in a style that was not quite French enough. In the words of one critic, Tissot had repeatedly painted the same English bar-maid and placed her in a variety of costumes and settings;[6] another talked of young misses who had been transported from Hyde Park to the Bois de Boulogne; whilst another thought them quite charming tourists, indeed English women in Paris.[7] For some commentators the very illustrative and literary nature of the project tied it more closely to English than to French precedents.[8] Some saw the series as offering nothing more than banal illustration, a manifestation of a particularly English disease with which Tissot had been infected, while others were willing to capitalize on the anecdotalism of the project by weaving their own elaborate yarns around these works.

Tissot was by no means the first nineteenth-century artist to aim at capturing the essence of the 'Parisienne'. Indeed in the same year as he exhibited his 'femme à Paris' the popular dramatist Henri Becque put on his play 'Parisienne' featuring a vain, self-centred manipulator of men.[9] Emerging as a type in the burgeoning print culture of the Restoration, the 'Parisienne' represented the quintessential image of a commodified femininity, one which was packaged to create an alluring, eroticised spectacle centring on the fetishised, fashionable body and flirtatious address of the female figure.[10] Such a figure was characteristically represented either adorning herself for public delectation, posing for public acclamation of her physical charms, or selling something, the elision between the merchandise on sale and the woman herself being easy to make.

The history of French popular imagery is full of representatives of Parisian womanhood whose sole purpose was to seduce men. The 'grisette' (from the 1820s), the 'lorette' (from the 1830s), and the 'cocotte' (from the Second Empire), all with their specific class connotations, formed stock representations of the 'Parisienne' who while not necessarily publicly and legally branded as prostitutes were nevertheless engaged in the trade in sex.[11] Such image-types were widespread in the popular press and contemporary broadsheets, eventually influencing the modern-life subject matter of realist and naturalist painting from the mid-century onwards.

The formulation of types had its origins in the classificatory systems of Johann Kaspar Lavater and his Enlightenment colleagues, keen to classify and codify human nature according to certain consistent rules and principles. It was alleged that physical appearance, when scientifically studied and observed, provided clues to character and conduct, and 'phrenology' evolved as the systematic reading of the inner essence of a person via external physical signs. The classificatory mentality of early nineteenth-century taxonomers found its consummate expression in the genre of the 'physiologie', the textual and iconic elaboration of stock characters or types, ranging from the rag-picker to the laundress, the blue-stocking to the 'lorette'.[12] The 'Parisienne' became the generic term for describing the essence of a particularly modern, peculiarly French form of femininity, which could, ostensibly, encompass women of all classes by a shared 'je ne sais quoi', a quality which none could put their finger on but all professed to recognise when they encountered it.[13] Far removed from the court beauty of the eighteenth century, the 'Parisienne' connoted an urban creature, whose tantalizing presence and mysterious allure was linked to the enchantment and potential dangers of the modern metropolis. Tied to the ascendancy of Paris as a cultural and commercial centre and of the urban bourgeoisie as the newly empowered ruling class, the 'Parisienne' had become one of France's principal exports by the 1880s. Frenchmen claimed that women were a hundred times more feminine in Paris than in any other city and a whole industry developed dedicated to spreading her charms abroad.[14]

By this time, the 'Parisienne' had not only been naturalised as *the* desirable representation of the feminine but 'she' had become necessary for the smooth functioning of the economy. The department stores and shopping arcades proffered an unprecedented array of goods aimed at seducing women and creating in them the desire to consume luxury goods indispensable to their identity as women. France's fashion industry and all its ancillary enterprises depended on the credibility of the 'Parisienne' as a living monument to modern femininity. Fashion plates, like those produced in *La Mode Illustré, La Gazette des Dames*, and *Le Bon Ton, Journal des Modes* (see fig. 3 on p. 7), were one of the major forums for the elaboration of the type. It was these images which reached every salon and boudoir in the capital and it was to the authorities that controlled these publications that women deferred. The Parisian woman was said to rule the salons of Europe, setting trends in fashion and etiquette to which all women would soon aspire. She represented novelty, modernity and style. Born of the modern metropolis, she embodied both its delicious allure and its deadly dangers. The city constituted her stage. It was here that she performed her part, always aware of being watched, always watching herself. Her appearance was her most precious possession and it was to her appearance that she devoted all her energy and attention.[15] Women were simultaneously deified and enslaved by a system of exchange which depended on their consumption of commodities while they themselves were commodified.[16]

It was in the urban spaces that she inhabited that Tissot situated his 'femmes à Paris'. There were, as some critics were quick to point out, no representatives of the 'femme au foyer', the mother or the devoted wife, in his series.[17] Conceived as belonging to the private sphere, these idealised types, widely promoted in Republican mythologies of femininity, operated as counter-discursive images aimed at promoting a wholesome, redemptive image of Woman in direct opposition to her commodified, carnal construction in the metropolis. Such women were neither sexy nor seductive and were certainly not associated with the mythic 'Parisienne' of the popular imagination. It was the public face of femininity that Tissot explored, not its hidden depths or private permutations. Here, wrote one critic, one could only find manifestations of 'la vie extérieure'. Nothing about the morals or manners of living women could be gleaned from these paintings. 'These were gracious puppets made mobile in the theatre in which they were accustomed to move about, calling for neither commentary nor annotation, neither inspiration nor admiration, neither repugnance nor desire, content with being interesting and pleasant to look at'.[18] Tissot's was the world of external appearances alone.

A number of artists before Tissot had tried to distil the image of the 'Parisienne' into a single icon. Indeed, some critics declared that any single artist who tried to represent the 'Parisienne' in her entirety was over-ambitious and foolish. It took the combined efforts of a wide range of artists to achieve this and viewers were advised to look to the forthcoming Salon for single representatives of the type rather than accept Tissot's array of fashionable women as a reliable overview.[19] In the 1885 Salon, which was open at the same time as Tissot's exhibition, for example, Ringel was showing a sculpture entitled *Parisienne* in which a single, seated figure dressed in low-cut evening dress, revealing ample heaving bosoms, swoons suggestively in her chair. Her semi-conscious state and languid limbs seem oddly juxtaposed with her tightly corseted bodice but the combination of these factors produces an image of Woman as seductive but only semi-conscious. Here the 'Parisienne' is condensed into a single allegorical figure, resonant with associations. Renoir's *La Parisienne* of 1874 (fig. 36) had also isolated the figure. Her packaged personage, her skilfully moulded and rigid silhouette, although represented on an indeterminate ground which speaks of no specific place or context, is already imbricated by an elaborate story about who she is.

All of Tissot's 'Femmes à Paris' are visibly haunted by a male presence. Not only are they themselves the products of male fantasy, both Tissot's and the numerous writers and image-makers to whom he was heir, but they are

36. Pierre-Auguste Renoir, *La Parisienne*, 1874, oil on canvas, 160 x 105.4 cm. National Museum of Wales, Cardiff

physically surrounded by the men to whom they are accountable and on whom they are dependent. Whether dressed up as *The Fashionable Beauty* (fig. 37) or undressed, as in *The Acrobat* (see fig. 64 on p. 160) as the lowly tight-rope walker, the least elevated of contemporary performing artists, women tightly held in by leotards or corsets, are watched, surrounded and admired by what is predominantly a chorus of men. They form the framing reference point for Woman's highly polished and packaged appearance, her erect stance and frontally lit, frozen rigidity. As such, Woman's physical presence in the paintings mirrors women's actual presence in the social and psychic economy of late nineteenth-century France. In the story commissioned from Ludovic Halévy to accompany *The Fashionable Beauty*, the main female character is shown to be dependent on the whim of an irresponsible young aristocrat who creates and destroys her

37. Tissot, *The Fashionable Beauty*, 1883–5, oil on canvas, 147.3 x 101.6 cm. Private Collection, Switzerland

reputation with impunity. Impressed by the appearance at the theatre of a modest young *bourgeoise*, wife of a lawyer of modest means, Prince Agénor, a promiscuous womaniser, declares her to be 'the most beautiful woman in Paris'. This is overheard by an ambitious gossip columnist who prints this information on the society page of his newspaper. The modest Mme. Derline is transformed after reading the column into a rapacious consumer of luxury goods who, in her attempt to live up to her new-found reputation, must buy compulsively. In order to present herself at a forthcoming ball she finds it necessary to order a sumptuous new ballgown and jewellery. In addition she persuades her husband to replace their old horse and carriage and hire an English coachman so that they can arrive in style. Mme. Derline makes an impressive entry at the ball, Halévy taking his cue from the scene depicted in Tissot's painting:

38. Tissot, *The Artists' Ladies,*
1885, oil on canvas, 146 x 101.6
cm. © Chrysler Museum,
Norfolk, VA

> She entered, and from the first minute she had the delicious sensation of her
> success. Throughout the long gallery of the Palmer's house it was a true tri-
> umphal march. She advanced with firm and precise step, erect, and head well
> held. She appeared to see nothing, to hear nothing, but how well she saw!
> How well she felt the fire of all those eyes on her shoulders! Around her arose
> a little murmur of admiration, and never had music been sweeter to her.[20]

Mme. Derline's triumph is short lived. To the horror of the heroine, the Prince is
not present to endorse her appearance at the ball and confirm his first impres-
sions. He has, by this time, already declared someone else to be 'the most beautiful woman in Paris' and Mme. Derline is left deflated and humiliated despite her
grand entry. While her beauty is, to a large extent, dependent on her elaborate
toilette, she is nevertheless punished for her vanity and susceptibility to flattery.
The 'woman of fashion' falls as quickly as she has risen. The ambivalent feelings

39. Tissot, *The Ladies of the Cars*, 1883–5, oil on canvas, 144.7 x 100 cm. Museum of Art, Rhode Island School of Design, Providence, RI, Gift of Walter Lowry, photography by Cathy Carver

of society towards the artificial beauty of the society woman is captured by Tissot in the way in which a number of the men surrounding the beauty seem to recoil with repugnance even as they gaze surreptitiously at her charms.

In Tissot's series women either implicate the viewer in a suggestive exchange of looks or are ogled from inside the picture frame. In *The Shop Girl*, 1883-5 (pl. XXI) the enigmatic shop assistant locks eyes with the viewer/customer while the men outside, beyond the shop window, salute and peer at the ladies within.[21] The young wife in *The Artists' Ladies*, 1883–5 (fig. 38) looks around, quite unbelievably, her head turning impossibly on its axis as she strives to engage the look of the observer who is beyond the picture plane and about to take his seat at one of the empty tables in the forefront of the open-air restaurant. The extraordinary doll-like riders at the Hippodrome in *The Ladies of the Cars*, 1883–5 (fig. 39) are surveyed from an audience which is predominantly male with an odd smattering of brazen females who peer from behind their fans or cast sideward glances at the

40. Tissot, *La Mysterieuse*, 1883–5, oil on canvas, Private Collection

41. Tissot, *Without a Dowry*, 1883–5, oil on canvas, 147.3 x 101.6 cm. Private Collection, New York

performers.[22] Some women are mysteriously followed as in *La Mysterieuse*, 1883–5 (fig. 40) which has an odd cloaked figure, described by one critic as the woman's valet,[23] stalking her and her frisky little boudoir pups in an alley in the Bois de Boulogne. Others are surreptitiously glanced at as in the melancholy *Without a Dowry* (fig. 41) where two soldiers, set discreetly off-centre, seem quite distracted by a dreamy, demure young maiden, placed mischievously beneath the naked, muscular legs of a male statue in the centre of the picture. One coquettishly dressed young woman is even the object of a crude call by a young ragamuffin in *The Bridesmaid*, 1883–5 (fig. 42) at the same time as she receives the lascivious, sidewards leer of the best man whose face is dangerously close to hers. Her rigid, tight-laced appearance is offset only by her provocatively visible feet and suggestively gaping glove which proffers a tiny glimpse of her otherwise concealed and contained flesh. Even when no men are actually depicted in the paintings, as in *The Liar*, 1883–5 (see fig. 69 on p. 175) or *The Sphynx*, 1883–5 (see fig. 70 on p. 176), their hidden presence is invoked, in the one by the enigmatic

42. Tissot, *The Bridesmaid,*
1883–5, oil on canvas, 147.3
x 101.6 cm. Leeds City Art
Gallery

title which leads one to wonder about the nature of the lie and the possibility
that it concerns a lover, perhaps the man responsible for financing the suffocat-
ing luxury of the gilded cage in which the woman is enclosed, the other by the
strategic placing of the cane and hat on the provocatively splayed out tiger
skin, recognised by a number of contemporary reviewers as metonymic references to a hastily departed or hurriedly hidden male figure, perhaps mauled,
metaphorically of course, by the tigress within.[24] Most reviewers thought the
narrative overkill of these paintings ludicrous, and poked fun at the over-blown
pretensions of paintings that strove to tell a tale in so elaborate a way.[25] If the
figure of the 'Parisienne' herself was already the repository of elaborate narrative
projection, then her placement in an enigmatic narrative setting seemed gratu-
itous, artificial and outside of the remit of painting.[26]

43. Tissot, *The Circle of the Rue Royale*, 1868, oil on canvas, 215.9 x 330.2 cm. Private Collection, London, UK / Bridgeman Art Library, London/New York

In 1868 Tissot had executed a painting, *The Circle of the Rue Royale* (pl. XV and fig. 43) showing upper-class gentlemen relaxing at their exclusive gentleman's club in which hats and canes and discarded overcoats make unambiguous references to the men themselves. While some of these men seem to have just arrived, still wearing their full outdoor apparel, others have settled in and signify their attitudes of relaxed sociability by their bare heads and casual attitudes. It was men like these, the same men who had accompanied the so-called 'political woman' in the first painting of the series, who comically chose to undress themselves at the Circus featured in the extraordinary *The Sporting Ladies*, 1883–5 (pl. XXIII). Here '*clubmen*' as the critic for *La Gazette de France* called them, who do not need to earn a living, remnants of the declining aristocratic class, could rough it by divesting themselves of their penguin suits under which their bodies were usually concealed and make a spectacle of themselves.[27] The monocled face of the central trapeze artist establishes his class position. He has been identified as Count Hubert de la Rochefoucaud, a regular performer at the Cirque Molier, an amateur circus with a majority of performers drawn from the aristocracy; he and his fellow trapeze artist, reputedly the painter Théophile Wagner, were depicted by Henri Gerbault in a programme for the Cirque Molier in 1886.[28] In Tissot's painting, they are watched by a rather dour bunch of top-hatted gentlemen and a most animated crowd of ogling female spectators. While they have stripped themselves of their gentleman's garb in order to play out a forbidden form of male display, the women have dressed themselves up in their best clothes to come and stare. Their brazen looking gives them away as demi-mondaines who titter and giggle at the indecorous oozing of male flesh (the swollen buttocks of the central figure positively spill over the thin bar on which he dangles so comically while the bar of the distant figure cuts into his meaty thighs) or look solicitously out of the picture at the spectator, perhaps at a male occupant of the front gallery. Women who look too boldly, like the intent spectators in this painting, risk contravening the codes of female modesty and reveal themselves as demi-mondaines rather than respectable ladies. Demure young ladies were required to satisfy their curiosity by concealing their *lorgnettes* behind their fans while looking surreptitiously through them. Nor should they be visibly gesturing or applauding too ostentatiously. Most importantly, they should not be seen to be looking.[29] The ogling women of *The Sporting Ladies* (pl. XXIII) are dressed like respectable *hautes bourgeoises*, with their demure necklines, elaborate headgear and gloved hands, but their animated poses, rampant gazes and flamboyantly waving fans suggest that they are the coquettish creatures of public life: solicitous, sexualized and seductive.

The female figures in *The Sporting Ladies* give off confusing signals about their social origins and seem to be dressed in an elaborate disguise. Their flesh is contained and constrained by their bourgeois costume at the same time as their gestures and gazes reach beyond the confines of good manners. The trapeze artists, on the other hand, are isolated from their top-hatted class allies by their state of semi-undress and unseemly fleshly excess. Their aging bodies are encased in wrinkled silk, forming puckers and pleats of fabric which stand in for skin and flesh in an outrageously provocative way. The effect is discomforting, even, in the words of one critic, 'embarrassing'.[30] These men transgress codes of class and gender decorum. It is the licence that this context gives to such transgression that allows them to glory in the spectacle that they present. For a time, they find themselves allied with those (foreign) men who are permitted to adopt the conventionally feminine role of self-display, such as the English military men pompously strutting about in the lower men's gallery or the clown curiously dressed in a Union flag costume who looks up, plaintively, from the circus ring.[31] For the representatives of the army, this renunciation is replaced by an even more elaborate form of defensive armoury than the obligatory, anonymous black male costume while the bathetic English clown, by contrast, is left looking rather vulnerable and pathetic with his garish make-up, ridiculous hat, carrot-coloured hair and frilly collar. He does not cut an impressive figure. Indeed his very renunciation of masculinity contributes to making him a figure of fun. Foreign, English, an outsider who comments on society without being properly of it, his position mirrors that of Tissot himself, so resolutely defined as English by many of his French contemporaries. The clown as obvious figure of fun deflects the humour away from the posturing aristocrats but at the same time serves as an ominous pointer to a well-known contemporary literary topos, the impoverished gentleman forced, through financial hardship, to become a circus performer and play the professional fool.[32]

The juxtaposition of the clown, the trapeze artists and the gentlemen in the crowd offers a tantalizing image of class and gender construction. While normative masculinity is embodied by the suited spectators, their compatriots exploit their own privileged position by taking on a less decorous, performative subjectivity, which was ruled out of court in the mundane contexts of daily life but which was licensed in the arena of the circus, while the clown stands as a tragi-comic reminder that this is a dangerous game, one which could all too easily become real and thereby divest the sport of its playful, fanciful allure. The aristocratic trapeze artist renounces his masculine costume in an exhibitionistic display which allows him to overstep traditional gender roles. But this game is not without its dangers. The potential feminization of such a position is poignantly rendered in a watercolour by Théophile Wagner (fig. 44) himself in which he renders himself in his costume in front of a mirror in a dressing room, accompanied by a female nude. The effect produced by the conventionally feminine setting, the pose in front of the mirror and the costume of leotard and tights is of a castrated man, one who aligns himself with the feminine at some cost.

It is the play with gender and class identities that *The Sporting Ladies* (pl. XXIII) articulates. The picture is structured around a series of conventional oppositions which are both staged and overturned. The juxtaposition between masculinity and femininity, France and England, the upper and lower classes is interrogated and explored here in a potentially open-ended way. But the punishment of male transgression remains hinted at by the comic presence of the clown, while the proper place of Woman as exclusive object of display is crucially maintained by the central importance of the pink-clad woman in the forefront who turns around to catch our attention and secure her position as the focus of our desiring gaze. She serves to remind us that it is *her* elaborate costume and finely wrought *toilette* which is, for the viewer at least, the principal object on

44. Théophile Pierre Wagner, *Self-portrait of T.P. Wagner in the Dressing Room of the Cirque Molier*, watercolour on paper. Jane Voorhees Zimmerli Art Museum, Rutgers, The State University of New Jersey, David and Mildred H. Morse Art Acquisition Fund

display in the modern city, despite the complex games of renunciation and exhibitionism that the picture articulates.

Unlike the performers in *The Sporting Ladies* the charioteers at the Hippodrome who feature in *The Ladies of the Cars* (fig. 39 on p. 103) were drawn from the lower ends of the class hierarchy. While the circus could offer an arena for the enactment of marginal masculine subjectivities, and the figures of the clown and the trapeze artist could stand for the renunciation of prescribed roles in favour of liminal, licensed forms of male deviance, it did not provide such a space for female performers. The female acrobats, tight-rope walkers and horse-riders of the fairgrounds and circuses which multiplied in the modern city were the least revered of performers, the least well-paid and the most exploited. In the garish artificial spotlight of the performance, their bodies shone and glowed in a mesmerising splendour creating a veneer of perfection and an impression of unblemished surface beauty which belied the actual conditions of their labour and the stresses to which their bodies were subjected. The duped crowd at the Hippodrome was, according to at least one critic, hypnotised by the sight of so much flesh and gold. The seduction of surface glitter hid the stupidity and vacuousness of the performers and their false glamour.[33] The massive arena of the Hippodrome provided entertainment on a grand scale. The hall could hold up to ten thousand spectators.[34] The sheer numbers are evoked in Tissot's painting by the sea of minute top hats and bonnets which are dotted in the distant raked seats. In the ring, the riders perform impassively on their chariots, their faces expressionless, their statuesque presences providing a marked contrast to the movement and animation of the galloping horses. These stiff, frozen figures, with their scaled armour, padded hips, piercing headdresses and erect and upright carriage seemed like puppets[35] polished to reflect the garish electric light and gilded surface excesses of the massive entertainment hall. They are monuments to modernity, reminiscent of lofty allegories of liberty, justice and peace, but here reduced to mindless mannequins signifying nothing more elevated than the glitter of gold and the passing pleasures of empty pageantry. The audiences at the Hippodrome came to be amused rather than edified. As such, they regularly feasted their eyes on a diet of female flesh, spectacularly displayed, perfectly packaged and easily consumed.

The association between looking and consuming which was so crucial a part of the spectacle of modernity is brilliantly thematised in Tissot's *The Shop Girl* (pl. XXI) where a series of enigmatic looks is exchanged in the quintessential modern and commercial context of shopping. Here the bustling boulevard and the intimate feminine interior of the dressmaker's shop come dangerously close together.[36] The transparency of the glass shop front provides a barrier which while forbidding entry facilitates the interchange of looks, indeed places the interior on display for the passer-by and potential customer. Prominently displayed in the window is a headless and limbless shop-dummy sporting a tightly fitting bodice over a stylishly hour-glassed body. This doll is moulded to present the ideal shape that only the tight-lacing of the corset could produce in actual women's bodies. The bodice hugs the body forming its own curvaceous carapace for the corseted figure beneath.

The rigid scaffolding which the corset provided produced a stiff structure onto which clothing could be placed. The ideal figure of fashion was the shop mannequin, headless, lifeless and available for perpetual scrutiny. In Tissot's painting the dummy's contours are mirrored by the severely moulded shapes of the shop assistants whose frames were expected to conform to the rigid requirements of fashion. These women, demurely clad in their black uniforms, are both involved in exchanging glances. The one that holds open the door looks at the viewer, here conceived perhaps, as a woman who has completed her purchase and is about to be handed her neatly wrapped pink parcel as she leaves. Her coachman and horse await her outside. Already she appears to be being hailed, through the window by the top-hatted gentleman behind the shop girl. Her purchase over, she herself re-enters the world of exchange in which she is pursued, assessed and, if she's lucky, desired. Indeed the possibility that it is the viewer herself who may be incorporated into this drama of sexual exchange is disquieting. To look at the picture is to be subsumed into its narrative possibilities and this position, for a female viewer in particular, is unnerving. While this invisible drama is suggested in the right-hand half of the painting, a more explicit exchange is enacted on the left. Here another top-hatted gentleman penetrates the interior with his stare. He, according to contemporary critics,[37] is exchanging a furtive glance with the left-hand shop-girl, a movement which seems echoed by the two chairs in front of the table which exactly duplicate the stance of these two figures.[38]

The association of sex and shopping is perfectly articulated in French by the word for that novel experience, window-shopping, 'lèche vitrine', or literally, licking the window. Women were thought to have a voracious and uncontrollable appetite for shopping which novelists like Emile Zola represented in highly sexualized terms.[39] Describing a crowd of women before the shop window of the department store which is at the centre of his novel about modern consumerism *Au Bonheur des Dames*, he writes:

> groups of women [were] pushing and squeezing, devouring the finery with loving, covetous eyes. And the stuffs became animated in this passionate atmosphere . . . , even the pieces of cloth, thick and heavy, exhaled a tempting odour, the dresses threw out their folds over the dummies which assumed a soul, the great mantle particularly supple and warm as if on real fleshly shoulders, heaved, panted and expanded its limbs.[40]

'Lèche vitrine': consumption of goods and consumption of bodies amounts to the same thing here. The delicious sensation of looking at desirable objects is akin to licking, a very physical way of describing the eroticised pleasures of looking. But it is not only the looking at goods on sale which is thematised here. For Tissot, more important than the desiring look of the female commodity fetishist is the lecherous looking which is directed at women themselves. Indeed the penetration of the interior by the licking of the external looking is symbolised in the interior by the curious little griffin so conspicuously placed at the corner of the table. This masculine presence, its columnar shape comically echoing that of the coachman, is shown with a long curled tongue which is positively lewd in its associations. Vulgar, bawdy and mischievous, its intrusion into the feminine indoor space seems almost an affront, but it serves as a salutary reminder that even the realm of the intimate interior is circumscribed in relation to a public to which it owes its existence. Furthermore, Art itself was implicated in the eroticised commercialism of the day by the manner in which Tissot's paintings were exhibited. Placed under glass at eye level, they themselves become seen through windows invoking objects for sale in 'vitrines'. To see these works the viewer had to 'lick the window', to engage in a sensory experience which is figured in the body rather than in the disembodied eye of disinterested contemplation. He/she was constantly reminded by the glass that these works were objects for sale, commodities like the goods they represented.

Tissot's interest in the packaging of femininity in the context of the modern metropolis is articulated in a very different way in the curious *The Artists' Ladies* (see fig. 38 on p. 102) which also formed part of the *Femme à Paris* series. In *The Shop Girl* (pl. XXI) Tissot had painted those young women of humble birth who learned to adopt the behaviour and mannerisms of their clientèle in the course of their work. Their demure uniforms obviated the necessity for dressing up and their perfect demeanours and learned manners served to hide their crude beginnings. The artist's wives, on the other hand, were dressed up in the fashionable regalia of the urban bourgeoisie. These women are consummate representatives of the new-found fashionable femininity available from the department store, 'the sham elegance born of the shop' of which Alphonse Daudet wrote. They come, wrote one critic, in all colours and in a number of different moulds.[41] Tissot paid minute attention to the details of their costume. Their hats are veritable bouquets over their swept-up coiffures, their dresses busily patterned and dotted and their hour-glass figures are as tightly laced as any shop mannequin's of the period. Indeed one critic described them as 'gracious puppets', content to be manipulated so that they became an agreeable spectacle for passing viewers.[42] Their taut torsos which seem to strain at the seams are suggestively juxtaposed with the rounded contours of the lightly draped caryatids of the building in the background. Here the classical coverings seem to express the lines of the figure's monumental bodies rather than transform or restrict them. Two of the 'artist's wives' are demurely gloved so that the hand belonging to the central female figure seems ostentatiously bare and exposed. The wedding ring on her finger, placed prominently in the foreground and framed in the starchy whiteness of the table linen, gives ample evidence that these dressed-up ladies are indeed wives. Out lunching flamboyantly 'chez Ledoyen', a fashionable open-air restaurant, on 'le jour de vernissage,'[43] they are keen to be seen, in their splendid outdoor regalia, at the fashionable watering hole where *le tout Paris* has gathered to gossip and gawp in the bright spring sunlight.

The pretensions and disappointments of 'artist's wives' had been the subject of some satire in the 1870s. Alphonse Daudet's collection of stories entitled *Les Femmes d'artistes*, published in 1876, chronicled a number of disastrous marriages in which artists, fragile nervous creatures ('child-men', as he called them) whose talent needed to be nurtured and nourished, were destroyed by the rapacious appetites and superficial concerns of their status-seeking wives.[44] For Daudet and many of his contemporaries, artists made lousy husbands. Genius was all-consuming and it left no room for the mediocre pleasures of the hearth. Artists' wives, Daudet concluded, would inevitably end up embittered and disappointed and were bound to pull their unfortunate husbands down with them. Daudet's characters constantly advise artists not to marry. Marriage led to 'the degradation of one's talent' on the part of the artist and misery on the part of the wife: 'It cannot be very amusing to be the wife of a genius. There are plenty of labourer's wives who are happier', he wrote.[45] A classic Daudet example of the unfortunate artist's wife is Mme. Heurtebise, a shopwoman of modest income who marries a writer. 'What pleased her in this marriage', wrote Daudet, 'was the idea of wedding an author, a well known man who would take her to the theatre as often as she wished. As for him, I verily believe that her sham elegance born of the shop, her pretentious manners, pursed up mouth and affectedly uplifted little finger, fascinated him and appeared to him the height of Parisian refinement, for he was a born peasant and in spite of his intelligence remained one to the end of his days.'[46] The 'Parisienne' confers status and style on her country bumpkin of a spouse whilst his literary pretensions are expected to lend substance to her superficial, rather shallow existence. In the end neither one satisfies the other and the marriage, like all Daudet's scenarios, ends in disaster.

There were some critics who recognised in Tissot's painting the, by now familiar, juxtaposition of anxious artists and upwardly mobile wives.[47] One critic, writing for *Le Figaro,* saw the exhibition of Tissot's picture as the perfect opportunity to contribute to the expanding discourse on a new social type.[48] To be married to an artist, he/she claimed, was a dubious pleasure: 'If the Parisienne was the bravest of women then the artist's wife was the bravest of Parisiennes'. The phenomenon of 'the artist's wife', wrote this critic, was, in any case, a new one. Any self-respecting artist of the 1830s would rather have been guillotined than married but bohemian culture was a thing of the past and artists now sought respectability via the most conventional channels. Since the Franco-Prussian war, he/she declared, artists had seen fit to set themselves up in intimate *ménages* and were now lamentably bourgeois. Wives still had to put up with much eccentric behaviour from their artist-husbands (the very term seemed oxymoronic), but artists were no longer paupers and some could receive incomes of a hundred thousand francs a year for 'oiling a canvas'. As such they were good catches for grocers' daughters and other women with aspirations to rise above their station. But artists were always going to be disappointments to such women. Their eccentricities, penchants for fads and aberrant crazes — they would raise bears, keep lions, smoke pipes — would drive all but the most heroic and brave creatures to despair and it was only amongst 'Parisiennes' that such noble, brave and absolutely contemporary creatures were to be found. It was these unlikely heroines of modern life that Tissot had captured and it was to them that critics paid a rather mocking homage.

There is something pathetically perky about the way the stiff figure in the brown dress in *The Artists' Ladies* cranes her head to see who is looking at her in her feathers and finery. She seems to look out of the picture to proclaim her good fortune and revel in the limelight or perhaps to check on which renowned artist or critic is about to take his seat at the front table. Of course the viewer (another artist or perhaps a critic) is interpolated as just such a character, hailed by the solicitous glance of the over-eager young woman in the foreground. Across the table from her sits the only recognisable artist in the picture, John Lewis Brown.[49] The choice of this top-hatted, ruddy faced gentleman for the image of the artist underlines the new-found respectability, even stuffiness, of the profession while invoking Tissot's own reputation as an 'anglicised Frenchman' functioning within the exclusive and jealously guarded networks of the Parisian art-world.

The Artists' Ladies brings up questions about the legibility of class, gender and national signs as they are inscribed on the body in modern life painting. Contemporary critical accounts provide an indispensable resource for reading beyond surface appearance and revealing the anxieties that attend attempts to fix identity and secure it for interpretation. The outer packaging of a woman did not, as we have seen throughout this chapter, necessarily reveal who she was or where she came from. The idea of disguise and display was at the heart of the modern construction of femininity which the figure of the 'Parisienne' articulated. Ostensibly egalitarian, one did not need to be born in Paris to be a 'Parisienne'. Equally, birth in that city did not guarantee the possession of those enigmatic qualities, that 'je ne sais quoi' that was said to characterise the 'Parisienne'. Part of her allure was the mystery in which she was veiled. What lay beneath the veil was an object of unending curiosity but the risks of looking too closely at her were always present.

The venal power of Woman was only constrained by her costume, it was not vanquished by it. Woman, in nineteenth-century mythologies, always exceeds the parameters of her performance. Like the android of modern science-fiction, her careful programming cannot always be controlled and the dazzling spectacle of her sexuality, however contained and packaged, can threaten her admirer with blindness or even death. It was this danger that was so enigmatically thematised in the first painting of the series, *The Political Lady* (pl. XXII). Here the excessively pink and pleated 'Parisienne' with her outdated black girdle, large presence and false smile,[50] sweeps into a full room causing psychic havoc as she enters. The monocle of the elderly man placed in front of her commanding presence is transformed to an opaque eye patch at the sight of the resplendent striding Woman, an event which is mirrored by the sinister blinding of the figure in the violent scene depicted in the background sculpture where a man's face is shown to be penetrated by a horrific spear. Danger lurks beneath the resplendent surface of this glittering occasion. Unwittingly, Tissot had, from the start, articulated the double-edged nature of the fantasy of femininity which the 'Parisienne' embodied. Her fetishised body held in a nature and a sexuality which was deemed dangerous and threatening. Her beauty, alleged some commentators, was the 'beauty of the devil' concealing a duplicitous and deceptive nature.[51] The mask was indispensable to stave off the fear of castration and death which the spectre of femininity invoked.

But, as the misogynist pornographer Felicien Rops pointed out in *Coin de Rue* (fig. 45), the mask of femininity could easily be peeled back to reveal the hideous face of Death. Woman was positioned as tantalising temptress while being the source of syphilis, disease and ultimately death. The fascination with the mysterious allure of femininity was always, therefore, permeated by fear. The *Femme à Paris* series with its cheerful banality and wooden female characters represents the mask of femininity without, for the most part, dwelling on the anxieties which were at the source of this elaborate masquerade. Only unwittingly in small asides like that provided by the blinding spear does the threat of castration which fuels this fantasy of femininity find its place. And it is details like this one that suggest that it is the fear of women that produces the hypostesization of Woman as type. The *Femme à Paris* series deals in just such a type. To remove the mask would be to unleash the hideous monster which fuels the fetishised image of Woman known as the 'Parisienne'.

45. Felicien Rops, *Coin de Rue*, 1880s, lithograph. Private Collection

A longer version of this essay has been published in my book *Bodies of Modernity: Figure and Flesh in Fin de Siècle France* (London: Thames and Hudson, 1998). I am grateful to Katharine Lochnan whose invitation to me to participate in the Tissot Symposium at the Art Gallery of Ontario prompted me to undertake this study and to Caroline Arscott who shared the 'journey' with me.

1. Nestor Roqueplan, *Parisine* (Paris: Hetzel 1869), 43. Quoted in and translated by D. Roche, *The Culture of Clothing, Dress and Fashion in the 'ancien régime'* (pub. in French 1989; Cambridge: Cambridge University Press, 1994), 61.

2. The literature on woman as 'object of the gaze' is now extensive. Crucial for this formulation was Laura Mulvey's essay, 'Visual Pleasure and Narrative Cinema' in *Visual and Other Pleasures* (Basingstoke: 1989).

3. For biographies of Tissot, see W.E. Misfeldt, *J.J. Tissot: A Bio-Critical Study* (Ann Arbor: University of Michigan Press, 1991); M. Wentworth, *James Tissot* (Oxford: Clarendon Press, 1984). Most reviewers commented on the English filter through which Tissot observed Parisian life. In the words of one critic: 'C'est à travers le brouillard de Londres qu'il s'est mis à regarder de côté de Paris avec cet attendrissement que donnent les souvenirs et les regrets. Et maintenant il s'est fait l'historiographe au pinceau de cette vie parisienne dont il fut si longtemps privé' 'Courrier de Paris', *Le Monde Illustré* (25 April 1885), 266.

4. For a detailed discussion of the project, see M.J. Wentworth, *James Tissot, Catalogue Raisonné of his Prints* (Minneapolis, 1978), 300–25.

5. I am grateful to Juliet Hacking for her help in tracking down some of the reviews of the London exhibition.

6. 'La Femme à Paris', *La Vie parisienne* (2 May 1885), 255.

7. See A. Georget, 'Deux expositions', *L'Echo de Paris*, 2 April 1885, 2.

8. See, for example, F. Javel, 'M. James Tissot', *L'Evénement* (19 April 1885), 2; G. Dargenty, 'Exposition de J.J. Tissot', *Courrier de l'art* (24 April 1885), 200; R. dos Santos, 'Chronique', *Moniteur des arts* (24 April 1885), 1.

9 See Henry Becque, *Parisienne* (Paris, 1885). I am grateful to Ann Saddlemyer for bringing this play to my attention.

10. For a discussion of the relationship between commodity fetishism and the development of an eroticised, spectacular femininity, see A. Solomon-Godeau, 'The Other Side of Venus; The Visual Economy of Feminine Display', in *The Sex of Things; Gender and Consumption in Historical Perspective* ed. V. de Grazia, E. Furlough (Berkeley and Los Angeles: University of California Press), 113–50.

11. For a detailed discussion and illustration of these types, see B. Farwell, *French Popular Lithographic Imagery, 1815–1878*, vol. 2, 'Portraits and Types', 12–17.

12. The classic example of the 'physiologie' is of course the nine-volume work *Les francais peints par eux-mêmes* published in the 1830s and 1840s.

13. The enigmatic character of the 'Parisienne' permeates much of the literature and the critical reception of Tissot's paintings. By painting this figure in all her guises he claimed the capacity to represent her. As she was so mysterious and elusive a figure, though, his efforts were bound to be read as a failure. See, for example, 'Courrier de Paris', *Le Monde Illustré* (25 April 1885), 266.

14. For an elaboration of such a claim, see Octave Uzanne, *The Modern Parisienne* (London, 1912), 2.

15. See Arsène Houssaye's *Les Parisiennes* (Paris, 1869) for an elaboration of 'her' obsession with personal appearance.

16. In a very revealing paragraph from *Au Bonheur des Dames*, Emile Zola describes the activities of Mouret, the department store owner: 'He raised a temple to her [Woman], had her covered with incense by a legion of shopmen; he created the rite of a new religion thinking of nothing but her, continually seeking to imagine more powerful seductions; and behind her back, when he had emptied her purse and shattered her nerves, he was full of the secret scorn of a man to whom a woman had just been stupid enough to yield herself'. See *The Ladies Paradise*, trans. Frank Belmont (London, 1883), 128.

17. See the review by H. Havard, *Le Siècle* (21 April 1885), 2.

18 See G. Dargenty, 'Exposition de J.J. Tissot', *Courrier de l'art*, no. 17 (24 April 1885), 200.

19 For the clearest expression of this view, see Colombine, 'Chronique', *Gil Blas* (20 April 1885), 1.

20. L. Halévy, 'The Most Beautiful Woman in Paris' in *Parisian Points of View* (New York and London: Harper and Bros., 1894), 108.

21. For an interesting reading of the exchange of looks in this picture, see Hollis Clayson, *Painted Love: Prostitution in French Art of the Impressionist Era* (New Haven and London, 1991), 124.

22. The ratio of men to women in the audience seems roughly to duplicate that which prevailed at masked balls during the period. According to *The Parisian*, an Anglo-American journal that provided a chronicle of the week's events in Paris covering items from fashion to finance, the number of persons attending one masked ball at the Opera was 3,968, comprised of 2,239 'gentlemen in evening dress', 688 men in costume, and 1,041 women in costume or domino. See *The Parisian* (24 January 1882), 1.

23. See 'La Femme à Paris', *La Vie parisienne* (2 May 1885), 255.

24. See, for example, Meurville, 'La Femme à Paris', *La Gazette de France* (22 April 1885), 2.

25. See, for example, Colombine, 'Chronique', *Gil Blas* (20 April 1885), 1; *Moniteur des arts* (24 April 1885), 1.

26. Such anecdotal preoccupations were identified as English, the English being associated with an altogether too literary approach to painting. Tissot was described as having returned to Paris *résolument anglicisé* and incapable either of understanding the niceties of Parisian society or of representing these in an appropriately French way. See G. Dargenty, 'Exposition de J.J. Tissot', *Courrier de l'art*, no. 17 (24 April 1885), 200. Another critic wrote: 'Anglais par le style, par le facteur, et dans le choix même tant soit prétentieux de titres', *Moniteur des arts* (24 April 1885), 1. Yet another compared him to Hogarth and accused him of becoming a 'caricaturist', Colombine, 'Chronique' *Gil Blas* (20 April 1885), 1.

27. See *La Gazette de France* (22 April 1885), 2.

28. See *Pleasures of Paris: Daumier to Picasso*, exh. cat. (Museum of Fine Arts, Boston, 1991), 43–4 and 167–71.

29. For a late nineteenth-century discussion on decorum and the *lorgnette* see O. Uzanne, *Les Ornaments de la femme* (Paris, 1892), 79. For an earlier account of modesty and female spectatorship, see L. d'Amboise, 'Physiologie de la spectatrice' in *Physiologie du parterre* (1841), 10:103–5.

30. 'Voici le *Cirque Mollier* avec son public de femmes du monde … où de demi-monde, la nuance n'est pas très bien marquée, — avec ses clubman [sic] perchés sur des trapèzes, le monocle dans l'oeil, montrant leurs formes un peu vieillottes et … l'embarras d'une fausse position.' Meurville, 'La Femme à Paris', *La Gazette de France* (22 April 1885), 2.

31. I am grateful to Christopher Wilson and Tom Gretton for discussions about the identity of the soldiers.

32. Such figures featured in posters such as Jules Claretie's *Le Train 17*, 1877, and Gustave Kahn's *Le Cirque solaire*, 1898. For a discussion of this phenomenon see M. Verhagen, 'The Poster in Fin-de Siècle Paris: "That Mobile and Degenerate Art"' in *Cinema and the Invention of Modern Art,* ed. L. Charney and V. Schwartz (Berkeley, Los Angeles and London: University of California Press, 1995), 122.

33. See Meurville, 'La Femme à Paris', *La Gazette de France* (22 April 1885), 2.

34. For a brief discussion of the Hippodrome see *Pleasures of Paris: Daumier to Picasso*, 39–40 and 168.

35. The idea that Tissot had created 'dolls' not 'women' appears in a number of critical accounts of the show. See for example, Columbine, 'Chronique', *Gil Blas* (20 April 1885), 1.

36. I am indebted to Hollis Clayson's reading of this painting in *Painted Love*, 124–5.

37. As Alexander Gourget described it: 'le boulevard joyeux et animé vu au travers des glaces de l'étroite boutique, et le vieux beau qui lorgne le petit modillon', *L'Echo de Paris* (21 April 1885), 2.

38. I am grateful to Caroline Arscott for discussions with her on the symbolic role of chairs in Tissot's paintings. It was her observations in relation to a number of other Tissot's that lead me to see the relationship of these two chairs as anything but innocent.

39. Critics like Meurville noticed the link between this painting and Zola in their reviews. See 'La Femme à Paris', *La Gazette de France* (22 April 1885), 2.

40. Emile Zola, *The Ladies' Paradise*, (1883; English trans., London, 1883), 24.

41. See Meurville, 'La Femme à Paris', *La Gazette de France* (22 April 1885), 2.

42. G. Dargenty, 'Exposition de J.J.Tissot', *Courrier de l'art* (24 April 1885), 200.

43. A number of critics describe this as the location. See: Meurville, 'La Femme à Paris', *La Gazette de France* (22 April 1885), 2; Alexandre Georget, 'Deux Expositions', *L'Echo de Paris* (21 April 1885), 2; G. Dargenty, 'Exposition de J.J. Tissot', *Courrier de l'art* (24 April 1885), 200.

44. See A. Daudet, *Les Femmes d'artistes* (Paris, 1876), trans. as *Artists' Wives*, 1890.

45. Daudet, *Artists' Wives*, 13.

46. Daudet, *Artists' Wives,* 24.

47. Alexandre Georget describes the artists as 'nerveaux et maussades', 'Deux Expositions', *L'Echo de Paris* (21 April 1885), 2.

48. See Caliban, 'La Femme d'Artiste', *Le Figaro* (26 April 1885), 1.

49. He is identified as such by Alexander Georget, 'Deux Expositions', *L'Echo de Paris* (21 April 1885), 2. Although John Lewis Brown was of Irish origin, he was born in Bordeaux and spent all his life in France. A French artist with an English name, Brown must have provoked curious parallels with James Tissot.

50. Described as such by Meurville, 'La Femme à Paris', *La Gazette de France* (22 April 1885), 2.

51. See, for example, A. Houssaye, *Les Parisiennes* (Paris, 1869).

Tissot's Victorian Narratives: Allusion and Invention

Carole G. Silver

IN ALPHONSE DAUDET'S 1884 novel *Sapho*, the famous courtesan Fanny Legrand (also known as Sapho) hangs James Tissot's beautiful portrait of her in the boudoir of her Paris apartment. This is not in itself surprising for Tissot was, in the words of Philippe Jullian, 'the fashionable painter of actresses and *cocottes*'.[1] What is surprising is that both the lady and her picture are fictional and, moreover, that Daudet's book also spawned an actual Tissot painting and etching, *The Ladies of the Cars*, 1883–5 (see fig. 39 on p. 103). In *Sapho*, Fanny's imaginary portrait is her most valued possession, mentioned at several significant moments in the novel.[2] Far more than just Daudet's homage to a friend, the portrait is a paradigm for the coterie literary and visual commentaries—for a network of allusion—in which Tissot often participated.

Tissot's own use of literary allusions has made his painted narratives troublesome to twentieth-century critics bent on interpreting them. A variety of factors account for this difficulty: principal among them is the fact that Tissot occasionally originates an allusion and, more frequently, tends to refer to works written by people he knows rather than to the conventional sources one might expect. Then too, others of his allusions are *not* to specific literary works, although they appear to be, but are instead what I call 'visual invitations to narrative'—works that ask the viewer to create his or her own story. Moreover, in composing these visual pseudo-narratives, Tissot often alludes to other paintings of his own and/or creates deliberately ambiguous 'problem pictures'—depictions of situations whose resolutions remain uncertain. It is this constant tension between allusion and invention that makes so many of Tissot's pictures difficult to interpret.

It must also be noted that not all of Tissot's pictures are narrative in the first place, though many of the English paintings of the 1870s and most of the French paintings and etchings of the early 1880s are literary or pseudo-literary in this sense. Taken together, these paintings and etchings raise such characteristically Victorian issues as the presence of erotic subtexts in the pictures themselves or in the literary works to which they refer, the problematics of gender, narrative ambiguity, and the impact of coterie assumptions on cultural comment and in social satire. To return to my first point—the artist as creator of allusions—we can see that, in several pictures of *La Femme à Paris* series of 1883–5, Tissot, in an interesting inversion of the usual pattern, designs works of art for tales to be written subsequently by others. *Without a Dowry* (see fig. 41 on p. 104), for example, was provided with a text (published in 1888) by Georges Ohnet but, in this case, Tissot's picture came first and Ohnet's tale is a literary interpretation of a visual situation. Ohnet almost exactly describes the Tissot picture in his account of a pretty but dowerless colonel's daughter who spends the autumn after her father's death listening to the free concerts in the garden at Versailles under the chaperonage of her mother. The picture shows her smiling shyly, perhaps hoping to be approached by the officers to her right — potential suitors who are reluctant to involve themselves with a girl without a dowry. Ohnet's tale demonstrates that love can triumph when a young lieutenant once considered unsuitable by her father returns from abroad, having proved himself, and finds her still unmarried and himself still in love.[3]

In creating visual texts for which later verbal texts would serve as commentary, Tissot is not unlike Robert Seymour for whose sporting prints Charles Dickens was commissioned to write *The Pickwick Papers*. But on at least one occasion — in *The Gallery of HMS Calcutta (Portsmouth)*, c.1877 (pl. X), a study of flirtation and sexual selection among the elegantly dressed but obviously bored participants in a shipboard function — Tissot was unintentionally responsible for a subsequent literary reference: Henry James, briefly describing the painting in 'The Picture Season in London,' (1877) complained that Tissot paid too much painterly attention to the garb of 'women of high fashion,' yet he himself borrowed both the dress — 'of white muslin, with a hundred frills and flounces, and knots of pale coloured ribbon' — and the traits of the lady wearing it for his *Daisy Miller*, published one year later.[4]

In his mature works, Tissot seldom appears to utilize conventional or canonical novels, plays or poems. Interestingly, he instead refers to books written by friends and acquaintances, to 'society' novels and tales popular in his time and largely forgotten in ours. His allusions are to such figures as Daudet, Ouida, and Whyte-Melville rather than to Shakespeare, Homer, or even Dickens.

When Tissot chooses to illustrate (and it is worth remembering that he produced ten illustrations for his friends' Edmond and Jules de Goncourt's novel, *Renée Mauperin*) he can do so with precision — creating a visual commentary on his literary source. Look, for example, at his *Femme à Paris* paintings and etchings, acknowledged by most critics to be literary in their referents.[5] *The Ladies of the Cars* (see fig. 39 on p. 103) visually records a conversation detailed in Daudet's *Sapho*. When Fanny Legrand and her lover Jean go to visit Rosa, once a chariot-driver, they encounter her in conversation with three aged friends: 'Three *élégantes*, as these high-class women call themselves, three old frumps reckoned among the glories of the Second Empire, whose names were as famous as that of a great poet or a successful general—Wilkie Cob, Sombreuse, Clara Desfous' (101).

Tatave de Potter, a famous composer[6] who has been Rosa's lover for many years, to the detriment of his family and career, tells Jean of the beginnings of his twenty-year liaison: 'I went to the Hippodrome one evening and saw her standing driving her little chariot above me, her whip in the air, with her barrel helmet and her coat of mail which fitted her tightly to the hips' (106). Tissot's picture is a replication of the incident even to the fact that the viewer, like de Potter, is almost in the ring of the Hippodrome and must look up to see the chariot-driver—clad in her sensuous mail corselet, with her whip in the air, and a provocative smile on her face—ride past him out of the picture. Two of her fellow chariot drivers follow her and can perhaps be identified as youthful versions of Rosa's friends: the thin, fair Cob (who rides last) and the sultry Sombreuse.

In the same way, Tissot's *La Mystérieuse*, 1883–5 (see fig. 40 on p. 104) is an homage through allusion to Ouida and her novel *Moths* (1880). Ouida, whose society novels were enormously popular, 'seems to have been one of Tissot's first friends in London' and there is a direct correspondence between the etching and an incident in this novel.[7] Though her favorite dog Loris, a Russian wolfhound, is missing, the etching depicts Princess Vere Zouroff viewed by the tenor Corrèze as he rides in the Bois: 'walking in one of the allées des piétons; she was in black, with some old white laces about her throat; before her were her dogs [in the oil sketch one of the dogs precedes the Princess] and behind her was a Russian servant.' As Corrèze, who loves her, waits for her to pass, 'she bowed without looking at him, and went onward between the stems of the leafless trees.'[8] The nun helping the old woman in the extreme background functions as a symbolic comment on Vere's character: she is a reference to the spiritual nature of this woman who is, indeed, a mystery to society. Cold and unhappy but faithful to a sadistic husband, one of the most colourful of Victorian villains, Vere is repeatedly described as a nun, a 'young saint,' and 'St. Elizabeth.' Depicted as looking like 'a Burne-Jones thing,'[9] only more spiritual, she dresses almost entirely in black or angelic white. In the etching we encounter her from the same angle that Corrèze does, as described in Ouida's novel, but to us she appears coy rather than tragic and isolated. The mysteriousness alluded to is not visually evident, but it lies in the 'world's' inability to comprehend Vere's otherworldliness, nobility and purity.

These are just two examples, and commentators on Tissot have located sources for other paintings and etchings of *La Femme à Paris* series.[10] Nevertheless, *The New York Times*'s often quoted statement[11] that there 'were to be stories written' based on the visual works, as well as in its ascription of the unwritten tales to specific authors, is not entirely accurate. Many of the stories to which the paintings allude already *had been* written, and not necessarily by the figures the *Times* believed were to be responsible for them.

The tale behind *The Liar*, 1883–5 (fig. 69 on p. 175) for instance, had been published in 1874 as part of Daudet's 'framed' collection of stories, *The Wives of the Artists* (Tissot's 1885 painting of the same name is, I believe, an allusion to the thesis of the volume). Once again, Tissot's *Liar* is a precise if fictional portrait of Clotilde Deloche, the liar of Daudet's story 'A Life's Lie' (the title as translated in the 1889 American edition), and she is surrounded by all of the paraphernalia of her mendacity. In this story, told by a painter of the woman he once loved and now hates, we catch a tone of cynical disillusionment, perhaps reinforced by the smile on the 'liar's' face. We are told of Clotilde's 'tall lissome figure, her pale complexion . . . , her regular, delicate features, with a look of the Eastern Jews in the swelling roundness of her face,'[12] and of her nature as 'a thorough Parisian, dressed in perfect taste' (179). Tissot's picture suggests these elements, but what the portrait best illuminates is Clotilde's 'life lie.' Earning her own money, ostensibly by giving piano lessons, she 'buys bouquets of rare flowers' (182) for her artist lover and fills his flat with them and with the costly and exotic little objects that she says are gifts from her rich pupils. She even shows him rings and bracelets these bankers' and stock-brokers' daughters have bestowed upon her. Tissot's picture catches her with a bouquet of flowers in one hand and books (either of music used in her 'lessons' or to be given as gifts) in the other; there is a smile on her face as she eagerly reenters the home she has made so pleasant for her lover. However, the tale reveals that when she does not return one night the painter discovers that all is a lie. There are no pupils, no lessons; the endless, irrelevant details she has fed him are all false. When he asks who she really is and where she has obtained her 'money and lace and jewels' (190) she gives him a look of inexpressible sorrow, turns her head to the wall and dies, 'liar to the bitter end' (191).

Still other subtler and more interesting allusions are imbedded in the *Femme à Paris* series; they are sometimes in-jokes or encoded references to literary works by Tissot's acquaintances, as in the paintings of the shop attendants and of the artists' wives. We may wonder about the interactions depicted in the splendid *Shop Girl,* 1883–5 (pl. XXI) ostensibly to be the painted equivalent of a tale by Emile Zola, but it is not clear whether the painting or the novel was the originating inspiration, whether Zola had not already written the story in *Au Bonheur des Dames* (1883), his novel of the first great Paris department store, Au Printemps, and of the conflict between the owner of an old-fashioned small shop and the manager of the new innovative merchandising mart. But I would argue that the rather elegant-looking bearded and spectacled gentleman ogling the second salesgirl (whose face we cannot see) through the window, does look remarkably like Zola himself. This may well be a Tissot aside, one of the coterie allusions he so enjoys, for the resemblance between the man in the *Shop Girl* and both the Manet portrait of a younger Zola (1868) and the Fantin-Latour image of him in the 1870 *Studio in Batignolles* seems too close to be merely coincidental. (An older, heavier, and less attractive Zola, photographed in about 1875, wears the spectacles of Tissot's picture, missing in the painted portraits.)[13]

Sometimes Tissot's allusions take the form of references to the title of a work. Tissot's own titles are more meaningful than many believe, as, for example, his calling one of the pictures in the *Femme à Paris* series, *The Artists' Ladies,* 1883–5 (fig. 38 on p. 102). Commentators have ignored the reference to Daudet's narrative in this painting, reading it simply as a depiction of a gathering of artists and their wives at the Paris Salon's equivalent of the Royal Academy's 'varnishing' day. The assembled group is at lunch at Ledoyen's restaurant and they are, indeed, excited and gay; however, it is neither misjudgment nor poor technique that makes the artists' wives in this picture appear, as Wentworth comments, 'commonplace, and more than a little vulgar.'[14] Nor is it accidental that the woman in the foreground of the painting looks somewhat arch, less elegant and attractive than most Tissot women;[15] it is the very point of the picture. This woman and many of the other wives—all tightly and correctly corseted, all slightly overdressed in their upholstered day-ensembles—are examples of the kinds of women that artists foolishly wed. Daudet's argument in *Wives of Men of Genius* is that in the first place artists should not marry, and in the second that, when they do, they wed the wrong sort of women. Their wives are conventional and empty-headed ('Madame Heurtebise'), or coarse and shrewish ('The Transteverina'), or else provincial Galateas who, though attractive, are materialists, unsympathetic to the arts ('A Misunderstanding: Husband's Version'). The woman with the arch expression, who stares out of the painting as if to see who

46. Tissot, *Berthe*, 1883, etching and drypoint, 35.7 x 27.7 cm. Art Gallery of Ontario, Toronto, Gift of Allan and Sondra Gotlieb

else is coming and to note what she is wearing, is of the bourgeois, conventional variety, or so her fashionable but overdone costume implies. The woman with the lovely profile in the right foreground may represent the models whom artists sometimes marry: these are the other sort of artists' wives whom, Daudet announces in 'A Misunderstanding: Wife's Version', the more 'respectable' female spouses despise. Perhaps deliberately, Tissot's women dominate this painting/etching, just as Daudet insists they dominate the painters' lives.[16]

While the *Femme à Paris* series is generally recognized as essentially literary in orientation,[17] the associations of other Tissot paintings and etchings with literary works are less recognized. Either their references are deliberately encoded because their sources hint at sexuality or their origins have been obscured because the works to which they allude have been forgotten. Such indirect literary references may colour portraits of young women like 'Berthe' and 'Miss Lloyd' and, perhaps, the pictures that include mysterious Tissot twins. The charming *Berthe*, 1883 (fig. 46) may just be a study of a young woman of that name (although commentators on the pastel and etching do not identify her),[18] or the image may allude to a De Maupassant tale. In a short story called 'At the Spa,' published in 1881, a Marquis records his need for a female companion, a temporary mistress, since he is to be confined to a spa for a month. A young woman named Berthe, 'pretty, just out of the Conservatoire, waiting around for a part, a future star' is selected on the basis of her 'excellent manners, poise, intelligence' and, of course, her availability for 'love.' When the Marquis meets her at the train station he is impressed, for she looks like a lady, 'and what a hat!' he murmurs. 'Quite divine, charming yet simple!'[19] The typically cynical tale ends with Berthe enjoying her respectability as the 'Marquise' and enchanting all who meet her, while her titled lover almost proposes, changes his mind, and discards her — only to recognize, too late, that he should have wed her.

Here, as in the earlier etching of Miss Lloyd titled *'Portrait of Miss L. . . . or A Door Must Be Open or Closed'*, 1876 (fig. 52 on p. 144), the implications of the reference are sexual and thus must be veiled. In this *Portrait of Miss L. . . .* a rather elegantly dressed, seductive young woman stands in a doorway (wearing a dress that appears in at least three other Tissot works) and the allusion in the subtitle is to a courtship comedy of the same name by Alfred de Musset. De Musset's playlet or *proverbe* for salon entertainment makes explicit what Tissot's picture suggests — that the witty and flirtatious lady (in the play a young, widowed Marquise) is telling a suitor who is half-heartedly wooing her either to 'put up or shut up.' The door in the play is both literal and metaphorical as the suitor, a Count, wavers, and the lady, unsure of her own feelings, reiterates that he must either stay or go. The moment Tissot depicts is when the Marquise decides to end the sexual duel by exiting her own house. As she does so, the Count proposes, and the lady, while accepting him, reminds him that 'a door has to be either open or shut'.[20]

Berthe and *Portrait of Miss L.* signal erotic subtexts, but the presence in Tissot's paintings of physical twins — or of attractive young women who appear nearly identical — while indirectly provocative, may be more directly connected to his use of a now nearly forgotten piece of literature by G.J. Whyte-Melville. The English Romantics had been fascinated with doppelgängers and Edgar Allan Poe had added his versions of the double to the literary repertoire, yet twins (especially attractive female ones) had not had much currency in Victorian literature, and even less in painting, until the 1860s. Wilkie Collins's popular sensation novel of 1860, *The Woman in White*, may have created a minor vogue for women who looked alike, though his Anne Catherick — the actual woman in white — is just a pale shadow copy of her beautiful half-sister Laura Fairlie.

However, G.J. Whyte-Melville, one of the figures Tissot caricatured for *Vanity Fair* and thus came to know, had in 1869 written a popular novel called *M. or N.* about two beautiful sisters who look strikingly similar. Whyte-Melville, a gentleman author and expert foxhunter was 'a great favorite with readers of his own class,' and had an 'intimate acquaintance with . . . fashionable life.' Thus he 'could deal with it in fiction without any risk of falling into the ludicrous exaggerations and blunders which beset many writers who attempted to do so.'[21] His entertaining society novel with its portraits of Maude and Nina, nearly identical, though 'one [Maude] was a costly artificial flower, the other [Nina] a real garden rose'[22] may well have amused Tissot into visually representing such young ladies.

Indeed, Maude, the fashionable beauty, is a typical Tissot woman, impassive in face and cool and poised in gesture; while powerful in effect, she appears emotionless. Her 'pale delicate features,' 'graceful form,' 'dark eyes and glossy raven hair' (82) resemble those of the lady in Tissot's painting, *The Letter*, c.1876–8 (pl. XVII). Nina Algernon, 'as like Maude Bruce in form and feature, as though she had been her twin sister' (82) although she is in fact the slightly older 'natural' child of the same aristocratic parents, is different in temperament — fresh, kindly and unselfish. The two sisters are, of course, mistaken for each other. Maude is almost ruined in an elaborate blackmail scheme involving a letter she must destroy, while Nina's portrait as the 'Fairy Queen', shown at the Royal Academy and loved by the public, is panned by a critic whose negative review sounds remarkably like the reception which Tissot's paintings of the next few years would receive: 'flesh tints infamous, chiaroscuro grossly muddled; no breadth; not much story in it; badly composed' (208). Whyte-Melville's novel ends with the two sisters happily married, becoming fast friends and forming a bond that unites them both personally and socially. Is it, therefore, just coincidence that twins appear in Tissot's *Ball on Shipboard*, 1873 (pl. XII) just a few years later and that they are precisely the type — attractive, upper-middle-class young ladies — that Maude Bruce and Nina Algernon personify? Is the presence in the painting of three sets of nearly identical young women perhaps a comment on or an aside directed to Whyte-Melville?[23] Does the allusion help explain the twins in blue gowns who are seated with another set of twins at a table in the left background of *The Ball on Shipboard* but who take the foreground in *In The Conservatory (The Rivals)*, c.1875–8 (pl. VII) and are now major players in a scene rendered deliberately ambiguous? In this second picture, one twin holds a teacup and the other puts hers down, while both chat with a young man and with a woman who

47. Tissot, *The Portico of the National Gallery, London,* 1878, etching, 37.8 x 21.1 cm. Art Gallery of Ontario, Toronto, Gift of Allan and Sondra Gotlieb

was also present at the ball on shipboard where, set off from but near the twins, she engages with a naval officer.

Whether or not Tissot specifically refers here to Whyte-Melville, the recurrence of these figures points to an internal narrative, a structure of self-allusion that makes his works unusually rich in implications. For ultimately the most complex of Tissot's allusions are self-referential. His paintings, like such Victorian fictions as Anthony Trollope's Barchester or Palliser novels, comment on each other through repeated characters, situations, or settings. These paintings, pseudo-literary in a way, invite the viewer to write the stories that connect the images and situations. Again, like Trollope whose hallmark is to use the same characters and settings in related works but to shift them back and forth into major and minor positions of interest, Tissot will foreground a minor figure in

48. Tissot, *Ramsgate*, 1876, drypoint, 24.9 x 34.7 cm. Art Gallery of Ontario, Toronto, Gift of Allan and Sondra Gotlieb

one painting to a major role in another or relegate a major figure in one work to a background position in another. As in Trollope's Barchester series, so in Tissot the same setting may hold different figures. Thus, the National Gallery and St. Martin's-in-the-Field first frame the tourist couple in the painting *London Visitors*, c.1874 (pl. XVIII) while in the later etching, *The Portico of the National Gallery, London*, 1878 (fig. 47), Kathleen Newton, holding her artist's portfolio, is placed in the foreground and the tourist couple are reduced and relegated to the upper right-hand corner. In a similar way, the same room seen from a slightly different angle holds first the quarrelling couple of *A Passing Storm*, c.1876 (pl. VI), then the quiet readers relaxing in the *Room Overlooking the Harbour*, c.1876–7 (fig. 28 on p. 69) and finally the neutral scene suggested in the etching *Ramsgate*, 1876 (fig. 48).[24]

In yet other works, Trollope the literary artist and Tissot the painter are clearly involved in depicting the same world. This is most obvious in such pictures as *Too Early* , 1873 (pl. I) and *Hush!*, c.1875 (pl. XIII), works that satirize 'the way we live now,' as does Trollope's novel of the same name. The two men may well have met each other,[25] but, more important, for a few years in the 1870s they utilize the same sort of realism, strikingly similar subject matter, related techniques of depiction, and a nearly identical comic and satiric tone.[26]

Whether these similarities stem from allusions to each other or from a similar view of social realities, both men are deeply involved in narratives that illustrate the ways of the contemporary world. *The Way We Live Now*, written in 1873 and published in instalments from 1874 to 1875, then in volume form, is Trollope's indictment of the vulgarity, commercialism, and moral and financial corruption of the *nouveaux riches*, of a rising middle class turned social-climbers, and of a fading gentry and aristocracy. In this sharply comic but detached exploration of the moral climate of the 1870s, Trollope depicts dishonesty permeating every rank of society. Aristocrats are lazy, greedy do-nothings, lounging about like the young man near the stairwell in *Too Early* (pl. I), while the 'wrong people' successfully buy their way into society; women are concerned only with their appearance and their prospects in the marriage market; gossip is the universal occupation; faux pas, like arriving at a ball 'too early,' are equated with moral lapses; everyone dislikes everyone else, and the omnipresent emotion is boredom.[27]

Like Trollope in *The Way We Live Now*, Tissot depicts with comic detachment the most characteristic and colourful events of the 1873–5 London social seasons — elaborate balls and parties and public and private festivities in honour of foreign dignitaries. In Trollope's novel, a great and utterly fraudulent financier, Augustus Melmotte, entertains the Emperor of China in an incident based on the celebrations ordered for the Shah of Persia's three-week visit to England.[28] In a wonderful comic scene, Melmotte provides a dinner and reception for the Chinese Emperor in his own home and in the presence of English royalty; Tissot's *Hush!* (pl. XIII) creates a similar scene, substituting a concert for the dinner and an Indian Rajah for the Persian Shah. The short rather rotund lady in the doorway is reminiscent of Queen Victoria; adorned with diamond tiara, earrings, and necklace (the only lady guest so abundantly decorated) she may be Tissot's joking reference to English royalty.

But the strongest resemblances between the novel and the painting lie in their shared tones and common satiric targets. In *Hush!* as in *The Way We Live Now*, the collective pastime is gossip and the dominant affectation, so brilliantly epitomized in the languid back of the elegant lady in black, is boredom: the same is true of most of the spectators in the *The Ball on Shipboard*, c.1874 (pl. XII). Among the few people who seem even remotely prepared to listen to the music, whether or not it is to be played by Neruda (the second Lady Hallé), are the

Indian royal family. A foreground group is shown chatting, many spectators have their backs to the violinist, and active gossiping is suggested by those in the picture who shield their mouths like the man standing against the wall or the dowager only partially visible in the foreground, who almost commits the unpardonable sin of pointing. Ambiguities abound and certain questions remain unanswered, revealing *Hush!* as a problem picture. Who are these guests? What is the subject of their gossip? For whom is the empty chair reserved? Tissot's social conversation paintings are his comic novels. Like Trollope's *The Way We Live Now* they were criticised for their satiric edge and 'the oppressive vulgarity of . . . [their] characters'[29] and they are perhaps the most topical of all Tissot's works.

Interestingly, during the same period of time, he was also painting his equivalent of the tragic novel—pseudo-narratives that appear to allude to fiction but are actually his inventions. *The Letter* (pl. XVII) for example is a painting that *should* be based upon a literary work but does not appear to be. For letters—especially letters of love or of rejection—are so much a convention of the Victorian novel that they are difficult to identify with any one work of fiction. In this painting, as in others such as *Lovers' Quarrel*, 1876 (for etching, see fig. 54 on p. 146) or *The Stairs*, 1869 (fig. 49), the internal narrative is ambiguous, capable of multiple interpretations, and redolent of problems in heterosexual relations. Tissot is often compared to the Scottish painter William Orchardson in his choice of subject matter, especially in his depiction of the Victorian rich and bored, but an even closer relationship is suggested by their common attitude toward the 'meaning' of a given picture. Tissot's works are of a slightly earlier date but the same questions asked about Orchardson's studies of marital dishar-mony or sexual tension, such as *Mariage de Convenance* (1883) or *An Enigma* (1891), could well be asked about Tissot's enigmatic studies of separated or unhappy lovers. When Orchardson was asked if the couple in *An Enigma* were quarrelling, whether the man had proposed and been rejected, or wanted to pro-pose but feared rejection, he answered that 'any of these interpretations would be equally valid.'[30]

If asked to explain the 'meaning' of *The Letter* (pl. XVII) Tissot might well have answered in the same words. The painting bears the scent of mystery, as Tissot invites us to write and read our own letter and thus imagine our own nar-rative. The lady who stares out at the viewer, an active participant in rather than a victim of the spectator's gaze, could be a character from a novel by Ouida or Whyte-Melville or Trollope. Elegantly but soberly dressed for autumn, her black

49. Tissot, *The Stairs*, 1869,
oil on canvas, 50.8 x 35.5 cm.
Private Collection

outfit broken only by her steel grey overskirt and fawn-coloured gloves,[31] she has
the expressionless visage found among the heroines of society novels, a face
which manifests indifference based on superiority. Haughty and cold, a study in
well-dressed alienation, she seems larger than life, and her surroundings are
clearly symbolic of her condition. As she tears up a letter we wish we could read
and its pieces flutter down among the autumn foliage, we notice that her gloved
fingers are similar in form and colour to the chestnut leaves that surround her.
We scrutinize her, but the servant avoids looking directly at her as he takes away
the tray on which tea would have been or has been served. The lady's air of somewhat inexpressive grief (or is it anger?) tells us less than do the paths that lead out
of the picture — paths that signal separation or departure. We cannot be certain
(for the lady's controlled features conceal emotion) but we can guess that the
letter announces that someone (a lover?) either cannot or will not join her.
Though the sombre tones and erotic intensity of the painting powerfully convey
its mood, manifold possibilities of interpretation remain. Who is the letter from?

Does it announce a death or a desertion? Has he, whoever he is, been expected at the tea? Where does this scene take place? Is this an English garden or a French one? Where is the lady now going? The painting certainly hints at a canceled meeting, at the end of an affair, and the dead leaves suggest dead letters. Yet even the clues that Tissot offers the viewer remain mysterious. Perhaps it is significant that the goddesses or nymphs carved on the large urn at the lady's right appear to hold back or to intercept the chariot depicted next to them. Are they too victimized by time and change? Or perhaps the urn is simply an urn, the sort of ornament that this kind of formal garden would contain.

In *Sapho,* his friend Daudet creates and gives significance to an imaginary Tissot portrait; so in *The Letter,* Tissot invents and builds upon an imaginary work of fiction. Raising as many questions as he answers, he pulls us into his painted narratives and teases us into and 'out of thought'. This way of working, combined with the private nature of his allusions and the sophistication of his internal and serial narratives, makes him an endlessly fascinating but at times impenetrable chronicler of Victorian manners and mores.

1. *Dreamers of Decadence: Symbolist Painters of the 1890s,* trans. Robert Baldick (New York: Praeger, 1971), 137.

2. Alphonse Daudet, *Sapho: Parisian Manners* (Boston: L.C. Page, 1906). Hereafter all citations in my text are to this edition. The portrait seems to be the only significant object Fanny takes with her in the several residential moves she makes during the novel. First described at the beginning of the book, it is not included when Fanny, proving her fidelity to Jean, destroys the other relics of artists and novelists who have been her lovers. When, to save money, Fanny goes off to manage a boarding house for a rich woman (none other than Rosa, the former chariot-driver) she removes her belongings from Jean's flat, leaving only the Tissot picture and the following note: 'You will only find my portrait, which will not cost you anything, only the kind looks which I would bespeak on its behalf' (82–3). Later, when the couple move to the country, they bring only a few possessions with them but 'to embellish the frightful green paper in the bed-room,' they take 'Fanny's portrait' (111). Finally, when Jean returns to Fanny, after briefly attempting to terminate the affair, he awakes after a night of passion to 'the large portrait of Fanny [which] rose opposite him' (196).

3. I am indebted to Willard E. Misfeldt, *J.J. Tissot: Prints From the Gotlieb Collection* (Alexandria, Va.: Art Services International, 1991), 166, for much of this plot summary.

4. James's review is in *The Painter's Eye: Notes and Essays on the Pictorial Arts by Henry James,* ed. John L. Sweeney (Cambridge, Mass.: Harvard University Press, 1956), 140. Although implying that the lady's dress in Tissot's painting, while 'a triumph of

perception and taste' (141) reveals more character than the lady's face, James goes on to use Daisy Miller's gown as an index of her personality. He indicates that her dress *is* her character. See *Daisy Miller: A Study* in *The Norton Anthology of American Literature*, 4th ed., vol. 2, ed. Nina Bayme et al. (New York: W.W. Norton, 1994): 279–80. All quotations below are to this edition. Introduced to the reader as 'strikingly, admirably pretty,' Daisy is constantly 'smooth[ing] out a knot or two of ribbon,' 'inspect[ing] her flounces and smooth[ing] her ribbons again,' 'examining her bows,' and drawing up her 'muslin furbelows.' Her gown and her self-conscious toying with it reveal her, James tells the reader, as 'a pretty American flirt' (280–5).

5. See Michael Wentworth, *James Tissot*. (Oxford: Clarendon Press, 1984), 168–9, and Misfeldt, *J.J. Tissot*, 161.

6. De Potter may be based on Jules Massenet who turned Daudet's novel into a successful opera in 1897 and was apparently involved in a long liaison (despite his marriage and family) with one of his singers.

7. Misfeldt, *J.J. Tissot*, 168; Michael Justin Wentworth, *James Tissot: Catalogue Raisonné of His Prints* (Minneapolis, Minn.: Minneapolis Institute of Arts, 1978), 318.

8. Ouida, *Moths* (London: Chatto and Windus, [1880]), 195.

9. Ouida, *Moths,* 97 and passim.

10. For example, *The Fashionable Beauty* (fig. 37 on p. 101) is a visual depiction of a tale called 'La Plus Belle' and published in 1892 by another of Tissot's friends, Ludovic Halévy, which tells of the transient night of fame of a pretty bourgeois lawyer's wife, Madame Derline, who holds the title only for a moment. See Wentworth, *Catalogue Raisonné*, 317; Misfeldt, *J.J. Tissot*, 170.

11. *New York Times* (10 May 1885), 10.

12. 'A Life's Lie' in *Wives of Men of Genius* (New York: Worthington, 1889), 178. All references to this work in my text are to this translation.

13. See Manet, *Portrait of Emile Zola*, 1868; Henri Fantin-Latour, *A Studio in Batignolles*, 1870, and the photograph, 'Emile Zola at his desk,' c.1875. I am indebted to Prof. Pauline Kra for first noticing the resemblance. Moreover, Frederick Brown's recent biography, *Zola: A Life* (Baltimore: John Hopkins University Press, 1995) discusses a voyeuristic tendency in Zola that was partially manifested in a fascination with windows both in his art and his life. Brown comments on a letter written by the young Zola about his 'wildly Platonic love' for a young florist whom he watched from his window; he notes that Zola's experience 'ultimately furnished material for numerous scenes in his novels involving people who peer through windows . . . at unfaithful mistresses, unpossessable bodies, phantomatic lovers' (71). Later in his life, comments Brown, 'Zola struggled against the voyeurism in himself . . . who had on various occasions pictured himself and real and imaginary windows, yearning for some unpossessable woman or seeing her possessed by another man' (180). This trait might well have been sensed by his friends and acquaintances.

14. Wentworth, *Tissot*, 175.

15. Christopher Wood, *The Life and Work of Jacques Joseph Tissot 1836–1902* (London: Wiedenfeld and Nicolson, 1986), 141.

16. Guy de Maupassant agrees with Daudet on the foolishness of artists marrying. See 'The Artist's Wife' in *The Complete Short Stories of Guy de Maupassant* (Garden City, New York: Hanover House, 1955) in which de Maupassant advises his readers to read Daudet's book, 'so true, so cruel, and so beautiful' (788) before going on to tell of yet another painter's foolish union. The tale's narrator comments that 'painters make a specialty of ridiculous marriages' (788) and notes that they often wed their models, their former mistresses or just about any woman they happen to encounter.

17. Wentworth, *Tissot*, 168.

18. The same model appears in *Sunday Morning*, wearing another charming hat.

19. De Maupassant, 'At the Spa: Diary of the Marquis de Roseveyre' in *Complete Short Stories*, 90.

20. Alfred de Musset, *Comedies and Proverbs*, trans. David Sices (Baltimore: Johns Hopkins University Press, 1994), 239. First published in 1845, the play was performed in 1848 and reprinted in 1853,

21. See 'Whyte-Melville, George John' in *Dictionary of National Biography*, ed. Leslie Stephen et al., vol. 20 (London and New York: Oxford University Press, 1885–1993): 173–4.

22. G.J. Whyte-Melville, *M. or N.* (London: Ward Lock, [1869]), 82. Hereafter all citations in my text are to this edition.

23. Another possible answer, however, may lie in a fact even more obvious than a literary allusion, that is, the presence or availability of a pair of twin models. Two females described by Henry James as 'two young girls of eighteen or twenty stiffly posed and drawn, but very freely painted, and looking out of the canvas as Mr. Millais can so often teach his figures to look' (*The Painter's Eye*, 166) are the subjects of an 1876 portrait called *Twins*. See Peter Funnell et al. *Millais: Portraits*, exh. cat. (London: National Portrait Gallery, 1999), no. 51.

24. Tissot's use of this internal cross-referencing is too extensive to discuss in detail here. But in addition to the obviously related internal narratives suggested by such paintings as *An Interesting Story*, *Le Thé*, etc., it is worth noticing that he develops, reuses, and subordinates figures like that of the elderly woman in *The Convalescent* (1876) and *Holyday* (1877).

25. It is highly probable that Tissot met Anthony Trollope; both were living and socializing in London at the same time and both were good, even intimate, friends of the painter John Everett Millais. Moreover, Trollope was an avid gallery goer, much interested in the art scene, while both men were involved in magazine work: Trollope was writing for and editing *St. Pauls* when Tissot, through Bowles, was producing caricatures for *Vanity Fair*.

26. Some of Tissot's women may accurately be described as Trollopian, beautiful and cool, assertive and self-confident, aristocratic or trying to appear so — they seem similar to the female characters of the Palliser novels, especially *Phineas Finn* (1869), for example.

27. See Anthony Trollope, *The Way We Live Now* (New York: Modern Library, 1996), 489 and passim. Trollope's Augustus Melmotte, 'the Great Financier' is a parvenu, swindler

and forger of dubious background and criminal behaviour, but a sponsor of brilliant festivities. His original, John Sadleir, also dealt fraudulently in railways and estates, gave brilliant parties and, like Melmotte, committed suicide by taking prussic acid when found out.

28. See N. John Hall, *Trollope: A Biography* (Oxford: Clarendon Press, 1991), 385. The Shah was feted in the City and entertained at the Guildhall with a concert and a dinner for some ninety people.

29. A reviewer in the *Spectator* complained of 'the oppressive vulgarity of the characters' and other critics joined in attacking the harshness of the novel's satire, labeling the work and its author misanthropic. The *Times* however described the book as 'only too faithful a portraiture' of present-day manners. For reviews of Trollope's *The Way We Live Now* and suggestions about its impact see Hall, *Trollope: A Biography,* 387–8. It is worth noting that some of Tissot's paintings of the same period were attacked for the same reasons.

30. Quoted in Pamela Gerrish Nunn, *Problem Pictures: Women and Men in Victorian Painting* (Brookfield, Vt.: Ashgate, 1996), 63. For Orchardson see Jeremy Maas, *Victorian Painters* (New York: G.P. Putnam's Sons, 1969), 245–6.

31. Although soberly dressed, the lady does not appear to be in half-mourning, as has been suggested. Such colour combinations as steel-gray and black were popular during the mid-1870s. I am indebted to the curatorial staff of the Costume Institute of the Metropolitan Museum of Art, New York, for their help.

Spirits in Space: Theatricality and the Occult in Tissot's Life and Art

Ann Saddlemyer

O SCAR WILDE once described the paradox as forcing the verities to walk a tightrope.[1] James Joseph Tissot continues to be something of a paradox, and he seems perpetually to have walked a tightrope: in life the permanent outsider, methodically courting success both in Paris and London, making all the right gestures yet at the same time almost deliberately establishing obstacles in the way of social acceptance; in his art lovingly capturing minute details of dress and manners against a background of secret gardens, boldly inviting us in only to bar the entrance. Never entirely escaping from the medieval and Romantic idealism of his first masters, he yet took pains to announce himself an ironic modernist; teetering perilously between realism and symbolism, he embraced many of the naturalist techniques of his contemporaries while at the same time he was deeply committed to the occult and the unexpressed.

Such delicate balancing encourages theatricality, and one might even go so far as to say that Tissot anticipated many of the movements in the arts that were to mark the final decades of the nineteenth century, especially the shifting borders between realism and symbolism. His arrival in Paris in the mid-1850s coincided with a fertile period of critical and philosophical revolt, a struggle between the measured and the immeasurable, material outer reality and inner truth, the objective and the subjective, fact and intuition, definition and allusion, representation and transfiguration, the perpetual tension between science and belief. The use of the term Realism to describe a general anti-Romantic tendency with an emphasis on capturing external reality, be it nature or humanity, had long been current; now it became a battleground. The influence of Positivist philosophy, with its conviction that heredity, environment and the historical moment are the three forces determining one's life, was so pervasive that Ernest Renan (later to become notorious for his book disclaiming the divinity of Jesus) proclaimed science the new religion. Darwin's *On the Origin of Species*, Marx's *Critique of Political Economy* and Claude Bernard's *Introduction to the Study of Experimental Medicine* confirmed the ascendancy of materialist philosophy and led inexorably to Emile Zola's theory of Naturalism as he attempted to express it in his 'experimental novels', essays and plays. Indeed, for Zola imagination—so essential to the Romantics and earlier Realists—may even be a distraction to the artist.

Zola's challenge 'The theatre will be Naturalist or it will not be!'[2] would eventually be taken up in the 1890s by André Antoine and his Théâtre Libre, which was to be a laboratory for authors and actors. Antoine's productions accepted the concept of the 'fourth wall' through which the audience peered to observe the 'slice of life' enacted before them; one is reminded of Degas' keyhole. Acting must be based on 'truth, observation, and the direct study of nature', portraying 'the verities of everyday life.'[3] 'Antoine's back' became the byword for a new, understated and more intimate style of performance; ensemble playing challenged the convention of the heroic star. Stage setting too became more realistic: genuine meat hanging in the butcher's window, doorknobs on solid doors, windows that opened, properties and costumes that came from real life. One of Antoine's first productions was, not unexpectedly, *Thérèse Raquin*, adapted from Zola's novel.

But the playwright who caused the most controversy, and whose works became synonymous with the new theatre, was the Norwegian Henrik Ibsen. Ibsen too was impressed by the scientific and psychological theories of the time, but practised a more selective, heightened realism rather than Zola's uncompromising naturalism, suggesting rather than underlining the accumulation of experience which leads his characters to their fate. With the works of Ibsen the concept of what has come to be known as subtext, the message underneath the stage action and scrupulous setting which provides the ultimate truth of character, entered critical discourse. But Ibsen insisted that everything he created had its origin in a frame of mind and a situation in life; characters must be true to their time and situation. The door slammed by Nora in *A Doll's House* in 1879 reverberated throughout Europe, nowhere more loudly than in Paris and London. Not only Antoine but other 'free theatres' of Europe saw Ibsen as the banner of a new Realism. At least a decade earlier, in the clues that suggest rather than tell the narrative, Tissot seems independently to have discovered not only the impact of the 'subtext' but the 'fourth wall' as essential aspects of realism.

Equally noisy were the protests against the Naturalists' qualification of art. Courbet's *pavillon du réalisme* at the Universal Exhibition in 1855 would later be challenged by the Goncourt brothers in their novel *Manette Solomon,* with its demand for a more *selective* realism, a more sensitive style, to redeem the ugliness they saw. (Oscar Wilde's dismissal of the Naturalists would be even more sweeping: 'they find life crude and leave it raw'.[4]) In 1856, the year Tissot met Whistler, Baudelaire published his translation of Edgar Allan Poe's *Tales of Mystery and Imagination*, initiating an enthusiasm for imaginative correspondences and images emerging from the depths of the subconscious. In 1857, the year Tissot entered the École des Beaux Arts, Flaubert's *Madame Bovary* and Baudelaire's *Les fleurs de mal*, both celebrations of style over their contemporary subjects, were prosecuted for 'outrage of public morals and religions'. And in 1859, the year Darwin and Marx stormed the barricades of organized religion and social norms, Wagner, influenced by the pessimist philosophy of Schopenhauer, completed *Tristan und Isolde*, while Gounod's opera *Faust,* exploring the struggle between good and evil, nature and philosophy, was first seen in Paris. (The story of Marguerite and Faust, the subject of Tissot's early medieval phase, had long been popular in the theatre.)

In that eventful year, 1859, Tissot first exhibited in the Paris Salon, a year according to Baudelaire of 'a lot of know-how and skill, but very little genius'.[5] Tissot's skill would lead to an honourable mention two years later, and finally a medal in the Salon of 1866; but it did not lead to the kind of success, dubious or scandalous, which was to be achieved by his fellow artists Manet and Degas. Indeed, for Tissot, establishment approval (and some financial success) appears to have alienated rather than endeared him to his colleagues. How else are we to explain Manet and Degas' patrician disgust that Tissot should have made it his first priority to sketch — rather than retrieve — the corpse of their friend Cuvelier, *The First Slain Man that I Saw* , 1876 (fig. 50, etching)? Yet was that not precisely what Baudelaire had requested in his 1863 essay, 'The Painter of Modern Life'? Indeed by the time of his valiant engagement in the Franco-Prussian war Tissot seems with his own small sketch-book to have deliberately emulated the artist-journalist Constantin Guys, correspondent in the Crimean War for the *Illustrated London News*, who, Baudelaire claimed, captured 'elements of a valuable form of picturesque, which many well-known painters would have thoughtlessly neglected if they had found themselves in the same circumstances'. One can imagine the earnest young artist/stretcher-bearer pausing for breath on the second floor of the renowned Comédie Française, whipping out his sketchbook, and recording *Foyer of the Comédie-Française: Recollection of the Siege of Paris*, 1877 (fig. 51, etching) a moment of theatrical history and, with its grand parade of France's literary heroes, a preview of his own method. It would not be difficult to assume that Tissot saw himself as the next guardian of Baudelaire's 'precious archives of civilized life', the recorder of 'the idiom of beauty' of every age and profession, exemplified in the soldier, the dandy, and most particularly in the 'woman and the dress, an indivisible whole'.[6]

50. Tissot, *The First Slain Man that I Saw: Recollection of the Siege of Paris*, 1876, etching and drypoint, 45.4 x 29.4 cm. Art Gallery of Ontario, Toronto, Gift of Allan and Sondra Gotlieb

But poetry had not been permanently banished from the stage. Two new theatre companies in succession, the Théâtre d'Art, established by the poet Paul Fort, and the Théâtre de l'Oeuvre, founded by an actor whose surname acknowledges his allegiance to Edgar Allan Poe, challenged Antoine's Realist Théâtre Libre. Lugné-Poe's Théâtre de l'Oeuvre produced Ibsen's poetic dramas, but Paul Fort introduced the work of the Belgian symbolist Maurice Maeterlinck (the opening production in May 1891 a benefit for Gauguin and Verlaine). With Maeterlinck, mystery was to return once again to the theatre in the form of symbolism and ritual. He too was writing in reaction to the techniques of classical and Romantic drama. But, unlike the Naturalists, he advocated a return to tragedies without movement altogether, a static drama with detached, almost trance-like acting which would throw emphasis upon the inner dialogue of silence: a theatre of the unexpressed, even the inexpressible, which

51. Tissot, *Foyer of the Comédie-Française: Recollection of the Siege of Paris*, 1877, etching, 37.7 x 27.6 cm. Art Gallery of Ontario, Toronto, Gift of Allan and Sondra Gotlieb

depended upon the imagination of the viewer to fill in the gaps. He, like the symbolist poet Mallarmé, preferred allusion and suggestion to direct statements of fact. These, Maeterlinck felt, expressed a greater reality:

> I have grown to believe that an old man, seated in his armchair, waiting patiently, with his lamp beside him, giving unconscious ear to all the eternal laws that reign about his house, interpreting without comprehending, the silence of doors and windows and the quivering voice of the light, submitting with bent head to the presence of his soul and his destiny . . . he, motionless as he is, does yet live in reality a deeper, more human and more universal life than the lover who strangles his mistress, the captain who conquers in battle, or 'the husband who avenges his honour.'[7]

Again, in Tissot's 'frozen moments' of tableau, we recognize the same impulse at work at least a decade earlier.

Yet one more influence had entered the theatre earlier in the nineteenth century. In fact, even before Tissot had arrived in Paris, the Comédie Française restored to the stage the delicate, understated psychological sketches of Alfred de

52. Tissot, *Portrait of Miss L. . . . or A Door Must be Open or Closed,* 1876, drypoint, 36.8 x 20.6 cm. Art Gallery of Ontario, Toronto, Gift of Allan and Sondra Gotlieb

Musset, friend of Victor Hugo and Sainte-Beuve and one of the early repudiators of French Classicism. Showing no concern for either theory or moral purpose, intended to be read as much as acted, Musset's 'armchair theatre' — short scenes of social and salon life culminating in well-known sayings or 'Proverbs' — blended playful fantasy with lyrical language. From 1847 on Musset's plays were to be regularly performed in France: his plays became part of the repertoire of both Paul Fort and André Antoine, and he is known to be one of the few playwrights Ibsen openly admired.

No door slams in Tissot's etchings, but it is I think significant that one of his few works to bear a theatrical title, *'Portrait of Miss L. . . . or A Door Must be Open or Closed,* 1876 (fig. 52), refers to Musset. The play *A Door Must be Kept Open or Shut,* first produced in 1848, is a witty dialogue between two characters in a Paris drawing-room, perhaps based on Musset's love affair with George Sand; certainly the Marquise is too knowledgeable to accept without ironical

53. Tissot, *Trafalgar Tavern (Greenwich)*, 1878, etching, 35 x 24.7 cm. Art Gallery of Ontario, Toronto, Gift of Allan and Sondra Gotlieb

debate the Baron's courtship (although she does in the end), and the door of the title suggests not only the play's action but the witty thrust and parry between the couple. It is tempting to read into Tissot's title a private joke with either 'Miss L', or his domestic muse. It is possible also that the ironic detachment of an amused dandy's observations on society—as in *Hush!*, c. 1875 (pl. XIII), *Too Early*, 1873 (pl. I), or *The Confessional*, 1866 (fig. 2 on p. 6), for example—owes as much to Musset as to Baudelaire.

Whatever drew Tissot to London in 1871, his continued stay there produced works which not only reflect his own continuing need to walk the tightrope between subtext and surface realism, romance and modernity, but foreshadow these contraries in the theatre. His use of superficial realism as signifier of character is analogous to theatrical 'realism': costume, properties, setting are all lovingly elaborated with the utmost precision, whether it be the wooden figure-heads behind the traditional romantic triangle of *Portsmouth Dockyard (How Happy I could be with Either)*, 1877 (pl. XI), the duplicate dresses of *The Ball on Shipboard*, c.1874 (pl. XII) which force the viewer to travel with the costume across the stage, or the table setting of *Trafalgar Tavern (Greenwich)*, 1878 (fig. 53).

54. Tissot, *Lovers' Quarrel*, 1876,
etching, 30.4 x 18.1 cm. Art
Gallery of Ontario, Toronto, Gift
of Allan and Sondra Gotlieb

The narrative, however, especially in *Trafalgar Tavern*, carries us beyond these
details in the manner of Ibsen and Maeterlinck to the suggestion of a subtext or
'second dialogue' which is just out of earshot. And here the viewer is called upon
to complete the picture: it is we who are at the deserted table, looking through
an open window to the next balcony, occupied by a group of gentlemen alert to
the urchin life on the streets below, while further away strollers pause on the
bridge to observe them—and us. One of the gentlemen's party returns our gaze,
thus widening the circle further.

Doors, windows and railings are a constant preoccupation in these etchings
and paintings. They are used, as Ibsen was to use them later, to suggest psychic
or emotional as well as physical distancing, an invisible barrier between the

55. Tissot, *The Three Crows Inn*, 1877, etching, 20.5 x 29.5 cm. Art Gallery of Ontario, Toronto, Gift of Allan and Sondra Gotlieb

characters and between them and us. *A Passing Storm* , c. 1876 (pl. VI), with the gentleman outside between railing and window and only one cup and saucer set before the lady, suggests a narrative which is more subtle and ambiguous than *Lover's Quarrel* (fig. 54); despite its almost ominous quiet, the related scene in the etching *Ramsgate* , 1876 (fig. 48 on p. 130) implies more psychological turbulence than *The Thames*, c.1876 (fig. 71 on p. 177). The railing is again structurally significant in *The Three Crows Inn*, 1877 (fig. 55) where the men and boy watch the lady while she looks beyond the frame altogether.

Windows serve as blocking devices as well as suggestive 'other' boundaries, not only creating frameworks within frames, but deterring as they invite, much as the proscenium arch in a theatre allows us to peer through the 'fourth wall' but restrains us to the role of voyeurs. This was a device later frequently employed by Maeterlinck to achieve 'le nouveau frisson' so admired by the symbolists. *The Organ Grinder*, 1878 (fig. 22 on p. 56) plays longingly to a window that remains stubbornly dark above; the woman in *At the Seaside* , 1880 (fig. 56) actually has to climb a chair to sit on the window ledge; the protagonist in *'Portrait of Miss L. . . . or A Door Must be Open or Closed'* (fig. 52 on p. 144) almost saucily dares us to enter, while book, umbrella and arm firmly block the way. *Woman at the Window* , 1875 (fig. 57) offers the reverse situation: we are on the inside, with chairs hindering our answering her call; intriguingly, the chairs face opposite ways, suggesting further ambiguity. Later works from the *Femme à Paris* series, *Without a Dowry*, 1883–5 (fig. 41 on p. 104) and *The Shop Girl*, 1883–5 (pl. XXI), take us out of doors but not into the bright sunlight of certainty: the young widow and her uncaring chaperone are hemmed in by empty chairs and imprisoned by trees; the sales clerk may be offering an exit to the invisible buyer (the viewer?) as passers-by freely gaze in through the window, but carpet within and coachman outside block a swift getaway. *Morning,* 1886 (fig. 76 on p. 187) further intensifies the stillness of an immovable object: is she coming in or going out? Her fixed gaze meets ours but we are also invited to look to the window reflected in the mirror behind her. Chairs can also suggest absence, as in *Dreaming*, 1881 (fig. 58) where the subjects sit on the lower steps and, ominously towering over them in the background, is the wicker chair which so often accommodated Kathleen Newton — here empty.

Furniture and railings are not the only barriers: plants, hammock and parasol, a croquet mallet behind the

56. Tissot, *At the Seaside*, 1880, etching and drypoint, 38 x 13.7 cm. Art Gallery of Ontario, Toronto, Gift of Allan and Sondra Gotlieb

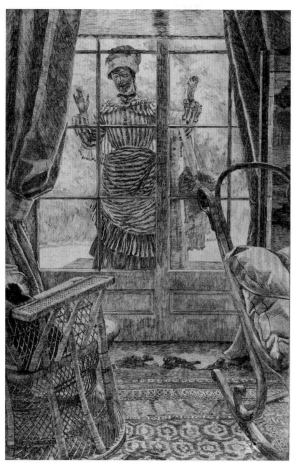

57. Tissot, *Woman at the Window*, 1875, etching, 55.5 x 35 cm. Art Gallery of Ontario, Toronto, Gift of Allan and Sondra Gotlieb

58. Tissot, *Dreaming*, 1881, etching and drypoint, 22.7 x 11.3 cm. Art Gallery of Ontario, Toronto, Gift of Allan and Sondra Gotlieb

back (as in *Croquet*, c.1878, fig. 27 on p. 68), even a direct conquering gaze — all can bar the viewer from entry into the magic garden portrayed so tantalizingly in the background. We are forced to hover, just outside; the promised land of permanent felicity is not for all.

Reactions to Tissot's realism during the 1870s would be paralleled in England two decades later by the critics of Ibsen who, coining the term 'ibscenity', castigated the playwright for, among other improprieties, ludicrous amateurishness, vulgarity, egotism, coarseness and suburban values. Admittedly Tissot did not go as far as Ibsen in his choice of subject; most of this virulence was directed at the

59. Tissot, *The Widower*, 1876, etching and drypoint, 35.2 x 22.9 cm. Art Gallery of Ontario, Toronto, Gift of Allan and Sondra Gotlieb

play *Ghosts,* which dealt in barely disguised manner with the subject of syphilis. But Ruskin dismissed Tissot's canvases as 'mere coloured photographs of vulgar society', while Wilde found all but the conventional *The Widower*, 1876 (fig. 59) in the 1877 Grosvenor Gallery exhibition 'deficient in feeling and depth' and lamented the choice of 'over-dressed, common-looking people' and 'the ugly, painfully accurate representation of modern soda water bottles'. We can imagine the exquisite shudder if this Baudelairean dandy were to encounter Andy Warhol's soup cans. *The Spectator* was especially shocked by images of 'ladies in hammocks, showing a very unnecessary amount of petticoat and stocking, and remarkable for little save their indolence and insolence', while the *Athenaeum* scornfully dismissed the oil painting *Rivals*, 1878–9 (fig. 73 on p. 180): 'a clever but rather coarse painting of unpleasant persons seated at afternoon tea.' Novelist and critic Henry James, objecting to 'hard, vulgar and banal' painting,

The Annunciation. J.-J. T.

60. Tissot, *The Annunciation* from *The Life of our Saviour Jesus Christ* (1897–8), chromolithograph, 11.3 x 14.9 cm. (image). Gift of Allan and Sondra Gotlieb. Photograph courtesy The Edward P. Taylor Reference Library and Archives, Art Gallery of Ontario, Toronto

'trivial' humour and 'stale' sentiment, wailed, 'Is there to be no more *delightful* realism? I sometimes fear it'. Twenty years later, after attending the first performance of Alfred Jarry's savagely symbolist *Ubu Roi* in 1896, the poet W.B. Yeats would answer, 'After us, the Savage God'.

One can see in objections to Tissot's realism both a desire for the completed narrative and an unease concerning the subtext. While Tissot, ever alert to public taste as we have seen with his overt reference to Musset in *Portrait of Miss L.* (fig. 52 on p. 144), occasionally obliged with conventional even melodramatic groupings, as in *A Boring Story, Lovers' Quarrel, The Widower, Orphan, Emigrants*, on the whole he frustrated expectations of closure. As late as 1896 Edward Burne-Jones objected to the illustration of the *Annunciation* (fig. 60) in Tissot's Bible series, 'I want to see the Virgin's face and her little expression, I'm not to be put off with turban and burnous instead. That won't do — it is not enough.'[8]

As we know, Tissot's fascination with the subtext and unspoken dialogue eventually led him to a belief in the hidden world of the supernatural, a step I suspect he would have taken even without the impetus of Kathleen Newton's death. For, attuned to the preoccupations and passions of the time, he could not be unaware of the growing interest in Spiritualism and the occult that took place in the latter half of the century. Occultism, the study of things hidden or mysterious, an acknowledgement of the secret forces of nature beyond the range of ordinary knowledge, has of course a long history. Alchemy, astrology, witchcraft and magic were all practices seeking for keys to the supernatural and spiritual reassurance. The symbolist plays of Maeterlinck, with their emphasis on the contemplative life of the soul, their preoccupation with the mystery of life and death and the haunting shadow of Fate, were but the culmination in the theatre of a fascination that was, more even than a rejection of philosophical materialism, a need for renewed guarantee that life continues beyond bodily death. The 1850s saw the establishment of the Swedenborgian New Church, founded on the writings of the Swedish mystic; there was a revival of mesmerism — celebrated by, amongst others, Charles Dickens — which had been popular in France in the previous century, the practice of healing by controlling the body's 'animal magnetism', often by inducing a hypnotic trance; and Walt Whitman was not alone in consulting a phrenologist.

Second sight, clairvoyance and clairaudience, and what is now referred to as telepathy had long been acknowledged as gifts possessed by the select, and strange, few. But the phenomenon that now swept North America and Europe claimed to be a science, a philosophy, and a religion all in one. Spiritualists believe in the continuity of personality after death, and that spirits of the departed communicate through a living person who is sensitive to these forces. Their belief is also democratic, for everyone has the potential to be a medium; however, spirits will be naturally attracted to those individuals whose qualities resemble their own. Eventually most spirits progress to a higher plane and lose contact altogether with the earthbound, although they can continue to watch over and even influence the living through 'controls', spirits on a less advanced level.

It is commonly accepted that Spiritualism originated in strange rappings heard by the New England Fox family; once decoded, the messages showed an impressive knowledge of a body in the cellar, and much less remarkable information about the neighbours. Although the Fox sisters later admitted the strange knocking was the result of talented joint-snapping, table rapping spread like wildfire as séances bred further mediums who in turn developed greater powers: such improvements as table-turning, automatic writing, direct writing, slate writing, spirit music, voice through trance, direct voice, speaking in tongues, apports, teleportation, levitation, materialisation. New professions arose to accommodate the phenomena: spirit photography, astral projection, and spirit healing. Within four years Spiritualism had arrived in England and a new generation of mediums emerged, many of them remaining within the privacy of the family circle but also including professionals who travelled a fairly extensive circuit and were frequently subjected to tests devised by scientists and other sceptics. Table turning and tilting reached epidemic proportions not only in England; it is reported that in France those in the know enquired not after one's health but one's table manners ('Thank you, mine turns beautifully — how goes yours?'). Fraud was frequently detected, especially among nubile young mediums from whose darkened cabinets emerged charming, often mischievous and flirtatious controls, but the movement advanced notwithstanding. The clientele for professional séances included members of the aristocracy and royalty as well as a considerable number of professionals, artists and writers. Abraham Lincoln, Elizabeth Barrett Browning, Harriet Beecher Stowe, Bulwer Lytton, Dion Boucicault, John Ruskin, the entire Rossetti circle, all frequented the tables. Victor Hugo in exile in Jersey was greatly impressed by table turning; perhaps not unexpectedly, the messages received were of a high literary calibre, including a challenge by Shakespeare to a literary competition and, again not surprisingly, the spirit of Hugo himself briefly took control of a medium seven years after his death. Victorien Sardou, whose 'well-made plays' made him one of the most popular playwrights in France and (in adaptations) England, was himself a medium, his most impressive achievement automatic drawings of dwellings on the planet Jupiter.

Spiritualism in England and North America preferred to ally itself with Christianity despite warnings of demonic possession. In France, although Spiritualism had its adherents, Spiritism, which denied certain basic Christian tenets, gradually became the ascendant belief. Under the leadership of the French educator Allan Kardec (Hippolyte Rivail) who had previously been interested in mesmerism and phrenology, the doctrine of reincarnation and a belief in the astral body were added to the Spiritualists' belief in physical phenomena. Basing his teachings on spirit messages received through clairvoyants, Kardec tended to play down aspects such as materialization in favour of more direct contact through automatic writing, during which the subject holding pen or pencil is not necessarily conscious. A series of works published by Kardec in the 1850s and 1860s became the standard textbooks of Spiritism. Frequent visits of British mediums did, however, continue to keep French interest in Spiritualism alive.

61. Tissot, *William Eglinton*, 1885,
etching in black ink, 15.6 x 10.1 cm.
Art Gallery of Ontario, Toronto, Gift
of Allan and Sondra Gotlieb

Two of the most impressive visitors, both in the range of their achievements
and in their willingness to be tested, were Daniel Dunglas Home, whose
unblemished career extended from 1850 to his death on the Continent in 1886,
and William Eglinton, Tissot's mentor (*William Eglinton,* 1885, fig. 61).
Although Home's remarkable mediumship included nearly all forms of phenomena, he was never detected in fraud—perhaps because of his engaging personality which seems to have won over sceptics and believers alike. His younger
affiliate, Eglinton, had a much briefer career and was even more closely examined: he was inspected with his sleeves sewn to his knees or behind his back, his
wrists and ankles were tied or held, his sittings were frequently held in daylight
and, for the first nine years of his mediumship, never in his own rooms.
Outraged conjurors, some hired by the Society for Psychical Research, more
than once acknowledged their bafflement. With over three thousand five hundred recorded sittings, Eglinton was detected in fraud only three times, the most
outrageous as an accomplice for a trick by Madame Blavatsky, the charismatic
founder of Theosophy. Like Home, Eglinton while in trance was noted for

62. Tissot, *Mediumistic Apparition*,
1885, mezzotint, 48.9 x 34.2 cm. Art
Gallery of Ontario, Toronto, Gift
of Allan and Sondra Gotlieb

transportation of objects, levitation and, most amazing of all, materializations of one or more spirits while remaining in full sight of the sitters. There exists a spirit photograph of Eglinton—a short small man—being almost lifted off the ground by a much taller, muscular spirit (*The Medium Eglington . . . with the phantom in white*, fig. 95 on p. 215).[9] Among the many notable figures who were convinced of the genuineness of these materializations was the scientist Alfred Russel Wallace, who had simultaneously with Darwin developed the theory of evolution, and the statesman Gladstone who, after a session with Eglinton, was sufficiently impressed to join the Society for Psychical Research.

Although it is highly unlikely that anyone interested in Spiritualist phenomena—as we know Tissot was—would *not* have heard of Eglinton, the artist apparently first met him in Paris in February 1885. Having already travelled throughout Europe, South Africa, the United States and India with resounding success, Eglinton was in Paris on his way to Vienna; after a number of séances it was agreed that Tissot should attend further sittings in England on Eglinton's return there. The final séance, memorialized in *Mediumistic Apparition*, 1885 (fig. 62), took place on 20 May 1885 in the London home of the artist Albert Besnard. We have two conflicting reports of the occasion, one by the charming and unreliable gossip Jacques-Emile Blanche, who writes in his memoirs, *Portraits of a Lifetime,*

> In utter darkness, essential for such a manifestation, we were breathless with excitement. An ethereal and vaporous form glided on to the scene. A voice uttered words and groans. Tissot hurried forward as if to seize this spirit from the tomb. At that moment a joker — no one ever knew who it was — turned up the gas behind and in front of the stage. We then saw Annie Jones, Besnard's red-haired model.[10]

In contrast, here is the (much abridged) account by John S. Farmer, Eglinton's biographer:

> there were present, besides M. Tissot and the medium, three ladies and one gentleman. After the usual preliminaries of a dark *seance*, Mr. Eglinton took his place in an easy chair close to M. Tissot's right hand, and so remained the whole time. The doors were all locked, and the room otherwise secured. After conversing for a time two figures were seen standing side by side on M. Tissot's left hand. They were at first seen very indistinctly, but gradually they became more and more plainly visible, until those nearest could distinguish every feature. The light carried by the male figure [the spirit] ('Ernest') was exceptionally bright, and was so used as to light up in a most effective manner the features of his companion. M. Tissot, looking into her face, immediately recognised the latter, and, much overcome, asked her to kiss him. This she did several times, the lips being observed to move. One of the sitters distinctly saw 'Ernest' place the light in such a position that while M. Tissot was gazing at the face of the female form her features were 'brilliantly illuminated'; it also lighted M. Tissot's face. After staying with him for some minutes, she again kissed him, shook hands, and vanished.[11]

Blanche's testimony is made questionable by a number of other factual errors in his book, the most glaring his claim that Eglinton was later imprisoned for fraud.[12] But no matter which version we choose, Tissot's own version coincides with Farmer's. In fact, he presented his portrait of an entranced Eglinton holding the famous slates used for spirit-writing as a frontispiece to Farmer's book, while a print of *Mediumistic Apparition* hung in the office of the London Spiritualist Alliance.

63. Tissot, *Way of Flowers, Way of Tears*, 1859, oil on panel, 34.3 x 97.8 cm. Museum of Art, Rhode Island School of Design, Providence, RI

Tissot's spiritual journey had, however, just begun. Barely six months after the momentous séance, while attending mass as part of his research for one of his *La Femme à Paris* series, he experienced another vision and re-entered an old familiar Mystery, Roman Catholicism. In some ways he had never completely discarded the faith of the early painting, *Way of Flowers, Way of Tears*, 1860 (fig. 63) which was patterned on the medieval morality Dance of Death. Tissot's religious conversion again anticipated the theatre, this time the revival of religious mystery plays: this was inaugurated during Holy Week in 1890 when Sarah Bernhardt and two other players recited a dramatization of the Passion, and culminated in the religious plays of Paul Claudel (whose own conversion occurred a year after Tissot's) and Vollmüller's *The Miracle* for which in 1911 Max Reinhardt converted London's Olympia stadium into a vast flamboyant Gothic cathedral and claimed numerous religious conversions. The enormous popularity of Tissot's illustrations of the Bible was thus reinforced by a popular movement in theatre as well.

On his return to Paris, theatre had caught up with Tissot yet again. His projected series *La Femme à Paris*, with its literary accompaniments sometimes by dramatists or librettists, coincided with the introduction of the cynical *comédies rosses*. Henry Becque's play *La Parisienne* (concerning a *ménage à trois*) was performed in Paris in 1885. Naturalistic in intention and photographic in manner, containing little action, Becque emphasised the contrast between appearance (what the characters think of themselves) and reality (what the audience recognizes about the characters). Many of Becque's plays, in fact, play upon the ironic themes we recognize in the projected *La Femme à Paris* series and indeed, in Tissot's earlier works.

Yet despite this worldliness, Tissot had no difficulty reconciling his return to Christianity with his continuing interest in Spiritualism and in the occult. Edmond de Goncourt's journal of 1 February 1890 reports an evening visit during which Tissot showed him a ball of rock crystal and an enamel tray 'qui servent à des evocations, où l'on entend, assure-t-il, des voix qui se disputent'.[13] Again, he walks the tightrope between the real and the ideal.[14] As early as 1892 William Butler Yeats wrote firmly to a well-intentioned but concerned friend, 'The mystical life is the centre of all that I do and all that I think and all that I write';[15] in 1917 his wife would produce by automatic writing the basis of his philosophical study, *A Vision*. But let me close with, once again, a theatrical parallel to Tissot's final position, this time a passage from T.S. Eliot's *The Cocktail Party*, a play considered by some to represent an occult belief in otherworldly guardians:

'He could hear the cry of bats.'

'But how do you know he could hear the cry of bats?'

'Because he said so. And I believed him.'[16]

1. *The Picture of Dorian Gray*, in *Oscar Wilde's Plays, Prose Writings and Poems* (London: Dent, Everyman, 1955), 102–3.

2. 'Le Naturalisme au Théâtre', *Le Roman experimental*, 2nd ed. (Paris: G. Charpentier, 1880), 118.

3. *Le Théatre-Libre*, a pamphlet published privately by Antoine in May 1890 for his subscribers.

4. 'The Decay of Lying', *Oscar Wilde, Selected Writings*, ed. Richard Ellmann (London: Oxford University Press, 1961), 7.

5. 'The Salon of 1859', *Baudelaire: Selected Writings on Art and Artists*, trans. P.E. Charvet (Harmondsworth: Penguin, 1972), 324.

6. Baudelaire, 'The Painter of Modern Life', in *Baudelaire: Selected Writings*.

7. Maurice Maeterlinck, 'The Tragical in Daily Life', *Treasure of the Humble*, trans. Alfred Sutro (London: George Allen, 1897), 101–3.

8. G.B-J [Burne-Jones], *Memorials of Edward Burne-Jones* (New York: Macmillan, 1906), 281–2.

9. Fred Gettings, *Ghosts in Photographs: The Extraordinary Story of Spirit Photography* (New York: Harmony Books, 1978), 50.

10. Jacques-Emile Blanche, *Portraits of a Lifetime: the Late Victorian Era, the Edwardian Pageant 1870–1914* (London: Dent, 1933), 65–6.

11. John S. Farmer, *'Twixt Two Worlds: A Narrative of the Life and Work of William Eglinton* (London: The Psychological Press, 1886), 186–7. Of *Mediumistic Apparition,* Farmer goes on to say that ' "Ernest's" face reveals the noble spirit he is — full of solicitude and compassionate love for his kind. The ideal which those who have come in contact with him must have formed (I can speak for myself) is here fully portrayed.'

12. Two years after this momentous séance, Eglinton travelled to Russia where his distinguished sitters included Emperor Alexander III. On his return to England he decided against a projected Australian tour, married, and abandoned mediumship for a successful career in journalism which included spells as editor of *The New Age* and *The Tatler*. He did return to South Africa, but this time to indulge a passion for big-game hunting. By the time he died in 1933 the entry in *Who's Who* makes no reference to his earlier career as a medium. 'William Eglington' [*sic*], *Who Was Who, 1929–40*, 409.

13. Edmond and Jules de Goncourt, *Journal* vol. III (1879–90), ed. Robert Ricatte (Paris: Fasquelle et Flammarion, 1956), 1118.

14. Canadians should not be too surprised at this odd synthesis. Few any longer question the efficacy of acupuncture or dowsing; and have they not had their own Spiritualist statesman in Mackenzie King? Journalism, William Eglinton's chosen second career, has recently brought two events to world attention: in 1996 scientists in Sydney, Australia discovered a 'mind switch' somewhere between relaxation and drowsiness, which can harness voltage from brain waves to turn on and off household appliances across the room; while just four months later an Angus Reid poll reported that 70% of Canadians believe it is likely there is intelligent life elsewhere in the universe; 55% believed earth had already been visited by extraterrestials ('Brain power truly brings enlightenment', Victoria *Times Colonist,* 17 May 1996, C9; 'Alberta leads in belief of UFOs', Toronto *Globe and Mail,* 11 September 1996). Belief is, after all, a matter of choice. William Gaunt queried in his memoirs, 'Perhaps true occultism and mysticism are merely two different approaches to the same goal. The path of occultism is more circuitous, but not so steep. It is possible by the use of the appropriate techniques to enlarge the borders of apprehension, to obtain a glimpse, if only a glimpse, of the mystery of Being.' William Gaunt, *Museum Piece* (London: André Deutsch, 1963), 231–2.

15. W.B. Yeats to John O'Leary, c.23 July 1892, *The Collected Letters of W.B Yeats*, vol.1 1865–1895, ed. John Kelly and Eric Domville (Oxford: Oxford University Press, 1986), 303.

16. T.S. Eliot, *The Cocktail Party* (London: Faber and Faber, 1950), 14.

64. Tissot, *The Acrobat*, c.1882, oil painting, location unknown, reproduced in James Laver, *Vulgar Society: The Romantic Career of James Tissot* (London, 1936), pl. XXVIII. Photograph courtesy The Edward P. Taylor Reference Library and Archives, Art Gallery of Ontario, Toronto

The Conservatory in St. John's Wood

Margaret Flanders Darby

THE ESSAYS throughout this volume explore Tissot's commitment to paradox. In quoting Oscar Wilde that paradox 'forc[es] the verities to walk a tightrope,' Ann Saddlemyer acknowledges the way paradox requires a light-footed but uneasy balance between opposing forces, competing free falls. Paradox places the tightrope walker on a risky high wire; for truths to survive they must neither be over-generalized nor spread too thin. 'Verities' they may be, but only along the narrowest of lines.

The circus image does not seem overextended when we consider Tissot's confident showmanship, his many reflective surfaces and bright colours, his dramatic compositions, his readiness to place his figures on narrow thresholds of every kind. Having selected *The Acrobat*, 1883–5 (fig. 64) as one of his 'parisiennes', Tissot portrays her balanced on the wire high above the sea of masculine faces that comprise her audience. Moreover, in a way perhaps self-parodied by the clown dressed in the Union flag in *The Sporting Ladies*, 1883–5 (pl. XXIII), ringmaster Tissot often provides his figures, trapeze artists all, with the ambiguous safety nets of various kinds of background webbing: the slats of venetian blinds, ships' rigging, networks of frills, ribbons, stripes, backlighted chestnut leaves in autumn, or, in the case of nearly a dozen paintings, the cast iron bars of a conservatory.

As Baudelaire demanded in 'The Painter of Modern Life,' Tissot's paradoxes found expression through the spaces, social events, people and objects of contemporary urban life. During his sojourn in London during the 1870s, Tissot created a particularly modern, fashionable environment to support his pursuit of favoured themes: his studio, conservatory, and garden at 17 Grove End Road in the London suburb of St. John's Wood, itself an ambiguous neighbourhood, opulent and yet risqué, often home to the privileged demi-mondaine kept in discreet comfort by her bourgeois gentleman lover. As Nancy Marshall makes clear in this volume, to the contemporary critics of Tissot's garden paintings, St. John's Wood was itself a high wire act, its female inhabitants balanced precariously between respectability and its opposite.

New glasshouse technology in the second half of the nineteenth century made possible horticultural paradoxes that parallel with remarkable affinity Tissot's artistic ones, especially those concerning femininity as defined in an androcentric world: here nature is also artifice, nurture is also control, the exotic is also the familiar, protection is imprisonment, sickness is health, fantasy is reality. To use his own conservatory in his paintings was to include a subtle resonance in his art; I hope to show that Tissot did not prove indifferent to its rich implications. Grounded as it is in the material facts of industrial life, the iron and glass structure of his conservatory rises from the literal to the metaphoric in a way especially well suited to Tissot's factually precise imagination.

We are not surprised to discover that Tissot's 1874 renovations to his house and garden in Grove End Road were very fashionable: the colonnade round the garden pool replicated one in Paris and the conservatory was furnished in the European style. During the late 1860s, English fashion in conservatory planting began to follow the French practice of a naturalistic enclosed landscape, complete with winding paths and rocky elevations, the larger plants set into soil at or just above floor level, as if planted in the ground. Earlier British taste had been more botanically minded, with plants displayed as individual specimens and set on stages in pots.[1] Writing about conservatories abroad, William Robinson was critical of English ones: 'Winter-gardens in [France, Belgium, and Russia] are usually verdant at all times, being filled with handsome exotic evergreens, planted and arranged so as to present the appearance of a small garden of luxuriant vegetation, and not that of the glass shed filled with red pots and prim plants. We build more glass houses than any other nation, but have as yet nearly everything to learn.'[2] According to Mireille Galinou, Tissot used his own property in his art so consistently, and from such varying viewpoints, that the layout of his studio, conservatory, and garden can be reliably reconstructed from the paintings themselves.[3] We are also aided by architect J.M. Brydon's drawing of Tissot's studio (fig. 65), which shows the conservatory opening the full length of one wall. When published in *The Building News*, it was accompanied by the following note: 'As will be seen from the drawing, [the studio] is a large apartment, amply lighted, principally from the north and east. The whole of one side (the right in the view) is open to a large conservatory, from which it is separated by an arrangement of glass screens and curtains. The floor is laid with oak parquet, and the walls are hung with a kind of tapestry cloth of a greenish blue colour.'[4]

65. J.M. Brydon, *Studio for James Tissot, Esquire, Grove End Road*, lithograph in *The Building News* (15 May 1874). Photograph courtesy Cornell University Library

Among Tissot's London paintings, *In the Conservatory (The Rivals)*, c.1875–8 (pl. VII) most clearly shows the boundary described between studio and conservatory. Galinou's own diagram of the property, based on the art since the property itself was long ago completely altered, shows that the conservatory was at least as big as the studio, and the two together were bigger than the house. An examination of the 1884 architectural drawings made when the Dutch artist Alma-Tadema renovated and extended the house reveals how dramatic the conservatory had been in Tissot's day—Alma-Tadema made it smaller while making the house and studio much bigger. He kept a number of Tissot's most characteristic architectural devices, however: the sweeping curvilinear outer glass wall, the weblike trellis on the inner wall that is clearly visible in *In the Conservatory* (pl. VII), and the classical pilasters one can see in *Rivals* (see fig. 73 on p. 180). Alma-Tadema also saved the mirrors which ran from nearly floor to ceiling and, in a different part of the house, an equally long bay window that was nearly all glass.[5] Clearly Alma-Tadema appreciated Tissot's sensitivity to the ambivalence of glass, its capacity for both transparency and reflection, and the many variations possible in such visual play. Tissot's unique blend of architectural and horticultural elements created endless possibilities for his themes of boundary, threshold and enclosure, for his meticulous attention to contrasting surfaces and textures, and above all for his fascination with ironic social situations.

66. *Completed Transept of Joseph Paxton's The Crystal Palace* in *Illustrated London News* (25 January 1851), p. 57. Photograph courtesy Yale University Library

The Paradoxes of Nineteenth-Century Glasshouse Technology

In allocating so much money and space to his conservatory, Tissot supported his artistic paradoxes with a showcase that embodies in its technology and horticultural history a wide range of nineteenth-century cultural paradoxes. The repeal of the glass tax in 1845 made experimentation worthwhile, and soon better quality glass was being manufactured in quantity, clearer and less distorted, in larger sized panes, and cheaply enough to become available to the middle classes. At the same time iron manufacture was improving, making it possible to support greater expanses of glass roof on narrower cast iron columns. The new strength of cast iron made possible decorative casting of greater and greater delicacy, enabling the illusion of fantasy worlds, and producing ornate exhibition buildings, shopping arcades and railway stations, as well as the domestic conservatory.

From the beginning of the century, garden designers such as John Claudius Loudon had anticipated the paradox of domesticating the exotic—plants, animals, even human beings. He wrote in 1817: 'such artificial climates will not only

67. John Fiske Allen, *Victoria Regia* (underside of leaf and radiating cantilevers), chromo-lithograph, 68.6 x 54.6 cm, from *Victoria Regia or the Great Water Lily of America* (Boston: printed for the author, 1854). Mortimer Rare Book Room, Smith College

be stocked with appropriate birds, fishes and harmless animals, but with examples of the human species from the different countries imitated, habited in their particular costumes and who may serve as gardeners or curators of the different productions'.[6] Expert gardeners like Joseph Paxton developed many of the ideas first proposed by Loudon. Paxton's design for the Crystal Palace in 1851 (fig. 66) was inspired, as he told his Royal Society audience on 13 November 1850, by the properties of modern glass and the natural engineering of a tropical water lily leaf: 'In short, there is no limit to the uses to which this material [glass] may be applied — no foresight can define the limits where it will end; and we may congratulate ourselves that, in the nineteenth century, the progress of science and the spirit of manufacturers have placed at our disposal the application of materials which were unknown to the ancients, and thereby enabled us to erect such structures as would have been deemed impossible even in the early part of the present century.' In quoting Paxton, the secretary commented on the most interesting of his supporting illustrations: 'a specimen of the leaf of the *Victoria regia* [fig. 67], five feet in diameter, the growth of five days. The under side of the leaf presents a beautiful example of natural engineering in the cantilevers which radiate from the centre, where they are nearly two inches deep, with large bottom flanges and very thin middle ribs, and with cross girders between each pair to keep the middle ribs from buckling.'[7] Even in its native habitat, the leaf structure of *Victoria regia* reminded Englishmen of modern technology; Richard Spruce, writing from the Amazon on 15 November 1849, thinks in manufacturing terms: 'A leaf, turned up, suggests some strange fabric of cast-iron, just taken from the furnace, its ruddy colour, and the enormous ribs with which it is strengthened, increasing the similarity.'[8] To a mid-century Englishman, the underside of a tropical leaf is imagined as cast iron still hot from the furnace; the colour red is the glow of industrial fire. Raising exotic plants in British greenhouses was a paradoxical exercise in taming nature, controlling it within artificial limits, domesticating the foreign and industrializing the natural, making it familiar. At the same time, hothouse horticulture was a testament to the aggressive wealth, ingenuity and pride of the rising mercantile classes, an association with 'vulgarity' that may help explain the uneasy distaste in critical reception of paintings like *Rivals* (fig. 73 on p. 180).

Plant-hunting expeditions like the ones that found *Victoria regia* in the tributaries of the Amazon led to improvements, first in the glass-fronted collection boxes that enabled safe voyages home, then in heating technology, so that the new exotics could be protected under glass long enough to test their hardiness in England. The improved cast iron made possible not only visually delicate structures of great strength but more advanced heating systems, fueled by steam or hot water. In his renovations, Alma-Tadema kept Tissot's heating pipes along the outer conservatory wall.[9] Careful horticultural practice and abundant cheap labour made possible exact climate control, and it was not unusual on a large estate to have ranges of greenhouses, each maintained at a different temperature, one suitable for pineapples, one for grapes, another for orchids. Tissot's garden included a range of greenhouses probably used for this purpose; one with a shed roof is visible against the house on the opposite side from the conservatory in *A Quiet Afternoon*, 1879 (fig. 15 on p. 32).[10] The glasshouse, and in its more social aspect the conservatory, thus simultaneously nurtured and dominated nature, which was both constrained to unprecedented levels of artificiality and at the same time protected and preserved in an increasingly polluted environment. Gardening in a heated glasshouse sustains tropical growth, but also keeps it in check lest it become too rampant. The atmosphere is a hybrid of culture and nature; the environment is a fantasy, but one supported by the most mundane, painstaking work. Plants can be forced to bloom or fruit out of season, or put on display only at their peak of beauty and then replaced, or arranged in combinations impossible in the wild. Just as in Eden the lion lay down with the lamb, so in the glasshouse the Darwinian competition for light, air and soil, given sufficient effort, can be temporarily evaded.

Technical innovation having made it possible, and imperial plant collection, abundant servant labour, and new capitalist wealth having made it popular, the Victorian conservatory's horticultural paradoxes captured the Victorian imagination. The opposing implications for nurture and control of 'culture' expanded from horticulture to many circles in society, and the glasshouse became a metaphor for a range of social and political conflicts, but especially for sexual politics, given the association of women with 'nature,' with beautiful flowers, and given the patriarchal impulse to control those blooms while simultaneously nurturing them. Made intensely ambivalent by conflicted meanings, this modern space became available for discourses about femininity as well as social class, both materially to architects and metaphorically to writers and painters.

The Ambivalent Environment

For architects the conservatory was a feminine space, in spite of its masculinity as a workspace: men worked in the conservatory, women were at leisure in it. It was a very privileged space, costing so much to create and maintain that its very presence demonstrated the monetary power of the upper middle classes who supported Tissot's lifestyle by buying his work. No space in their houses better demonstrated the unceasing servant labour needed to support their conspicuous consumption. Usually attached to the more public reception rooms, the conservatory provided a contrasting zone between both the formal confinement of the house and the open, more natural informality of the garden. It was a half-domesticated space where the rigid social rules of the ballroom or drawing room might be temporarily suspended. The embarrassments of *Hush!* (pl. XIII) and *Too Early* (pl. I) would not have taken place in a conservatory, which, in contrast, offered an atmosphere of verdant growth, of 'Nature' as opposed to 'Society.' The moist heat necessary to exotic plants was beguiling; in stepping from the ballroom into the conservatory, people experienced a sudden invitation to relax into another world. Just as tropical hothouse plants are a fantasy of nature in England's cold climate, so the social activities of the Victorian conservatory were described as dangerous, magical, fantastic, even sometimes oppressive to the point of suffocation, where emotions tended to escape control.

In *The Gentleman's House* (1865) architect Robert Kerr finds the conservatory so feminine that he stresses its potential for private use in addition to its use for guests. He defines 'the proper character of a Boudoir . . . [as] a Private Parlor for the mistress of the house. It is the *Lady's Bower* of the olden time.. . . A *Conservatory* opening from the Boudoir is obviously a charming addition; so also is a *Balcony* when upstairs.'[11] We note the traditional floral associations of 'bower' with femininity, drawing on its connotations of privacy, greenery and courtship. But Kerr goes on to stress an important reservation about the domestic conservatory that underscores the artificiality of its link to women and their subtly foreign place in androcentric culture:

> It must never be lost sight of that for a Conservatory to be too directly *attached to a Dwelling-room* is unadvisable. The warm moist air, impregnated with vegetable matter and deteriorated by the organic action of the plants, is both unfit to breathe and destructive of the fabrics of furniture and decoration. On a small scale, however, and when used only for comparatively hardy plants, it may be a very pleasant adjunct, provided it be never overheated and always well ventilated.. . . The *intercommunication* most usual for a Conservatory is with either the Drawing-room, Boudoir, or Morning-room; or, what is probably better than all, with a Saloon, Vestibule, Gallery, or Corridor, immediately adjoining any of those apartments. The Staircase also may be connected with it so as to have a good effect. An *outer door* to the grounds is of course indispensable; indeed a small Conservatory is probably best of all when constituted to form a *floral porch*.
>
> After what has been said, it will at once suggest itself that the interposition of a *Lobby* or small *Ante-room*, or *Porch*, capable of thorough ventilation, may be made so serviceable in preventing ill effects, that it ought seldom if ever to be dispensed with.[12]

The idea that plants emit poisonous vapors was generally accepted at mid-century. The conservatory entry for *The Dictionary of Architecture* (1853) warns that 'illness of inhabitants' is possible when the conservatory is attached to a dwelling. It also notes the likely deterioration of furnishings: the 'vitiation of the atmosphere by the vegetation' and 'evaporation from the water daily given to the plants are sufficient causes for these evils.'[13] So the conservatory is both suitable and unsuitable for ladies and their comfortable furnishings; the atmosphere is both entrancing and toxic; women's health is both protected and endangered. This dilemma required the ingenious buffer zones in the architectural design outlined in Kerr; according to one modern historian, about a quarter of the country-houses of the second half of the century had conservatories attached, and of those about one-third had access to the conservatory directly from living rooms, another third were entered through anterooms or corridors, and the rest could be reached only from the garden.[14] As many exotic plants proved hardy by the century's close, the extreme artificiality of the hothouse intended as living space was tempered. The glasshouse heated to tropical temperatures became less popular, and gardening fashion shifted from entirely enclosed environments to ones that blurred the boundary to the out of doors, striving for the effect of nearly imperceptible gradations. Once again we note that Tissot was in the vanguard; his studio joins his conservatory and both join his garden in a series of steps or thresholds, some easy, some precipitous, seemingly natural but carefully calculated. In many of his St. John's Wood garden paintings, furniture, rugs and picnic paraphernalia bring the indoors out, as does the colonnade around the pool, crossing and recrossing the imaginative boundary between house and garden. It would seem no accident that two of his female convalescents are to be found in these transitional spaces, for example, *Woman in an Armchair*, 1870–2 (fig. 10 on p. 25) and *A Convalescent*, c.1876 (pl. XVI).[15]

The Conservatory as Metaphor

For writers, too, the conservatory became a paradoxical space, both literally as setting in fiction and symbolically in discussions about femininity. A wide range of fiction and nonfiction testifies to the potency of the conservatory setting as a space charged with metaphors of gender conflict. Michael Waters characterizes the action of conservatory scenes as 'reserved almost exclusively for the private meetings of lovers' who occasionally find themselves in the fairy-tale setting 'by mutual consent,' but more often act out a drama of seduction and resistance.[16] Emerging from the same dynamic of conflicting purposes—nurture and control—as the larger gender system, the transparent glass walls of the conservatory make both confinement and protection seem invisible. The plants appear to be growing in their natural environment—the glass shell and steam heat closely approximating that native habitat—but in fact the weather on the other side reveals the artificiality that enables the gardener to force them to bloom or to bear fruit unnaturally; most of all the heated glass cage assures their survival in inhospitable circumstances. These horticultural facts, necessitating environments that appeared to diminish yet in fact intensified the ambiguity of boundary zones, led Victorians who chose the metaphor to a consideration of the inhospitality of the larger culture to women's lives. The conservatory was such a vivid boundary zone that it seems to the modern sensibility a nearly perfect emblem of patriarchy, exposing the way in which Victorian culture organized both plants and women in terms of its impulse toward power and control over nature.

The traditional association of women with flowers was extended to include the new tender exotics under glass, so that ladylike womanhood could be reimagined as a delicate foreign import, a fragile-seeming oriental lily requiring protected surroundings and lavish care. The hothouse became suitable as a metaphor for privileged women because respectable femininity was defined as dependency, delicacy and fragility — highly decorative but always in need of protection. While today such protection suggests suffocation and imprisonment, to many Victorians it was the most efficacious nurturing, shielding women from the harsh conditions of industrial mercantilism and reinforcing the separation of spheres. Nead quotes Baptist Noel, an evangelical writing in 1860: 'women deserve all tenderness; and, made of a more delicate organisation, and of less strength, they need respect and courtesy, protection in danger, the supply of their wants, and, above all, affection to repay affection.'[17]

But from a woman novelist like Elizabeth Gaskell we get a very different use of the metaphor. Molly Gibson, her independent, strongminded heroine in *Wives and Daughters* (1866), finds herself as a child being taken to admire the gardens of a nearby country house, 'A Novice Amongst the Great Folks:' 'Presently they came to a long glittering range of greenhouses and hothouses, and an attendant gardener was there to admit the party. Molly did not care for this half so much as for the flowers in the open air; but Lady Agnes had a more scientific taste, she expatiated on the rarity of this plant, and the mode of cultivation required by that, till Molly began to feel very tired, and then very faint. She was too shy to speak for some time; but at length, afraid of making a greater sensation if she began to cry, or if she fell against the stands of precious flowers, she caught at Miss Browning's hand, and gasped out: "May I go back, out into the garden? I can't breathe here!" '[18] Still more ominously, and considerably earlier in 1847, Anne Bronte used the conservatory metaphor near the beginning of *The Tenant of Wildfell Hall* in an important debate concerning the education of girls compared with boys. The conventional Mr. Markham argues that 'if you were to rear an oak sapling in a hothouse, tending it carefully night and day, and shielding it from every breath of wind, you could not expect it to become a hardy tree.' Helen Graham, another independent-minded but much older and more disillusioned heroine, asks him why he would not do the same for a girl: 'No; you would have her to be tenderly and delicately nurtured, like a hothouse plant—taught to cling to others for direction and support, and guarded, as much as possible, from the very knowledge of evil.' She goes on to summarize Bronte's sense of injustice: 'You would have us encourage our sons to prove all things by their own experience, while our daughters must not even profit by the experience of others.'[19]

At least one masculine Victorian sensibility was attuned to the implications for feminists in the conservatory metaphor. John Stuart Mill used it in *On the Subjection of Women* (1869) to convey the unnatural pruning of women's vital power under patriarchy: 'What is now called the nature of women is an eminently artificial thing—the result of forced repression in some directions, unnatural stimulation in others . . . in the case of women, a hot-house . . . cultivation has always been carried on of some of the capabilities of their nature, for the benefit and pleasure of their masters. Then, because certain products of the general vital force sprout luxuriantly and reach a great development in this heated atmosphere and under this active nurture and watering, while other shoots from the same root, which are left outside in the wintry air . . . have a stunted growth . . . men, with that inability to recognise their own work which distinguishes the unanalytic mind, indolently believe that the tree grows of itself in the way they have made it grow.'[20] The analogy to artificially hastened growth under glass enabled Mill to distinguish the femininity encouraged by Victorian men for their convenience from an imaginable but unknowable truly natural feminine existence.

For painters, the conservatory could provide a lush background to complex portraits of women, thereby extending and intensifying the cultural values expressive of femininity usually delineated in Victorian art. Given the middle-class woman's domestic mission according to the ideology of separate spheres, we are not surprised to find innumerable presentations of feminine enclosure in paintings, yet these enclosures are qualified by their opposite: the woman is often found on the edge of the enclosing space. We consistently find her at a threshold, sometimes with a clear way out, sometimes not: in doorways, at windows, next to walls. The idea of enclosure is in this way undermined as it is presented, and made dramatic by the implication of choice: will she or will she not step across the threshold? The androcentric viewer also has a choice between two responses to the maiden on the boundary: chivalrous protection or lascivious appropriation. Both encompassed and threatened, she often stands poised at the threshold of the major decision of her life — choosing a mate — as surely as at the threshold of her parlour, balcony, window, bower, or walled garden, as in, to name only a few examples, Calderon's *Broken Vows* (1856), Millais' *Mariana* (1851), even perhaps *The Rector's Garden Queen of the Lilies* (1877) by Atkinson Grimshaw.[21] The ideology of domestic enclosure, with its paradoxical double meaning of protection and prison, was repeated and intensified emblematically by birds in cages and plants in pots, these also placed at thresholds. When living beings are confined, whether plant, bird, animal or woman, their needs must be met by their keepers; they must be nourished. To portray a beautiful woman against this background is to emphasize her vulnerability, inferiority, and subservience. According to Susan Casteras, the condition of the potted plant on the windowsill in many Victorian paintings of women, thriving or wilting, was an index of the health of the female protagonist.[22]

When a conservatory is the site of these images of women, its hothouse technology comments with a special urgency on the wider cultural issues of femininity, and the female protagonist is inevitably equated metaphorically, or ironically contrasted, with especially delicate, tender flowers. That commentary, no matter how indirect, was too urgent, perhaps, for widespread use in the visual arts, providing an interesting contrast with literature, where it became virtually a cliché. The conservatory setting carries the theme of protected enclosure in a direction at once both highly mechanical and highly symbolic; the technology was luxurious and modish, perhaps too much so for a public expecting serious moral narratives in traditional settings. The conservatory's highly artificial, fragile balance of natural growth and cultural control interrogates the ideologies of domesticity very darkly indeed. As a fantasy of nature, the conservatory places much pressure on the tenuous stasis of the contradictions in the ongoing cultural debate over the essential nature of womanhood. Victorian moral earnestness, whether feminist or anti-feminist, might be expected to have rejected images of the woman in the conservatory as at once vulgar, extravagant and ominous; if so, this would help to explain the negative critical response to Tissot's conservatory paintings.

All the more remarkable, then, that he both provided the generous space needed to pursue his exploration of what we call sexual politics, and persisted with his conservatory paintings in the face of critical disdain. He was not entirely alone in taking advantage of the conservatory's potential. In the disturbing portrait of his friends M. and Mme. Jules Guillemet, *In the Conservatory* (1879), Manet explores these possibilities at their most complex; W. H. Deverell's *A Pet* (1853) demonstrates similarly rich ironies. He places the female protagonist of *A*

Pet in the doorway of a greenhouse, with a dog at her feet, a caged bird at her hand, and other birds caged and free in the walled garden beyond. These animals, in combination with the potted plants, some looking healthy and some looking dead, make fully ominous the implications of the title, providing an ambiguous context for the figure of the woman at its centre. In a much more benign way, Alfred Stevens used a conservatory for one of his delicate portrayals of relationship between two women in *Consolation* (c.1875).[23]

Tissot's Conservatory Paintings

But it is with a complexity, subtlety and depth unmatched by any other nineteenth-century artist that Tissot used the conservatory as a symbolic setting for representations of femininity in fraught social circumstances. The particularities of his own glasshouse, its trellis and full-length mirrors, its contrasting angles and curves, its multiple levels and thresholds, were ideally suited to his most conflicted themes of artifice, social control and imprisonment on the one hand, and nature, beauty and sophistication on the other. Above all, the contradictions of the conservatory underscore his determination to delineate every nuance of the fashionable veneer of society in order to show ominous underlying realities: depths of feminine unease beneath frivolity, anxieties of entrapment beneath ennui. Moving across thresholds, levels and angles of vision, his feminine subjects are placed in a series of personal contexts each less familiar than the one before: from the comfortably furnished studio across the barrier of screens and shades to the mirror-hung terrace of the conservatory, then down several feet to the tropical jungle at planting level, enclosed within a wide curved shell of iron and glass. Each of these contexts suggests new ambiguities of meaning, or at most narrowed unstable truths rather than broadly assured ones. Clearly Tissot is never willing to come to rest on any generalization firmer than ambivalence; he suggests one narrative only to undermine it, one social drama only to balance it against opposite possibilities of interpretation. His evocative title 'Entre les deux mon coeur balance' seems to apply not only to gender triangles like *Portsmouth Dockyard (How Happy I could be with Either)*, 1877 (pl. XI), but to all possible readings of his feminine portrayals. He does not want us to be able to decide what a given image means, or what exactly is going on in it; he sees to it that we end in incomprehension.

We can examine seven paintings of women posed in or next to a conservatory in order of the decreasing familiarity of the social space and the increasing intensity of the atmospheric conditions, moving from the reassuringly bourgeois

68. Tissot, *Hide and Seek*,
c.1880–2, oil on panel, 73.9
x 53.3 cm. National Gallery
of Art, Washington, D.C.

opulence of Tissot's studio across the sliding glass barrier to the sociable warmth
of the conservatory terrace, and down several feet into the hothouse landscape of
the oversized plants themselves.

In *Hide and Seek*, 1877–82 (fig. 68) the woman engaged in the mundane
relaxation of reading the morning paper is illuminated by the shaft of light, daz-
zlingly bright in the largely dark painting, that streams in from the summer
garden, a shaft of light that highlights many of the luxurious textures and surfaces of the crowded rich furnishings of the studio: oversized overstuffed cush-
ions, exotic furs, gleaming brass, gilt, porcelain, polished wood. The picture
rewards a leisurely perusal as the viewer discovers the children hiding, one by
one. But their game expands metaphorically to the larger question of what is
being hidden here, and what sought? At the border of the comfortable repose are
several ominous even morbid masks hanging at the entrance to the dimly
translucent iron cage of the curved outer wall of the conservatory. The invitation

69. Tissot, *The Liar,* 1883–5, oil painting, whereabouts unknown. Reproduced from the albums of photographs Tissot kept of his own work. Private Collection

of the open door is belied by the frightening masks; the woman sits between them and the children's game. The heavy draperies covering both the french door and the glass wall between the studio and the conservatory control the light, giving it a fugitive quality as it flits from one reflective surface to another. The two picture frames enclose incomprehensible reflections.

Like *Hide and Seek*, two of the *Femme à Paris* series (1883–5) offer a luxurious interior space bordering a conservatory. *The Liar,* 1883–5 (fig. 69) smiles the greeting we know, from reading Alphonse Daudet's story intended to accompany the painting, is false. A classic tale of feminine inaccessibility,[24] of the dangerous muse whose inspiration turns out to be only a reflection of the masculine self, this drama is portrayed with the liar walking from a conservatory through a portière of heaving curtains printed with monstrous dragon faces, each with bulging simian eyes, a fabric repeated in the foreground on a cushion. The viewer stands in for the cuckolded artist of the story — and of the painting as

70. Tissot, *The Sphinx*, 1883–5, oil painting, whereabouts unknown. Reproduced from the albums of photographs Tissot kept of his own work. Private Collection

well? — who seems to have just risen from the tea tray and the 'open book.' The masculine presence satirized here remains, however, only a ghostly presence, its surveillance suggested rather than delineated.

Paul Bourget's accompanying story for *The Sphinx*, 1883–5 (fig. 70) was apparently never written. The model is perhaps Louise Riesener; a study for *The Sphinx*, now in the Tanenbaum Collection, was accompanied by the following information: 'According to a dealer's notation affixed to the back of the painting "this portrait is presumed to be of Mlle. Riesener to whom Tissot was engaged in 1882".'[25] The engagement is said to have been suddenly broken off, giving the man's top hat and walking stick all the more disembodied an air: another masculine ghost. Once again, the disillusioned man is presumably the viewer, and perhaps the artist, and once again the mysterious, unknowable and unreliable woman is backed by a lighted conservatory whose foliage is seen through the open glass doors.

71. Tissot, *The Thames*, c.1876, oil on canvas, 72.5 x 118 cm. Wakefield Art Gallery and Museums

In the famously uncomfortable social drama *In the Conservatory (The Rivals)*, 1875–8 (pl. VII), the dividing line between Tissot's studio and conservatory terrace takes on a central importance, stressed by the striped roman shades and the sliding glass partitions, closed to the left, open to the right. Overt social discomfort is restricted to the studio's drawing-room furnishings with its material comforts: oriental carpet, upholstered velvet. We are offered the interesting puzzle of the 'twins,' so often remarked on. Why did Tissot clothe multiple figures in the same costume? In a painting like *The Ball on Shipboard*, c.1874 (pl. XII) the repetition sets up strong compositional rhythms, but here the implications seem thoroughly social. The repeated costume encourages us to ask what the difference might be between these two women. Frilly young ladies seem to clone themselves, reproduced with no distinguishing characteristics. They are alike; individuality is denied them. As in *The Thames*, c.1876 (fig. 71) our gaze is uncompromisingly androcentric—a young man cannot choose because there is nothing to choose. Beyond the studio, however, on the conservatory terrace, the more distinctively dressed woman with the fan has crossed over into a very different stage of courtship; the couple in the artificial/natural world of the conservatory have escaped the proprieties in just the way we have examined from literature. The long mirror captures their *tête-à-tête*, and reflects it back into the studio, but like the framed reflections in *Hide and Seek* does not explain it. The 'twins' on the other hand, are stranded in their superficial social attitudes over the tea cups, caught in the embarrassments of the more formal studio. Although it insists on the boundary between Tissot's studio and his conservatory, this painting offers an easy crossing from the one to the other, since the terrace is exactly level with the studio, in contrast to the plantings behind and below. We have seen from Papworth's and Kerr's contemporary testimony how important this barrier was perceived to be—for both human health and the protection of furnishings. A lot of ominous social interaction stands between the viewer and the plants, but with the suggestion that successful courtship has passed the first social barrier onto the terrace. Successful, however, in what way? The neighbourhood is St. John's Wood; the proprieties are designed to protect vulnerable women as much as to imprison them. Too much depends on the men's intentions, and a woman's stake in the marriage game is always frighteningly high. The conservatory is too well marked as a zone where impulsive passion can overstep prudence for there to be any sense of comfort on either side of the sliding glass screens.

In *The Bunch of Lilacs*, 1875 (pl. X) we leave the questionable amenities of the studio behind. The tropical jungle, with its fertile greenish light, looms much closer in this painting, just kept at bay yet always threatening. We must look hard to be able to see through the plants to the iron ribs of the outer conservatory wall; the wooden sill alone, emphasized by the oriental art along its edge, keeps us from falling into the plantings. More than a third of the picture's surface is the polished floor of the terrace, as reflective as glass. Lilacs are not hothouse plants; they have been picked outside and brought in. Is the feminine here defined as a plucked and vased blossom from a hardy English shrub, or as a delicate exotic in a pot on an oriental table at the edge of the jungle? Tissot emphasizes the surfaces—from mirror-finish hard to the velvety softness of plant matter—surfaces as varied as stone, wood, fabric, flesh, leaf, frond, stem. This is a lush painting; the conservatory jungle grows in a heavy, dank atmosphere; the green light suggests a rankness almost on the edge of rot. Tissot takes risks with the conventional warnings about the dangers of plants in dwellings; the risktaking extends itself to the woman placed in its context. Just this side of the wooden sill are the materials that would not survive in the tropics: the fragile ruffles and pleats of the dress, dramatically contrasted with the polished tiles. The lady in blue looks back to the springing growth of the conservatory, not forward to our gaze from the studio. We wonder where she belongs.

72. Tissot, *A Young Lady Holding Japanese Objects*, 1865, oil on panel, 36.5 x 46 cm. Private collection

The varied implications of enclosure are stressed in *In the Conservatory* and *The Bunch of Lilacs* by including the ornate bird cage, or perhaps it is a lantern. Either way it is one glassed enclosure within another, doubling the impact in the same way as in Tissot's earliest conservatory painting, the *A Young Lady Holding Japanese Objects,* 1865 (fig. 72), where the fish tank establishes several major preoccupations with the glasshouse setting. Wentworth quotes a contemporary critic who complained that Tissot's series of young ladies looking at Japanese objects could perhaps just as accurately be called 'Japanese objects looking at young ladies,'[26] a suggestive comment, especially when they are looking at a masculine doll in a glass case which, for Caroline Arscott in this volume, has a corresponding 'opportunity for covert observation.' Clearly surveillance is yoked with dehumanization; the difficulty of 'looking at' through multiple, only semi-transparent, layers is at issue. The fish tank also raises the question of oxygen — is there sufficient air here? The fish can breathe only because the fountain of bubbling water at the top of their tank oxygenates their water. Both environments — water and jungle — are a murky green; we can just see, beyond the

73. Tissot, *Rivals*, 1878–9, oil painting, whereabouts unknown. Reproduced from the albums of photographs Tissot kept of his own work. Private Collection

thick curtain of leaves and fronds, the light on the other side of the glass, and we cannot see through the fish tank at all. Our visual outlook balances that of the fish, enclosing the young lady with her strangely animated expression and awkwardly raised arms. Wentworth tells us that Tissot used a Japanese doll as model for her head, which perhaps accounts for her disconnected air,[27] as well as our doubts of Tissot's sense of feminine integrity, of personhood. She occupies her conservatory even less comfortably than the lilac bearer, but seems to be just another object for displaying objects. As in *Lilacs* this painting illustrates well the primacy of texture, surface and atmosphere for Tissot; far from lacking imagination, as early critics such as Sitwell have claimed,[28] Tissot's imagination was firmly grounded in the physical, in a way not dissimilar to Dickens's capacity for animating objects to increase their metaphorical impact. Matching subject to setting, Tissot has assembled exotic objects and beings in a closely confined exotic space, and juxtaposed them in a strongly objective, almost noncommittal way.

With *Rivals*, 1878–9 (fig. 73) we drop down to plant level in Tissot's London conservatory; it is here that he sets one of his most controversial social dramas.

This unique angle contributes much to the claustrophobia of the triangular relationship which so exercised its first critics. Unlike *Lilacs* and *In the Conservatory* our viewpoint is from the far outer edge of the terrace. We look towards the long mirrors and classical pilasters set into the wall of the house to which Tissot's conservatory was attached. The plants and the lantern dwarf the figures, whom we view from above, looking down into the well that rings the plantings. The intense focus of the two men's gaze converges on the woman crocheting; their appraising look seems to push her back into her chair. The two-to-one masculine-to-feminine ratio in this social triangle is enclosed by markers of femininity, hothouse plants on one side, tea table on the other, a tea table that bars our way into the space. Tissot walks his by now familiar tightrope of uneasily balanced sexual politics: who is in control? To the contemporary *Times* reviewer it was clearly the lady who 'keep[s] a brace of rivals in play at five o'clock tea, playing [her] crochet pins the while as demurely as if men's affections were women's natural playthings.'[29] Perhaps neither man nor woman is in control but rather the tropical foliage; it and its reflection occupy more than half the picture's space; the human world is crowded by the insentient one. While admired for the technical skill with which they were painted, the looming plants probably contributed to the waspish reviews, since to emphasize the sheer size of tropical leaves and trunk-like stems was to remind critics of the aggressive capitalism that made such status symbols possible.

Towards the end of his life, Tissot hired his London architect to recreate the key elements of his house in St. John's Wood at the Abbaye de Buillon, the family estate in France where he eventually died: gardens, including a roserie, a large studio and an adjacent conservatory (fig. 74).[30] In the roserie, a domed iron filigree structure without glass, he was photographed with his grand-niece Simone (fig. 75). In this evocative image, they regard each other: an old man seated on a bench with his cane, and a young girl, weight on one foot and hand on hip in a mythic feminine pose, standing among the roses entwined on the narrow iron columns. Both man and girl express a pensive self-consciousness, especially young Simone.[31] For decades James Tissot has contemplated femininity in just this way: even when evocatively placed in the ambiguous setting midway between garden and room, even when seductively posed and surrounded by roses, she puzzles him; above all, her inaccessibility engages him. To portray the anxious boundaries of class and gender, to conquer that inaccessibility, Tissot used all the details of fashionable life at his command: the furniture, the clothes, the luxurious settings. Images of beautiful women set among the

74. J.M. Brydon, *Studio of Mr James Tissot, Chateau de Buillon, France*, lithograph in *The Builder* (15 June 1895), pp. 452–3. Photograph courtesy Yale University Library

75. *Tissot and his great niece Simone, the late Mme. Jean de Gournay.* Photograph courtesy M. Gérard Mantion

artist's own props — his clothes, his plants, his vases and statues, his conservatory — are emblematic of the surfaces of femininity, portrayed from a fascinated but finally frustrated masculine point of view. They can be precisely represented, they can be owned in a superficial sense, but they can never be fully possessed or understood.

Exquisitely beautiful, artificial to the point of imminent breakdown, delicately balanced on the tightrope between coming into flower and falling into decay, the enabling technology always well hidden, the conservatory enacts the paradox of the 'nature' of nineteenth-century women under patriarchy. It invites us to ask what might be a truly natural environment for women, and more, what 'true' nature might be. It suggests that nature requires human intervention to become intelligible. Above all, it shows us how evanescent that intelligibility must be. In doing so the conservatory both encourages and exposes the Victorian myth that women are 'naturally' suited to their femininity in an androcentric world.

1. Brent Elliott, *Victorian Gardens* (London: Batsford, 1986) 185–6.
2. William Robinson, *The Parks and Gardens of Paris* (London: Macmillan, 1878) 222.
3. Mireille Galinou, 'Green-finger Painting,' *Country Life*, 13 (July 1989): 120–3.
4. John M. Brydon, 'Studio in the House of James Tissot, Esq.' *The Building News* (15 May 1874), 526–7.
5. Royal Institute of British Architects (RIBA), Drawings Collection, London: WII/9 (1–30).
6. Quoted in Elliott, *Victorian Gardens,* 29.
7. *Transactions of the Royal Society of Art*, 57 (1850–1): 1–6.
8. Quoted in Walter Fitch, *Victoria Regia; or Illustrations of the Royal Water-Lily . . . with descriptions by Sir W.J. Hooker* (London: Reeve and Benham, 1851), 9.
9. RIBA drawing 7.
10. Galinou, 'Green-finger Painting,' 122.
11. Robert Kerr, *The Gentleman's House*, 2nd ed. (London: John Murray, 1865) 114–15.
12. Kerr, *Gentleman's House,* 127.
13. Wyatt Papworth, ed., *The Dictionary of Architecture, issued by the Architectural Publication Society* (London: Thomas Richards, 1853–92), 2:130.
14. Jill Franklin, *The Gentleman's Country House and its Plan: 1835–1914* (London: Routledge & Kegan Paul, 1981), 63–4.

15. Warmest thanks to colleagues in Manchester, England, John H.G.Archer and Joseph O.Marsh, for patient and careful coaching on the architecture and technology of the Victorian glasshouse; also to Tom Askey, Peter Day, and Michael Pearman of the Devonshire Collections at Chatsworth, Derbyshire, for their help with the Paxton materials.

16. Michael Waters, *The Garden in Victorian Literature* (Aldershot: Scolar, 1988), 270–2.

17. Lynda Nead, *Myths of Sexuality: Representations of Women in Victorian Britain* (Oxford: Basil Blackwell, 1988), 29.

18. Elizabeth Gaskell, *Wives and Daughters* (London: Penguin Classics, 1986), 45.

19. Anne Bronte, *The Tenant of Wildfell Hall* (London: Penguin Classics, 1979), 56–7.

20. John Stuart Mill, *The Subjection of Women* (London: Virago, 1983), 38–9.

21. Calderon's *Broken Vows* is reproduced in Graham Reynolds, *Victorian Painting*, 2nd ed. (New York: Harper, 1987), 181; Millais' *Mariana* in Susan P. Casteras, *English Pre-Raphaelitism and its Reception in America in the Nineteeth Century* (Rutherford, NJ: Fairleigh Dickinson University Press, 1990), 78; Grimshaw's *The Rector's Garden* in Alexander Robertson, *Atkinson Grimshaw* (Oxford: Phaidon, 1988), 70.

22. Susan P. Casteras, *Images of Victorian Womanhood in English Art* (Rutherford, NJ: Fairleigh Dickinson University Press, 1987) 38.

23. Manet's *In the Conservatory* is reproduced in Robert Rey, *Manet* (New York: Crown Art Library, 1986), 75; Deverell's *A Pet* in Casteras, *Images of Victorian Womanhood*; Stevens's *Consolation* in Louise d'Argencourt and Douglas Druick, eds., *The Other Nineteenth Century* (Ottawa: The National Gallery of Canada, 1978), 183.

24. The story's plot features a mysterious and paradoxical protagonist, Clothilde, who gave the narrator 'five years of perfect happiness;' an artist, he 'owed to her my present celebrity; work was so easy to me, inspiration so natural at her side. . . . Her beauty and her character fulfilled all my dreams' (307). Yet he goes on to speak of her with hatred because on her deathbed he discovers her perfidy, that all the money, laces and jewels must be the gifts of other lovers. When he begs for the truth, she turns her face to the wall, refusing all explanation to the end. In Alphonse Daudet, 'The Liar,' *Memories of a Man of Letters*, trans. George Burnham Ives (Boston: Little, Brown, 1900), 307–14.

25. Louise d'Argencourt and Douglas Druick, eds., *The Other Nineteenth Century* (Ottawa: The National Gallery of Canada, 1978), 192.

26. Michael Wentworth, *James Tissot* (Oxford: Oxford University Press, 1984), 71.

27. Wentworth, *James Tissot*, 70.

28. Sacheverell Sitwell, *Narrative Pictures: A Survey of English Genre and its Painters* (New York: Scribner's, 1938), 91.

29. 'The Grosvenor Gallery,' *The Times* (2 May 1879), 3.

30. John M. Brydon, 'Studio, Chateau de Buillon,' *The Builder* (15 June 1895), 452–3; and Brydon, 'Chateau de Buillon,' *The Builder* (1 May 1897), 400.

31. Willard E. Misfeldt, 'James Tissot's Abbaye de Buillon,' *Apollo* (January 1984), 24–9.

Tissot as Symbolist and Fetishist? A Surmise

Elizabeth Prelinger

Tissot as symbolist? It sounds odd, improbable. We think of him more as a realist, chronicler of the society and customs of the Paris and London of his era. Rich in nuance and detail, both narrative and stylistic, Tissot's pictures would seem on the surface far removed from the strain of idealism that pervaded fin-de-siècle culture. But such simplistic views of Tissot and his work were always in question even during his lifetime, and have been discounted by scholars for quite some time, largely since the 1940s, with the rediscovery of his oeuvre and new revelations about his relationship with his twenty-eight-year-old mistress Mrs. Kathleen Newton. As the artist's images have been scrutinized with increasing critical distance, the ambiguities and downright strangeness of many of his subjects and figures, as well as his technique, have become disturbingly evident.

This is especially true of Tissot's later works, not only the religious illustrations, which represent an obvious example of his mysticism, but also his series of fifteen paintings entitled *La Femme à Paris* (1883–5). Although Tissot had consistently spiced his apparently straightforward anecdotal subjects with subtexts throughout his entire career, there appears, however, to have been a palpable rupture in his approach after the death of Kathleen Newton in November 1882, bringing to an end his eleven-year sojourn in London and occasioning his return to Paris a few days after her burial. Tissot then experienced a conversion, like so many others who became part of the late nineteenth-century Catholic Revival (*ralliement*). They included the decadent novelist Joris-Karl Huysmans, with whom Tissot shared some startling commonalities. Tissot embraced mystical imagery and Bibilical themes as he simultaneously explored Spiritualism in a desperate attempt to make contact with Kathleen Newton. Thus, the oddities present in Tissot's work from the beginning ultimately achieved full-blown fruition in his late production, both painted and printed. Such oddities suggest kinship with, even prefiguration of, the ethos of Symbolism and of Decadence, among them the polyvalent meanings of the scenes, as well as a mesmerizing, obsessive focus on objects, which he depicted in profusion and with an intensity and repetitiveness that is virtually fetishistic. Many of Tissot's images so clearly reflect the visionary strain of fin-de-siècle culture running parallel to the concern with the representation of modern life that they demand alternative contexts in which to be considered. This essay will explore how the artist's complex oeuvre may be analyzed in terms of late nineteenth-century movements such as Symbolism and such related phenomena as bric-a-bracomania and other fetishisms, thus establishing Tissot's links with the idealist currents of his time.

During the course of Tissot's life (1836–1902), critics were consistently stymied and not infrequently irritated by the ambiguities inherent in the artist's pictures, whose resistance to easy categorization was troubling and destabilizing. Tissot has always been viewed as a link between England and France; although he adapted with success to life on both sides of the Channel, Tissot and his art remained resolutely unclassifiable—were he and his art English or French? was his art academic or avant-garde? Today we discern the peculiarities of his oeuvre with new clarity, recognizing that the *Femme à Paris* series and other prints and paintings of the 1880s, such as *Morning*, 1886 (fig. 76), *The Liar*, 1883–5 (fig. 69 on p. 175), and *The Sphinx*, 1883–5 (fig. 70 on p. 176), diverge significantly from the artist's earlier representations of social or private events, however problematized, such as *A Widow* (1868), *The Ball on Shipboard*, c.1874 (pl. XII), and *Too Early*, 1874 (pl. I).

How did Tissot come to his unique blend of the 'painting of modern life' on the one hand and his suggestive, indeterminate content on the other, a deliberate strangeness which conterpoints, if not subverts, the detailed, seemingly objective manner of presentation? For there is no one else who was working in the same way as Tissot. Tissot's real genius lay in his synthesizing of the different artistic currents of his time. From combined stimuli he fashioned an art that, however much it may have resembled the work of others in certain ways, was uniquely his own. Interestingly, Tissot was highly susceptible to influence; the development of his art seems frequently to have been swayed by the choice and course of his friendships with French and English artists in particular whose impact may be discerned in his visually and intellectually hybrid pictures. During his prolonged sojourns in Paris, Tissot became acquainted with Degas and Manet, and exhibited with them and with other Impressionists and Post-Impressionists starting in the late 1850s and 1860s. He also was well acquainted with English colleagues. By 1871 Tissot was in London, painting Victorian narratives according to his view, adapting his style and ideas to those of fashionable English painters as diverse as Whistler and Frederic, Lord Leighton, and Pre-Raphaelites such as Sir John Everett Millais and Edward Burne-Jones. The close parallels between Tissot's genre scenes like *Les Adieux,* reproduced by John Ballin in 1873 (fig. 8 on p. 15), and Millais' *A Huguenot, on Saint Bartholomew's Day,*

76. Tissot, *Morning*, 1886, mezzotint, 48.9 x 26 cm. Art Gallery of Ontario, Toronto, Gift of Allan and Sondra Gotlieb

Refusing to Shield Himself from Danger by Wearing the Roman Catholic Badge, 1851–4 (fig. 7 on p. 14) and works such as *The Convalescent (The Warrior's Daughter)*, c.1887 (fig. 77) and William Holman Hunt's *The Awakening Conscience,* 1851–2 (fig. 78) demonstrate Tissot's intimate acquaintance with the moralistic dramas filled with symbolic objects that characterised English painting of the Pre-Raphaelite decades. Michael Wentworth notes that

77. Tissot, *The Convalescent (The Warrior's Daughter)*, c.1887, oil on panel, 34.3 x 20.3 cm. © Manchester City Art Galleries

by the middle sixties, Tissot was poised between two distinct, if overlapping, groups. Part of a circle which included advanced painters like Monet, Renoir, Berthe Morisot, and Fantin-Latour, as well as Whistler, Degas, and Manet, he was also the familiar of conservatives like Meisonnier, Heilbuth, Gérôme, and Alfred Stevens. By that time, he was adept at combining such diverse models in his work, using the audacities of the avant-garde to give a piquant gloss of modernism to his otherwise academic canvases.[1]

78. William Holman Hunt,
The Awakening Conscience, 1853,
oil on canvas, 76.2 x 55.9 cm.
Tate Gallery, London

It is noteworthy, however, that the London works, and certainly the later
Paris series, were considered incomprehensible or at the very least open to an
extraordinary range of interpretations and opinions. In fact, many of the essays
in the present volume address this issue, and reproduce important examples of
critical reaction. For example, of the painting *London Visitors* of about 1874 (pl.
XVIII), an ostensibly uncomplicated representation of tourists poring over a
guidebook, a contemporary critic observed, 'The picture is without distinct and
intelligible meaning.'[2] The critic concluded that the image was therefore lacking
in 'the higher distinction of pictorial grace.'[3] Tissot's deliberate refusal to enlarge
upon the story sets him apart from the artists who illustrated their narratives and
compels us to consider his work in quite another context.

This context is that of a certain type of later nineteenth-century Symbolism
or Idealism, specifically a strain of 'literary' imagery which depended for its mysteriousness on the subject matter rather than on anti-naturalistic modes of representation. Although Tissot is not known to have associated explicitly with the

Symbolist milieux of Paris and London whose ideas were pervasive, there are intersections between the members of those milieux, and Tissot's own life and work that would not seem to have been sufficiently taken into account. The artistic centre for the kind of literary Symbolism to which Tissot's art relates — this blend of naturalistic rendering with improbable or deliberately ambiguous subject matter — was Belgium. With all the emphasis on Tissot's life in England and France, it suddenly becomes interesting to remember that the artist was exposed to Belgian influences early in his training, in the form of an apprenticeship with the Belgian historical and costume-piece painter Baron Henri Leys. As Wentworth has explained, it was through Leys that Tissot was introduced to the kind of narrative illustration that would be perpetuated in his preoccupation with Pre-Raphaelite painting, and from the 1850s onward he exploited his fascination with intricate archaeological detail and narrative subjects. Following Leys's example, Tissot launched his career with his illustrations of Goethe's *Faust*, a favorite subject of such Romantic artists as Delacroix. Henri Zerner draws a significant distinction between Leys's enterprise and Tissot's, which has important consequences for the latter's subsequent engagement with Idealist themes: he notes that Leys's 'imitation of earlier painters was the expression of a profound national consciousness, a will to resume a Flemish tradition. For Tissot, on the contrary, the interest could only be in the picturesque, the quaintness of the costumes, the estrangement.'[4] Zerner argues that there would have have been no lack of French models for costume-pieces (Gérôme, Delaroche) and thus this quality of distance, 'estrangement', must have been central to Tissot's project. Indeed, there was a certain disjunction between Tissot and virtually every style or influence with which he came into contact: he did not strictly follow the modernism of his friend Degas; his supposed English narrative paintings, as well as his Pre-Raphaelite-inspired images, were never accepted by the English critics; his late works of Parisian women, seemingly social documents, were fraught with psychological undercurrents; and, according to Zerner, his adaptation of Leys's historicism had quite other aims.[5]

However, I believe that Tissot's youthful engagement with Leys is more telling than previously acknowledged. His sensing of an emotional and psychological kinship was one of the factors that focused his attention on Belgium and more generally on Northern Europe. Brussels was the centre both of Belgian Realism, as exemplified by painters such as Tissot's acquaintance Alfred Stevens, and of the kind of synthetic Symbolism that combines naturalism and mysticism, as exemplified by the somewhat younger Belgian Symbolist painter

Fernand Khnopff and the printmaker Félicien Rops. Furthermore, Brussels and Antwerp were important exhibition cities: Tissot showed his work in both cities, in addition to visiting Leys, and was well acquainted with the cosmopolitan art world there. The Belgian artists' group Les XX, founded in 1883, sponsored international exhibitions that featured Khnopff and Rops and the German Max Klinger, and each would have been exposed to the others' works. In fact, in their blend of Realism and Symbolism, Tissot's works relate more closely to the paintings of Khnopff and to the prints of Klinger and Rops than to the work of such French Symbolists as Gustave Moreau, Odilon Redon, and Paul Gauguin, or to such painters of modern life as Manet, Degas, and Cassatt. By contrast, the connection with the English Pre-Raphaelites and such contemporaries as Whistler is more evident. Perhaps most significantly both Khnopff and Klinger (who, like Tissot, were profoundly influenced by the Pre-Raphaelites) shared Tissot's intense realism as well as his mesmeric obsession with objects, Klinger in his graphic work especially. Moreover, all these artists were showing their work in London, Paris and Brussels at the Salons and at private galleries in the 1870s and 1880s, and there is no question that they were known to each other. Klinger actually moved to Brussels in 1879 in order to study with Charles-Emile Wauters, painter of the 'neomedieval macabre,'[6] some two decades after Tissot's own sojourn with Leys.

All of these artists shared the late nineteenth-century's preoccupation with the female sex. 'Woman's' role as Virgin, Whore, Vampire, Idol, and Invalid in the fin-de-siècle has been well-rehearsed and needs no elaboration here. But Tissot's involvement seems to go further than the social episodes depicted by a painter such as Manet and to relate more to his personal perception of the symbolic role of the female, much like Khnopff's approach to the subject. In *Feminizing the Fetish*, Emily Apter observed of literature, and it is true of painting as well, that 'in the fin de siècle, we find a curious predilection on the part of male authors for writing femininity, that is, masquerading as a woman's consciousness.'[7] Even before his *Femme à Paris* series, Tissot demonstrated his preoccupation with his young mistress Kathleen Newton (see the essay by Marshall in this volume), with whom he lived clandestinely in London and who was wasting away from tuberculosis. At the risk of sounding hard-hearted, the situation was quite perfect: an artist prone to fetishizing, as we shall see later; a beloved, much younger mistress perishing from the disease of the century; and a slow death that permitted him to scrutinize every stage and indulge his obsession with looking and recording.[8] Tissot depicted Kathleen Newton repeatedly,

79. Tissot, *The Garden Bench*, 1883, mezzotint, 41.7 x 56 cm. Art Gallery of Ontario, Toronto, Gift of Allan and Sondra Gotlieb

80. Tissot, *Summer Evening*, 1881, etching and drypoint, 22.9 x 39.6 cm. Art Gallery of Ontario, Toronto, Gift of Allan and Sondra Gotlieb

81. *Tissot and Mrs. Newton*, c.1882, photograph. Private Collection

obsessively; we see her in numerous paintings, including the works made at the end of her life: *The Garden Bench*, 1883 (fig. 79), completed after her death in November 1882; etchings, such as *Summer Evening*, 1881 (fig. 80); and photographs (fig. 81). The degree of realism and engagement with detail in the artist's handling of paint and etching needle parallels the intensity of his process of looking, a kind of scopophilia, by which, in this case, he probably hoped at some level to keep Kathleen Newton alive.

This obsessive regard links Tissot's work to that of Khnopff, Rops, and Klinger. Khnopff was as preoccupied with Woman as Klinger and Tissot but he emphasised a Symbolist approach at the expense of the representation of modern life. Yet his work shares the qualities of obsessive realism and psychological intensity apparent in Tissot's art and the younger artist might have discerned the ambiguities in Tissot's work, which he surely knew, and recognized the kinship to his own. The Belgian was as obsessed with his sister as Tissot was obsessed with Kathleen Newton: Khnopff depicted Marguerite repeatedly, both in

82. Fernand Khnopff, *I Lock the Door Upon Myself*, 1891, oil on canvas, 72 x 140 cm. Bayerische Staatsgemäldesammlungen, Munich

portraiture, as in *Portrait of Marguerite Khnopff* of 1887 and as a symbolic figure, as in the seven-figure image entitled *Memories* (1889) and *I Lock My Door Upon Myself* , 1891 (fig. 82), an image whose connection to the Pre-Raphaelites is implicit in that the title comes from a poem by Christina Rossetti. In these works, however, unlike those of Tissot, Woman is spiritualized, somehow inaccessible and of another realm. Khnopff signifies this through her frontality or strong profile and through a certain rigidity that emphasizes her as an idea rather than as an individual. He cemented the reference to otherworldliness by surrounding her with objects like the bust of Hypnos, Sleep, that visually evoke ideas in the poem. Thus, Khnopff's 'symbolism' derives from the presence of symbolic features as well as a certain intangible sense of mystic urgency; while remaining wedded to a naturalistic style, he fully subscribed to trappings of the Symbolist aesthetic that Tissot never entirely embraced.

Rops too very likely made an impact on Tissot, both in terms of the media he used and his subject matter. For example, like Rops in Belgium, Tissot was an active member of the English etching revival and prints were central to his oeuvre. Second, the Belgian was infamous for his symbolic, explicitly sexual imagery and, at least on a few occasions, Tissot seems to have imitated him, though his notable avoidance of nude subjects was the opposite side of the coin of Rops's explicitness. It is surely no coincidence that, with the exception of a few

83. Tissot, *Second Frontispiece*, 1875, drypoint, 25.3 x 16.2 cm. Art Gallery of Ontario, Toronto, Gift of Allan and Sondra Gotlieb

84. Félicien Rops, *La Toilette à Cythère*, mixed media, 22.4 x 15.2 cm. Photograph courtesy Ministère des Affaires sociales et de la Communauté française de Belgique – Dépôt au musée Félicien Rops, Namur

paintings such as *Japanese Girl Bathing* of 1864, Tissot chose the intimate medium of drypoint for his three known representations of nude women (see fig. 83).[9] These nudes, which recall Rops's renderings (fig. 84) and which were made, and then rejected, as frontispieces for Tissot's 1877 portfolio entitled *Ten Etchings,* are however surprisingly awkward and somewhat distastefully coy; one infers that Tissot was as uncomfortable with them as the viewer. Indeed, the whole question of Tissot's printmaking needs reexamination. As Katharine Lochnan has remarked elsewhere in this volume, '[Tissot's] prints are generally much tougher than the paintings. . . . Far from being regressive, the proto-symbolist elements embodied in these works find their echo in the work of Symbolists such as Edvard Munch,' as in his lithograph of 1896 entitled *The Alley* (fig. 85).[10] But insofar as the prints do manifest 'proto-symbolist' character-

85. Edvard Munch, *The Alley*,
1895, lithograph, 55.9 x 71.1 cm.
Museum of Fine Arts, Boston,
William Francis Warden Fund

istics, one must look beyond the obvious influences, such as Whistler, to figures
like Rops and Klinger. The question about the relationship between their work
and Tissot's—even who influenced whom—remains a pressing topic for exploration.

Indeed, for the obvious reason of friendship, Tissot's debt to Whistler has
been much discussed in the literature on his graphic works, as has the role of
photography and Japanese prints.[11] However, Klinger's graphic series, with their
blend of everyday life and Symbolist meaning and their elaborated rendering,
seems even closer to Tissot's sheets. The duality of realism and symbolism seen in
Tissot's late images is evident in Klinger's etched portfolios such as *A Glove,* 1881
(fig. 86) and *A Love,* 1887 (fig. 87). Although the prints of *A Glove* were published
in 1881, they were based upon a series of ink drawings that Klinger exhibited at
the Art Union in Berlin as early as 1878, an exhibition that immediately established the artist's reputation. In this series, a man notices a woman at a Berlin

86. Max Klinger, *The Glove*, pl. 1, 1881, etching, 25.7 x 34.7 cm. The Art Institute of Chicago, H. Karl and Nancy von Maltitz Endowment

87. Max Klinger, *First Encounter*, pl. 2 from *A Love*, 1887, etching, engraving and aquatint, 40.5 x 23.5 cm. (image). Carus Gallery, New York

skating rink, picks up a glove she drops, and unleashes a chain of bizarre fantasies that unfold over the course of the ten images. The sheets are so detailed and realistic in style as to induce a terrifying disjunction between the contemporaneity and realism of the settings and an apparent state of heightened awareness produced by the utter improbability of a dream. To underscore this disjunction, *A Love* intersperses 'everyday' scenes of a couple falling in love with allegorical sheets that 'comment' on the action. Furthermore, as he discussed in his tract *Malerei und Zeichnung* (1891), Klinger, like many of his contemporaries, believed that the more intimate, black and white medium of the print could convey certain philosophical ideas and emotions in a manner impossible in coloured paintings. In a similar way, Lochnan has observed of Tissot, 'In the etchings made after paintings in the series *La Femme à Paris* in the mid-1880s, the powerful black and white patterns, the flattening of the picture space, and the use of violent perspective create claustrophobic images which are much more disturbing than their painted counterparts.'

It is true that Tissot never abandoned 'realistic' representations of urban public and private life. With the notable exceptions of his *Mediumistic Apparition*, 1885 (pl. XXIV) and late Biblical scenes such as *The Journey of the Magi*, c.1886–95 (fig. 88), the obvious visionary subjects depicted by Khnopff and Klinger, as well as Rops's sexual scenes, are lacking in his work. This accounts in part for the tendency of critics to describe his images in terms of their 'powerful psychological impact . . . neurotic intensity and their ambiguous situation,' reflections of the artist's 'strangely contradictory personality,'[12] but to fail to locate him in a specifically Symbolist context. However, Tissot intersects with the Symbolist aesthetic, particularly the Belgian and German formulation, in the way in which he, like Khnopff and Klinger, imbued his seemingly realistic objects with mystery and psychological tension, essentially animating the inanimate through a process of obsessive looking.

The series entitled *La Femme à Paris* (1883–5) is most revelatory of Tissot's realization of a strange blend of spurious realism and personal symbolism. It was this series of fifteen paintings (a number of which remain unlocated today, and five of which Tissot subsequently reconceived as etchings before abandoning the project), depicting scenes in the lives of a variety of French women, that Henri Zerner singled out for its bizarre qualities, going so far as to assert that 'with their violent perspective, their frozen atmosphere, their sharp decorative patterns, their artificial animation linked to a now radical typification and lack of expressiveness in their faces, *these paintings project something insane*' (italics mine).[13]

88. Tissot, *The Adoration of the Magi* from *The Life of our Saviour Jesus Christ* (1897–8), chromolithograph, 22 x 17.9 cm. (image). Gift of Allan and Sondra Gotlieb. Photograph courtesy The Edward P. Taylor Reference Library and Archives, Art Gallery of Ontario, Toronto

On the surface, the Paris series depicts a set of social interactions that might have occurred in the life of women from different class backgrounds, in different professions, and at different moments. This was a bold move on Tissot's part: the Parisian woman was the subject of countless painted and printed renderings by artists of every school, and a wealth of associations already accompanied her in her every guise. As Tamar Garb has pointed out in this volume, the reception of Tissot's fifteen large paintings, exhibited at the Galerie Sedelmeyer in Paris in 1885 and in London at the Arthur Tooth Gallery the following year, was not positive. On the one hand, critics were troubled by the 'Englishness' of their 'very illustrative and literary nature,' and on the other, by what seemed to be 'nothing more than banal illustration, a manifestation of a particularly English disease with which Tissot had been infected.' Still others saw the opportunity to extrapolate their own stories from the visual material provided by the artist.[14]

The strangeness of the images derives from a number of features. For example, they seem initially to be little more than versions of similar themes, such as intimate interiors and places of public spectacle, explored by artists as varied as

Stevens, Degas, Cassatt, Renoir and Seurat. However, there are significant, jarring differences between Tissot's images and those of the 'painters of modern life,' elements that are in consonance with the symbolism of Khnopff and Klinger. For example, in what other 'naturalistic' painter's images does one experience such an extensive concentration on objects and detail, in fetishistic profusion and repetitiveness? Which other artist forces the viewer in the same way to pore over the meticulously rendered elements of the composition with such attention, sensing concealed meanings that extend beyond simple glosses on the apparent narrative? Tissot infused the objects in his environments—virtual *cabinets de curiosité*—with such pulsating inner life that they exhibit incantatory power, much like the poetic word-choices and neologisms of poems by the Symbolist writer Stéphane Mallarmé. In 1874 Mallarmé himself founded and wrote many articles for a fashion magazine entitled *La Dernière Mode*. In this publication, the poet commented extensively on objects (*bibelots*), and fashion accessories such as feathers and other suggestive female ornaments that recur repeatedly in Tissot's own work and that were of consuming interest to artists and intellectuals of the time, including Rops and Baudelaire.[15] Tissot furthermore reinforced the power of the *thing* not only within a specific picture, but in the repeated use of the same props from his collection of costumes and accessories; whether fans, balls, or animal skins, they together comprise a set of mesmerizing internal cross-references. By means of such strategies of repetition—hothouse settings filled with *objets*, and a kind of hyperrealism—Tissot created a world of displaced desire, a complex of fetishisms lurking under the glossy veneers both of his subject matter and of the painted surfaces themselves. Ultimately, both his colour paintings and black and white prints (both original images and versions of his paintings) relate more to the syntheses effected in Belgian art than to the more mainstream English and French work; one can argue that Tissot thus trod a line between the rarefied intellectualism of Khnopff and, in a sublimated way, the quasi-pornography of Rops.

Other factors insist on the construction of Tissot's oeuvre as a nexus of many of the 'manias,' or 'fetishisms,' of this era, linking them to the prevailing ethos of 'decadence'. The abundance of detail in Tissot's work and his engagement with objects of all sorts, from Japonaiserie to costumes, animal skins, furs, fans, betray an obsession with collecting and with the things themselves that fits into a fin-de-siècle phenomenon called 'bric-a-bracomania,' an obsession that is but a short step to the eroticizing of objects and the sexualizing of sight. In his pictures, Tissot deploys strategies such as those mentioned above to confront the viewer

89. Tissot, *The Little Nimrod*, 1886, mezzotint, 42.5 x 56.7 cm. Art Gallery of Ontario, Toronto, Gift of Allan and Sondra Gotlieb

with his obsessive engagement with such common, yet uncommonly potent, fetishisms of clothing, bric-a-brac, women. To 'display' his objects—even women become commodities—Tissot represents spaces that evoke the hothouse environment of the private 'cabinet,' and consistently betrays his scopophilia, an extreme love of looking. He then artfully manipulates the voyeuristic gazes of artist, viewer-surrogate, and the figures in the pictures themselves, weaving an entangling web of intersecting social and psychological meanings. Again, what is astonishing about Tissot's accomplishment is that in Khnopff's *I Lock the Door Upon Myself* (fig. 82 on p. 194), for example, the objects focused upon are in themselves symbolic, while by contrast, in Tissot's paintings, the artist infuses 'ordinary objects' with an inner life that often exceeds that of his human figures, which become congealed cut-outs of commodification.

Over and over one sees the repetition of costumes, as in *The Ball on Shipboard* (pl. XII) where there are four sets of sartorial twins. The same red, blue and white-striped ball appears in *Hide and Seek,* c.1880–2 (fig. 68 on p. 174) and *The Little Nimrod*, 1886 (fig. 89). Tissot's ceramic fish ornaments the interior in the mezzotint of *Morning*, 1886 (fig. 76 on p. 187) and sits on the table in the lost painting of *The Sphinx*, 1883–5 (fig. 70 on p. 176). In the same way, the artist repeatedly portrayed women at evening soirées in certain poses: many are seen from the rear, as the artist directed his curious gaze to the napes of their necks, shoulder blades, and exposed bosoms; for example, one sees this stock figure in *The Fashionable Beauty*, 1883–5 (fig. 37 on p. 101) at lower left, as well as in *The Political Lady*, 1883–5 (pl. XXII). But what may be construed as a limited repertoire of motifs also suggests an obsessive repetitiveness that betrays Tissot's equivocal reaction to his world.

All of the above-mentioned features lurk within one or more of the images from the *Femme à Paris* series. In *The Liar* (fig. 69 on p. 175), a lost painting from the series, a malevolent female figure, clad in ruffly black, darkens the opening between heavy curtains embroidered with a motif of frightening Japanese dragons that exactly frame the woman's face. The threatening motif is continued on the pillow at left, which stares into the space of the viewer and of the unrepresented figure, whose open book and used teacup serve as metonymic indicators of his(?) presence and of us, the viewers. The room overflows with carefully observed and rendered Asian objects, exotic furniture, and furry animal skins. The claustrophobic interior of this image, as well as of *The Sphinx* (fig. 70 on p. 176) relate without question to settings described in what Apter has called a 'literary microgenre characterizable as "cabinet fiction".'[16] In these 'private places,' crammed with 'curios, antiques, and personal memorabilia,' there could unfold the most forbidden kinds of activities; one thinks of Joris-Karl Huysmans's *Against Nature* of 1883, in which an esthetic young man experiments with every kind of esoteric and erotic sensual stimulation from the confines of his exotically appointed chambers. And, like Tissot, after immersion in these preoccupations, Huysmans ultimately experienced a conversion and renounced his decadent writings.

Apter traces the progression of the later nineteenth-century mania for collecting, of which Tissot was so much a part. She observes that 'the mania of collecting and its increasingly refined, recherché developments—bric-a-bracomania, tableaumania[,] bibliophilia—seem to have merged in the 1870s with the newly minted sexual abberation of erotomania.'[17] Although it is extreme to attribute to Tissot the venality evident in many literary works of his era, it is not unreasonable to see the woman in *The Sphinx* as an elegant courtesan. Freudian fetish theory links fur and velvet with female genitals, and they appear here as they do regularly in Tissot's pictures. Furthermore, the point of view enhances the clandestine, surreptitious quality of *The Liar* and *The Sphinx*, which their titles themselves imply. Apter's description of these spaces evokes Tissot's settings: she refers to 'decadent cabinets, with their murky light, heavy crimson curtains, crevices, cavities, and plethora of "seeing eyes," [which] . . . already seem to theatricalize erotic fantasy, imaging, through decorative accoutrements . . . that facilitate the voyeuristic gaze, the "look" of the bordello client trained on feminine wares.'[18] Indeed, in images such as *The Fashionable Beauty* (fig. 37 on p. 101) the spectator's eye is drawn immediately to the three pairs of crossed hands, the woman's and those of the two men that flank her, that shield their sex while simultaneously drawing attention to it. The woman's fan lies at rest, black against the black of her dress; she has lowered her guard. Those sets of crossed hands, with the men concealing their arousal with their hats, constitute the real story of the image.

The 'theatricalization of erotic fantasy' occurs in public locations as well in Tissot's world. In *The Ladies of the Cars*, 1883–5 (fig. 39 on p. 103), the stiff figures guide their horses around the circus ring, their phallic headdresses pointing in the air in all directions. Aloof, remote, they are on parade as the blank eyes of the white lamps close in on them. The pink-clad woman in *The Sporting Ladies*, 1883–5 (pl. XXIII) makes erotic theatre even more obvious. Tapping her fan casually on her shoulder, she gazes outward shamelessly, as her companion leans voluptuously backward in her chair, the feathers of her black hat visually caressing the right foot of the trapeze performer. The nape of her neck, rendered in a suggestive triangle, presents a curly-haired erotic echo of the man's wide-open legs. Yet it is also the men, the aristocrats having their day at the circus, who perform and parade their wares to the female viewers. The monocled gentleman in red opens his legs wide to the viewer as a woman's head is framed between the crossed legs of the trapeze artist in blue. Tissot, 'writing femininity,' seems to portray the scene through the woman's gaze and seems to contrast the avid attention of the female spectators with the relative restraint (even distaste?) of the males.

Moreover, in images such as this, as well as *The Woman of Fashion*, 1883–5 (fig. 90), and *The Provincial Ladies*, 1883–5 (fig. 30 on p. 72), another theme of the *Femme à Paris* series is made clear, that is, the role of fashion and the way in which it complements the mania for collecting. In this volume Edward Maeder has discussed the costumes worn by Tissot's figures; yet they are even more significant than one might expect. Maeder mentions the etiquette of fans for example, noting how a nuanced flirtation was possible through different handling of the accoutrement. In the context which I attempt to suggest here, the fan, to

90. Tissot, *The Woman of Fashion*, 1883–5, oil on canvas, 148.3 x 103 cm. Photograph courtesy Christie's, London

take one aspect of fashion, fits in to Tissot's own obsessive and repetitive rendering of objects; to the notion that fashion defines femininity; and to the related desire for consumer goods and their eroticization that Tissot imaged in his *The Shop Girl,* 1883–5 (pl. XXI) as we shall see later.[19] In her discussion of the psychology of clothes and the ways in which late nineteenth-century French writers described their fetishistic qualities, Apter singles out the critic and writer Octave Uzanne, who actually wrote a history of the fan in addition to extraordinary ruminations on other female accessories in his book *Les Ornements de la femme* (1882).[20] A case in point are his musings about fur, which relate to Tissot's *The Woman of Fashion* (fig. 90 above) and *The Convalescent (The Warrior's Daughter)* (fig. 77 on p. 188), as well as any of the numerous images in which Kathleen Newton is posed against animal skins:

> Thus amid her furs, woman, this adorable plant, this *mimosa pudica*, releases a beauty more mysterious, more gentle, more alluring, more envelopped and

enveloping, as if the electricity of this furry skin were wafting into the air surrounding this provocative daughter of Eve, a sensuality enticing like a subtle caress that lightly brushes our senses as it passes.[21]

This astonishingly sensual passage forces reassessment of Tissot's women in quite a different context from that of contemporary fashion models and of mannequins for his extensive collection of garments and accessories. It would seem bizarre that virtually all of Tissot's women, with the exception of those in the etchings mentioned above, and against all contemporary trends in art, are so defiantly *clothed*. And clothed expressively and significantly. However, based upon Apter's work on clothing fetishism of this period, it is clear that Tissot's women exemplify the preoccupation with fashion and its social and sexual semiotics exhibited by the Goncourt brothers in their descriptions of eighteenth-century women and carried through in the literary and fashion writing of the nineteenth century. It is no accident that Tissot knew the Goncourts' work well and made illustrations of their novel *Renée Mauperin*. In Tissot's case, fashion accoutrements commodify the wearer and emblematize her, again linking his work to a broadly construed symbolic, if not Symbolist, approach. The women are somehow imprisoned yet also elevated by the insistence of fashion; it becomes a device to create a distancing process between artist/viewer and portrayed subject while simultaneously effectively heightening the sense of eroticism as well as reverence in the image. On the one hand, Tissot rendered the carefully defined articles of clothing more sensual through their provocative masking of the female body; as in a striptease where the strip never happens, he frustrated the viewer's vicarious climax, substituting the fetishistic pleasures of obsessive *looking*. On the other hand, Tissot's strategic use of fashion was curiously self-protective, coinciding with the goal of some of his contemporaries, including Octave Uzanne, to express a 'deep compulsion to keep the specter of the "essential" naked female body at bay. Pathologizing the nude was an ingenious technique for sustaining the fetishistic illusion of an idealized femininity.'[22] In *Quiet*, c.1881 (fig. 91), for example, Kathleen Newton glances out at the viewer while a tired child leans against her. Her decorated hat and cloak exude as much presence as she does and, along with the great furry animal skin, seem to ennoble her while at the same time subverting her apparent demureness and providing a symbolic substitute for her limited sexual powers due to her tuberculosis.

Fashion, collecting, and commerce intersect in *The Shop Girl* (pl. XXI). Here, the viewer-customer is about to depart from a Parisian luxury boutique

91. Tissot, *Quiet*, c.1881, oil on canvas, 68.8 x 91.4 cm. Private Collection, London

where ribbons and other feminine sartorial ornaments, the stuff of fetishistic obsession, are purveyed. A shopgirl, possibly the same model as the maid in *The Morning* (fig. 76 on p. 187), opens the door with one hand and holds our parcel with the other, her fingers contorted with baroque exaggeration. Tissot here exhibits the sense of *horror vacui* that characterizes so much of his work: the same scrupulous attention to detail, and the same uniform focus on people and objects, even the tangle of pink ribbon on the floor. A complex web of gazes bounces the eye from the viewer's position as departing customer to the face of the shopgirl and then to the male passerby gazing in. At the same time, the other shop assistant turns her head toward the display window, possibly responding to yet another gentleman, who touches his hat to her. As Tamar Garb has pointed out in her essay, the relationship between the commodification of objects and women at the end of the nineteenth century, extensively explored in recent literature, is made manifest by Tissot as he links the coveting and sale of luxury goods with the male gaze and as he displays the shop as locus of desire, desire that can be satisfied by money. Here, as Karl Marx foresaw, 'people and things exchange semblances: social relations take on the character of object relations, and commodities assume the active agency of people.'[23] Furthermore, Tissot has commented on the situation through the griffin that embellishes the edge of the sale counter; its lascivious tongue references the eroticization of looking, so remarked upon at the time, and so suggestive of the interchangeability between people and objects. An image of modern life, yes, but its documentary aspect emerges as so compromised that the viewer remains uneasy, our *desire* for certainties unsatisfied and unavailable at any *price*.

The issues of buying and selling, class and power, are explored further in one of the most disturbing images in Tissot's oeuvre, the carefully elaborated mezzotint of 1886 (fig. 76 on p. 187) after a lost painting entitled *The Morning*, which was probably part of a somewhat later incomplete series entitled *L'Etrangère*.[24] Looming above the viewer, the figure of a parlourmaid stares out at the viewer as she carries a breakfast tray from the morning room. Lit from below, the maid's face, teeth bared, glows demonically. Improbably elongated fingers curl around the tray like serpentine instruments of arcane erotic torture. Imposingly, even menacingly frontal, the figure wears a slightly glazed expression, directed at an unseen interlocutor — and the viewer — a gaze that is inviting as well and that corresponds to the coy placement of the tray slightly below hip level. On it, the remains of an appetizing meal and polished pots, cups, and toast rack have been artfully arranged and as minutely observed and rendered as the maid herself. Behind her, intricate objects, in equally sharp focus and practically animate, define an elegantly appointed interior: a clock with a sphinx and a phallic candlestick are perched on the mantlepiece and reflected in the mirror. Next to them, a leaping ceramic fish seems to gasp for air in this claustrophobic, tightly compressed scene with its vertiginously angled planes. At first glance, an innocent image; upon further scrutiny, uncomfortably ambiguous. The artist, whose obsession with detail leaves nothing visual to the imagination, has by contrast deliberately left any interpretation open-ended and unfixed.

This mezzotint appears to be based upon a watercolour documenting the missing painting which appears in one of Tissot's volumes of photographs recording his oeuvre.[25] The watercolour composition depicts a bright, airy room, with a gentleman at right apparently tying his shoes as the parlourmaid departs the room with the remains of the breakfast. The man's satisfied smile seems ominous in context both of the maid's frozen expression and the peculiar perspective of the room. There may be more to the scene than meets the eye, so to speak. First, Tissot intensified the effect of the image when he translated it from the brightness of the painting, or watercolour, to the moody shadows of the mezzotint. Most importantly, he eliminated the figure of the man in order to focus on the maid, insisting that we confront her. By adjusting the perspective so that she looks down upon us, we are 'supplicants,' she the dominatrix. Within Tissot's work, this is quite unusual; only the ladies of the cars (chariots) tower above the spectator in a similar way and their manner is sexually tempting through their suggestive costumes and seeming unavailability. By contrast, her monumental form filling up the vertical, compressed space, the maid leers down at us with an inviting, eyebrow-raised smirk that Kathleen Newton — ill, idealized, almost always reclining, *controllable* — certainly never wore. Moreover, in a world of shopgirls and bourgeois women, this is one of Tissot's few, if not only, representations of a maid, and it seems significant that she appears to be arguably the most powerful female presence in his oeuvre.

There exists an entire fin-de-siècle literature on the maid as a locus of fetishism. Apter has investigated at length the representation of the maid in texts by authors ranging from Flaubert to Freud. Through a selection of writings, she traces the role of the maid in the imaginary as well as actual lives of her male employers and her role as a target for sexual exploitation, fantasy, and fetishism. Class difference and power relations permit some of this response, as well as her position as a 'dispossessed yet self-reliant working woman.'[26] Indeed, Tissot's compositional strategies for depicting this servant are too marked to be passed over, much like his friend Manet's similar image *Bar at the Folies-Bergère,* 1882 (fig. 92). Her suggestive presentation of the food tray, balanced at the level of her genital area with the finger hole of the toast rack in the centre, the provocatively curved fingers, the voluminous apron which Apter describes as a common fetish garment,[27] the menacingly animate quality of the objects in the room, all point to the imposing, lusty figure of the maid as a provider of a service — other than that of bearing food. In titling the print *Morning* is a previous evening implied? Is this indeed the morning after?

To return to my initial proposition: was Tissot a Symbolist? For many of the reasons proposed above, this artist resists easy classification and his work introduces issues that expand the categories usually deployed to interpret his images. As even his own contemporaries understood, his subjects were not common narrative representations of modern life. In their manipulation of objects, compositional strategies and media, the images are often indeterminate and suggest far more than they ostensibly convey. In this sense, Tissot's images seem to relate most closely to Belgian and German Symbolist art, in particular the work of

92. Edouard Manet, *A Bar at the Folies-Bergère*, 1881–2, oil on canvas, 96 x 130 cm. Courtauld Institute Gallery, London

Khnopff, Klinger, and Rops. Moreover, his treatment of women and objects, his mania for collecting, and the fetishistic nature of the recurring objects and their presentation, point to a very modern, if very complex and somehow damaged personality, what Henri Zerner referred to discreetly as 'the subtle and disturbing interest of Tissot's troubled psychology.'[28] As one example, Tissot's devotion to Kathleen Newton was touching and admirable; nonetheless his scrutiny of her decline, his utilization of her illness to illustrate other stories, such as *Renée Mauperin*, and the fact that her illness probably prevented a 'normal' sexual relationship — which may in reality have been reassuring and acceptable to Tissot — indicate that he exploited her situation to his own purposes.

As I hope to have shown, or at least proposed, Tissot trained his eye obsessively on single objects and their details not just in order to provide commentary on the supposed narrative of the image, but in such a way as to create a relationship between looking and desiring that is unmistakeably erotic and that thus transforms the objects involved into instanciations of displaced desire, or fetishes. This goes beyond a 'commodification' of people in the economic sense, women in particular, to a psychoanalytically defined fixation that borders on perversion (perhaps that is what Zerner meant when he chose the word 'insane'?). The two processes—commodification and fetishization—are of course related, as Tamar Garb has indicated elsewhere in this volume. Furthermore, as Apter points out, 'late nineteenth-century bric-a-bracomania, with its domestic altars of eroticized things, brought Freud and Marx into collusion, and this connection, in turn, helped to explain the prevalent and subtly disquieting present-day consumerist practices of collecting, hoarding, displaying, desiring, fondling, possessing, and continually looking.'[29] This catalogue of activities in fact summarizes Tissot's enterprise quite succinctly. In other words, then, the primary function of much of Tissot's work, certainly that of the 1880s and beyond, is not description or chronicling; rather, the images subversively infiltrate the interstices between the seemingly objective painting of modern life (the world of surface appearances) and the subtext of symbolic (Symbolist?), sexual, and emotional significances (the world of underlying essences). In construing his pictures as suggestive, ultimately enigmatic, hardly documentary, Tissot's art acquires a new logic and conviction.

1. Michael Wentworth, *James Tissot* (Oxford: Clarendon Press, 1984), 17–18.
2. Unknown author, 'The Royal Academy,' *Art Journal* (June 1874), 164; cited in Wentworth, *James Tissot,* 94.
3. *Loc. cit.*
4. Henri Zerner, 'Introduction,' in David S. Brooke, Michael Wentworth and Henri Zerner, *J.J. Tissot: A Retrospective Exhibition* (Providence, Rhode Island: Museum of Art, Rhode Island School of Design and The Art Gallery of Ontario, 1968), n.p. See also the excellent discussion of Leys in Wentworth, *James Tissot,* 24ff.
5. Zerner, *J.J. Tissot,* n.p.
6. J. Kirk T. Varnedoe with Elizabeth Streicher, 'Introduction,' in *Graphic Works of Max Klinger* (New York: Dover Publications, Inc., 1977), xvii.
7. Emily Apter, *Feminizing the Fetish. Psychoanalysis and Narrative Obsession in Turn-of-the-Century France* (Ithaca and London: Cornell University Press, 1991), xv.
8. For the importance and prevalence of tuberculosis see Barbara Larson, 'Microbes and Maladies: Bacteriology and Health at the Fin de Siècle,' in *Lost Paradise: Symbolist Europe*, exh. cat. (Montreal: Montreal Museum of Fine Arts, 1995), 385–93.
9. I am grateful to Katharine Lochnan for her generosity in sharing with me information on Tissot's etchings of nudes and their possible relationship to the work of Rops.

10. See essay by Katharine Lochnan in this volume.
11. See Michael Justin Wentworth, *James Tissot. A Catalogue Raisonné of his Prints*, exh. cat. (The Minneapolis Institute of Arts and Sterling and Francine Clark Art Institute, 1978), 12–16.
12. Wentworth, *Catalogue Raisonné of his Prints*, 30.
13. Zerner, *J.J. Tissot,* n.p.
14. See essay by Tamar Garb in this volume.
15. See *Félicien Rops 1833–1898*, exh. cat. (Bruxelles: Centre culturel de la Communauté française et les Musées royaux des Beaux-Arts de Belgique; Paris: Musée des Arts Décoratifs; Nice: Musée des Beaux-Arts Jules Chéret, 1985), 54–5. This catalogue reproduces the cover of an issue of *La Dernière Mode* (Deuxième Livraison, Dimanche 20 Septembre 1874), which has an image entitled 'Toilettes de Promenade' by F. Pectueur (?). In subject and composition, the cover image bears an uncanny resemblance to Tissot's painting of about 1877, *The Gallery of H.M.S. Calcutta (Portsmouth)* in the Tate Gallery, London. This resemblance suggests that the connection between Tissot and Mallarmé's fashion publication needs further exploration. See also Rae Beth Gordon, 'Aboli Bibelot? The Influence of the Decorative Arts on Stéphane Mallarmé and Gustave Moreau,' *Art Journal,* 45 no. 2 (Summer 1985): 105–12.
16. Apter, *Feminizing the Fetish,* 39.
17. Apter, *Feminizing the Fetish,* 41.
18. Apter, *Feminizing the Fetish,* 45.
19. See Apter, chap. 4. Also Walter Benjamin, *Charles Baudelaire: A Lyric Poet in the Era of High Capitalism*, trans. Harry Zohn (London: New Left Books, 1973).
20. As Apter points out, Uzanne was taken aback by the success of his book *L'Eventail* [The Fan] (Paris: A. Quantin, 1882) and complained that his more 'serious' publications were undervalued in contrast. See Apter, *Feminizing the Fetish,* 81–2 and n26.
21. Octave Uzanne, in *Les Ornements de la Femme* (Paris: Librairies Imprimeries Réunies, 1892; orig. pub. 1882); cited in Apter, *Feminizing the Fetish,* 84 n33.
22. Apter, *Feminizing the Fetish,* 86.
23. Karl Marx, as paraphrased by Hal Foster in '(Dis)agreeable Objects,' in *Damaged Goods: Desire and the Economy of the Object*, exh. cat. (New York: New Museum of Contemporary Art, 1986), 13; cited in Apter, *Feminizing the Fetish,* 12.
24. See Wentworth, *Catalogue Raisonné of his Prints*, 326–9.
25. See Willard E. Misfeldt, *The Albums of James Tissot* (Bowling Green, Ohio: Bowling Green University Popular Press, 1982), 102, IV–3.
26. Apter, *Feminizing the Fetish,* 197.
27. Apter, *Feminizing the Fetish,* 177.
28. Zerner, *J.J. Tissot,* 25.
29. Apter, *Feminizing the Fetish,* x.

The 'Scientization' of Spirituality

Serena Keshavjee

> *Spiritualism is not a religion, but a science*, a science of which we as yet scarcely know the a,b,c.

S O WROTE the respected French astronomer Camille Flammarion (1842–1925)[1] near the end of the nineteenth century when metaphysical researchers still believed parapsychology would be accepted as science. Not only have parapsychological studies been ejected from the scientific canon since that time, they have virtually been expunged from history as well. The lack of a scholarly historicization of Spiritualism and parapsychology has been problematic for Tissot scholars because during the most successful artistic period of his life Tissot was immersed in Spiritualism and Neo-Catholicism. These religio-philosophies developed to prepare society for *la nouvelle ère* have been dismissed by some Tissot scholars as 'embarrassing,' 'irrational' and conservative,[2] yet the pan-Western critique of the Positivist world view—in which Tissot partook—was fundamental to emergent Symbolism. As has been argued in recent years, Modernism as a cultural movement involved both celebrating and critiquing the socio-political condition of modernity.[3] Tissot's desire to be modern was in no way contradicted by his investigation of Spiritualism which was being legitimized by some Western scientists at the turn of the century. Indeed 'New Age' religions that claimed to be based in contemporary scientific research were for this very reason perceived as modern.

My main interest in this paper is to examine the turn-of-the-century interpenetration of art and quasi-scientific religions of which Spiritualism is an example. The facts concerning Tissot's attendance at the séance of 20 May 1885 have been dealt with in this volume by Ann Saddlemyer and elsewhere by Michael Wentworth.[4] Here I will focus on the reception of the visual imagery produced by adherents of this popular religion. The late nineteenth-century Spiritualist revival differed from earlier Spiritualist outbreaks in that it employed visual material as a method of propaganda, and these images—including spirit photographs and 'automatic' drawings produced by mediums while in trance states—successfully promoted its tenets within elite culture. Tissot's mezzotint *Mediumistic Apparition*, 1885 (fig. 62 on p. 155 and pl. XXIV) is one of four prints by different authors that have survived, representing the medium William

93. J.G. Keulemans, *Apparition Formed in Full View*, c.1884–5, colour lithograph in *Twixt Two Worlds: A Narrative of the Life and Work of William Eglinton* (1886), pl. VIII. Department of Archives and Special Collections, University of Manitoba Libraries, Winnipeg

Eglinton invoking a phantom. These rare images, produced a few years apart and discussed here together for the first time, provide scholars with an unusual opportunity to examine the interaction between elite and common culture in fin-de-siècle Europe. Only one of the prints was made by an active Spiritualist: J.G. Keulemans' colour lithograph of his original watercolour produced around 1884–5 depicting Eglinton materializing a ghost, which was published in John S. Farmer's *Twixt Two Worlds: A Narrative of the Life and Work of William Eglinton* in 1886 (fig. 93).[5] The other images were made by professionally trained men, including the French academic artist Albert Besnard (1849–1934), whose little-known illustration of the 20 May 1885 séance depicts Tissot with Eglinton and the two ghosts and was published in the parapsychological publication *Force Psychique* (1889) by Yveling Rambaud (fig. 94),[6] and a so-called 'spirit' photograph taken in 1886 by the Russian scientist Alexander Aksákow (1832–1903) of Eglinton and his 'spirit guide Ernest,' published in an issue of the German metapsychical review *Psychische Studien* (fig. 95).[7] The appropriation of Spiritualist imagery by Tissot and Besnard introduced these images into Paris art circles, which, according to the art critic Jules Bois (1868–1943?), encouraged the

94. Wood engraving by Florian after a drawing by Albert Besnard, *En la voyant, il s'écria*, 1887, in Yveling Rambaud, *Force Psychique* (Paris, 1889). Bibliothèque Nationale, Paris

95. Alexander Aksákow, *The Medium Eglington in a trance with the phantom in white and a turban*, 1886, photograph, plate XI in Aksakow, *Animismus und Spiritismus* (Leipzig, 1919)

development of an avant-garde Symbolist style he labelled the 'Spirit Aesthetic,' best represented by the dream-like art of Eugène Carrière (1849–1906) and Odilon Redon (1840–1916).[8]

The Imaging of William Eglinton and his Ghosts

Spiritualists maintain that the human personality continues after bodily death and that it is possible to communicate with the surviving spirit through an intercessor.[9] Clark Garrett points out, furthermore that, 'most cultures . . . believe that sometimes supernatural spirits take possession of people on earth.'[10] By the end of the nineteenth century, materialistic 'clinical' analyses of 'spirit possession' such as those suggested by J.M. Charcot (1825–93), who defined possession as a form of 'hysteria,' were beginning to dominate. Alternative explanations persisted however. One of the most vital debates of the nineteenth century

96. Unknown, *Complete levitation of a table in Professor Flammarion's salon through mediumship of Eusapia Paladino*, 1898, photograph, G. Glendenning Hamilton Collection, Archives and Special Collections, University of Manitoba Libraries

revolved around whether the unconscious mind was 'closed' or 'open.'[11] The model of a 'closed' mind—which would only contain memories, daydreams and fantasies—was accepted by, for example, Charcot, Theodore Flournoy and Sigmund Freud. Other equally eminent scientists such as Sir William Crookes (1832–1919), Camille Flammarion, Gustave Geley (1868–1924) and later Carl Gustav Jung, asserted that the unconscious mind was 'open'; the unconscious was 'virtually in communication with an extra-individual and mysterious realm.'[12] The 'open' mind concept embraced a range of metaphysical ideas, such as the World Soul, the collective unconscious, and discarnate spirits, which the Spiritualists accepted. In this manner Spiritualism is typical of the other Neo-Romantic doctrines such as Vitalism, Monism and even Theosophy, whose main goals were to bring about a reconciliation between science and religion in preparation for *la nouvelle ère*—the twentieth century.

By the time that Tissot produced his apparition images in 1885, mediumship and séances were well integrated into the 'drawing rooms of the best society.'[13] The credibility of the Spiritualist doctrine had been boosted through the 1860s and 1870s in Paris and London by a number of high-profile scientists and literati

97. William Crookes, *Katie King*, c.1874, photograph. T. Glendenning Hamilton Collection, Department of Archives and Special Collections, University of Manitoba Libraries

who publicly endorsed its tenets. The astronomer Camille Flammarion began investigating the paranormal in his 1865 monograph on the Davenport brothers, and he soon put his knowledge of imaging techniques to use by photographing mediums in a trance state. Flammarion organized a series of evenings in Paris to investigate empirically the medium Eusapia Paladino's powers (fig. 96). He was aided in this endeavour by other savants including Jules Bois, Maria Caithness, the Duchess of Pomar, Jules Clarétie, Victorien Sardou and the investigator of hypnosis and future Nobel laureate Charles Richet. In 1874 the respected British scientists Alfred R. Wallace and William Crookes publicly defended the practise of photographing spirits: as with Aksákow's photograph of Eglinton with his familial spirit, Crookes produced forty-four photographs of the phantom 'Katie King' (fig. 97).[14]

The year that Tissot became involved in séances, the French Neo-Catholic writer René Caillié (1831–96) published his mediumistic writings entitled *La Vie de Jésus dictée par lui-même*, as a part of an ambitious project to initiate Catholics into Spiritualism. According to Eglinton's biographer, it was an article describing a séance with Eglinton by another Catholic Spiritualist, Florence Marryat (1837–99), which introduced Tissot to this medium.[15] If Tissot did indeed read Marryat's piece, he may have been struck by the similarity of his own relationship with the divorced Kathleen Newton, and Marryat's story of passion between a priest and a nun 'against the strictest rules of the church,' which ended in tragedy. Marryat's blend of Catholicism and Spiritualism would have been more attractive to Tissot than Alan Kardec's eastern-inspired Spiritism which, as Saddlemyer points out, had dominated the Parisian scene until this period. Along with Maria Caithness and René Caillié, Marryat belonged to a group of Catholics based in both Paris and London who were actively trying to reconcile these systems of belief. In her book *There is No Death* Marryat points out that despite its stated opposition, Christian doctrine accepts spirit communication: '[I]t seems strange to me that the Catholic Church, whose very doctrine is overlaid with Spiritualism and who makes it a matter of belief that the Saints hear and help us in our prayers and the daily actions of our lives, . . . should consider it unlawful for us to communicate with our departed relatives. I cannot see the difference in iniquity between speaking to John Powles, who was and is a dear and trusted friend of mine, and Saint Peter of Alcantara, who is an old man whom I never saw in this life.' She also wrote 'No greater proof can be brought forward of the truth of Spiritualism than the truth of the Bible, which teems and bristles with accounts of it from beginning to end.'[16]

René Caillié edited a number of socialistically oriented, Catholic Spiritualist journals, including *L'Etoile: kabbale messianique, de socialisme chrétien et de spiritualisme expérimental* (1889–95), whose secretary was Jules Bois and which promoted a mystical Catholicism. Maria Caithness, as President of the French Theosophical Society and as a friend of Helena Blavatsky, also enjoyed prominence in Parisian occult circles. She is credited with attracting Flammarion, Edouard Schuré, Richet and Bois to the Theosophical Society, and considering her longstanding belief, no doubt introduced them to Spiritualism. She engaged often with séances and automatic writing, all the while remaining 'on the right side of Rome' (fig. 98).[17]

At the midpoint in his life Tissot's world changed dramatically and he abandoned themes of leisure in his art for another, now equally fashionable theme,

98. Jean Buguet, *Spirit Photograph with Maria Caithness*, 1874, photograph. Bibliothèque Nationale, Paris

'New Age' religion. In 1885, the same year that he sought out a medium for the first time, Tissot experienced a vision of Christ at the moment of Transubstantiation during a mass at St. Sulpice Church in Paris. Some have speculated that his religious experience was due to the devastation he felt after the death of his brother in 1877, and then of Kathleen Newton, his partner of six years, in 1882.[18] I can only imagine that William Eglinton promised to invoke Newton's spirit on that evening of 20 May 1885, because the still vulnerable Tissot was all set up to paint the scene, as Besnard's illustration indicates (fig. 94 on p. 215).[19] Eglinton was a 'physical' medium and was said to be able to 'channel spirits' who provided proof of their existence by drawing and writing 'automatically' on modified chalk tablets (fig. 99). The frontispiece portrait of *William Eglinton* (1885) that Tissot provided for *Twixt Two Worlds* depicts the

99. William Eglinton, *A Direct Drawing (Automatic Drawing),* in *Twixt Two Worlds: A Narrative of the Life and Work of William Eglinton* (1886), fig. 12. Department of Archives and Special Collections, University of Manitoba Libraries

wide-eyed, hypnotized medium beside his tablet. This etching of Eglinton (pl. XXV), the original painting of Newton and Ernest's ghosts, and the mezzotint of the same scene, are the only Spiritualist work that Tissot is known to have produced, but the movement introduced him to the more mystical side of Catholicism, which he pursued for the rest of his life. Despite the visionary nature of his religious experiences, Tissot's projects illustrating the life of Christ, as well as the Old and New Testaments, were grounded in historicism and his style remained realistic even when he was reproducing his visions of Christ, as Edmond de Goncourt noted. While de Goncourt may have found this manner 'mediocre,' there was a mid-nineteenth century tradition of depicting visions illusionistically, with distinct black and white contrasts—both in automatic drawing, represented here by the work of the well-known Parisian mediumistic artist F. Hugo d'Alési (fig. 100), and in early spirit photographs (figs. 95, 97, 98).[20] Tissot may have chosen to reproduce *Mediumistic Apparition* as a mezzotint for its luminous, clear effect, which imitates the early spirit images. His

100. F. Hugo d'Alési, *Automatic
Drawing*, 1878, from J. Camille
Chaigneau, *Les Chrysanthèmes
de Marie* (Paris, 1880).
Bibliothèque Nationale, Paris

apparent ability to hypnotize himself and then accurately record his vision
before it faded from memory was promoted as an asset and used to advertise *The
Life of Our Saviour Jesus Christ* by the journalist Cleveland Moffett.[21] Art produced in a state of altered consciousness, in effect mediumistically, would
become increasingly admired as 'original' during the 1890s by the Symbolists.

On that day in May 1885 Eglinton was able to invoke two spirits, 'Kathleen
Newton' and 'Ernest.' The radiant, vaporous substance that enabled these apparitions to materialize was named 'ectoplasm' by Richet. Ectoplasm, or ideoplasm as
it was sometimes called, was the source of intense scientific study well into the
1920s. Its properties are similar to other now discredited substances — the 'ether' of
the nineteenth century physicists, the 'protoplasm' of the naive Vitalists, and the
occultists' 'astral light': all four were perceived as being 'intelligent' or 'directed'
invisible material forces which inhabited and surrounded living beings.[22] Ectoplasm was considered to be directed by 'psychic forces' and to be analogous to an
invisible, animating principle of life — the vital force. Nandor Fodor summarized

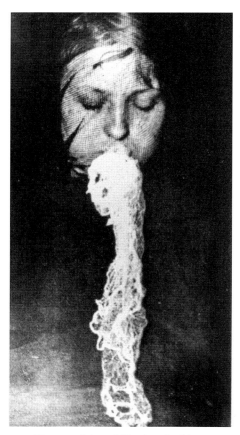

101. Albert von Schrenck Notzing, *Psychic Phenomena: "Ectoplasm"*, 1913, photograph. T. Glendenning Hamilton Collection, Department of Archives and Special Collections, University of Manitoba Libraries

102. Wood engraving by Florian after a drawing by Albert Besnard, *La fumée lumineuse*, 1887, in Yveling Rambaud, *Force Psychique* (Paris, 1889), Bibliothèque Nationale, Paris

the properties of the magic substance: 'ectoplasm is matter, invisible and intangible in its primary state but assuming vaporous, liquid or solid condition in various stages of condensation.'[23] Albert von Schrenck-Notzing (1862–1929) photographed ectoplasm extensively (fig. 101) and described it as a 'living substance' with the power of 'change, movement and assumption of definite forms.'[24]

Albert Besnard's drawing of the 20 May 1885 séance (fig. 94 on p. 215) and a second illustration of Eglinton with an ectoplasmic apparition (fig. 102) were produced in 1887 and published by Rambaud, who also accepted that the medium's psychic abilities were associated with vital forces.[25] Besnard's depiction accurately reflected the liquescent and dematerializing quality that the scientific

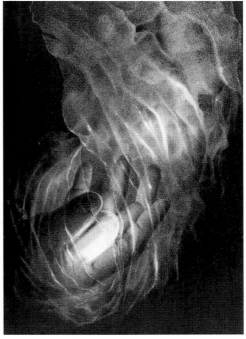

103. J.G. Keulemans, *Phases of Materialization no. 3*, c.1884–5, chromolithograph, in *Twixt Two Worlds: A Narrative of the Life and Work of William Eglinton* (1886), pl. VII. Department of Archives and Special Collections, University of Manitoba Libraries

104. J.G.Keulemans, *A Spirit Hand*, c.1884–5, chromolithograph, in *Twixt Two Worlds: A Narrative of the Life and Work of William Eglinton* (1886), pl. II. Department of Archives and Special Collections, University of Manitoba Libraries

and literary descriptions of ectoplasm conveyed. These images were stylistically prescient, in that they represented a less material, more 'otherworldly' mode of representation, which contrasted with Tissot's illusionistic manner of imaging his visions. In figure 94, while one can still recognize the drained and prostrate Eglinton with Tissot beside his easel, the impression of the ghosts is beginning to blur. Besnard depicts ectoplasm as vaporous and immaterial (fig. 102) in much the same way that the Symbolists Carrière and Redon chose to signify the unconscious state in their work. I will return to these artists later.

J. G. Keulemans' colour lithographs of Eglinton (fig. 103 and see fig. 93) were previously attributed to Tissot by Wentworth despite their naive style.[26] Of the four images discussed here, that of Keulemans is the most 'authentic,' in that it was produced by neither an academically trained artist, nor by a scientist, but by a steadfast believer who illustrated Spiritualist books. Keulemans was more involved with the Spiritualist movement than either Tissot or Besnard; he witnessed at least two séances with Eglinton between 1884 and 1885 and most likely produced these illustrations on one of these occasions.

As I have noted, the modern Spiritualist revival employed visual material as part of its promotional campaign but it also relied on written testimonies and descriptions of séances. Keulemans' plates, similarly to the high-art versions by Tissot and Besnard, closely follow the textual descriptions of Eglinton's séances: semi-opaque crystal which glowed with 'white-hot' phosphorescent light, and yards of white cloth which Eglinton's ghosts wove from ectoplasm (fig. 104):

> Mr. Eglinton appeared in the very midst of us in a trance. . . . As he stood thus, holding on to a chair for support, an airy mass like a cloud of tobacco smoke was seen on his left hip, his legs became illuminated by lights travelling up and down them, and a white film settled about his head and shoulders. The mass increased. . . , whilst invisible hands *pulled the filmy drapery out of his hip* in long strips, that amalgamated as soon as formed, and fell to the ground to be succeeded by others. The cloud continued to grow thicker and we were eagerly watching the process, when, in the twinkling of an eye, the mass had evaporated, and a spirit, full formed, stood beside him.[27]

The final image of Eglinton and the spectre is a spirit photograph taken by the parapsychologist Alexandre Aksákow (fig. 95 on p. 215). 'Transcendental' photographs, as 'photographic portraits of psychical entities not seen by normal vision' were called, began appearing very soon after Spiritualism took off in the United States.[28] There were both commercial and scientific uses for spirit photographs. The earliest photographs of ghosts were produced by entrepreneurs who sold these images at a profit as the Spiritualist movement grew in popularity. The first spirit photograph was exhibited at the 1860 meeting of the American Photographic Society; soon afterwards the genre was adopted by the engraver William Mulmer, who was able to make as much as ten dollars a photograph before he was tried for fraud in the late 1860s.[29] The demand for Mulmer's photographs encouraged other 'spectral' specialists to set up shop in Europe. Between 1873 and 1874, years during which Tissot lived in London, spirit photography was enthusiastically endorsed by a number of respected British scientists and professional photographers. Tissot, like anyone who was interested in photography, could not have missed the hoopla surrounding these developments.

In 1873, John Beattie, a prominent professional photographer, published the aesthetically pleasing results of his experiments with the mediumistic

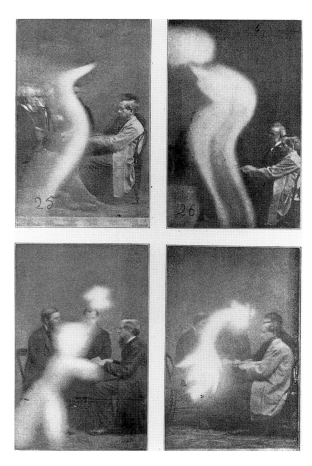

105. John Beattie, *Spirit Photograph*, c.1872–3, in *Animismus und Spiritismus* (Leipzig, 1919), pl. III

photographer Frederick Hudson in the *British Journal of Photography* (fig. 105).[30] Hudson's fame as a spirit photographer reached its peak when the well-known naturalist Alfred Russel Wallace accepted two spectral photographs of his deceased mother as genuine. Even more dramatic was the public 'love affair' enacted between William Crookes and the ghost 'Katie King.' Crookes, the English physicist who discovered the element thallium, invented the radiometer and pioneered the study of cathode rays, also had a life-long commitment to applying the positivistic paradigm to transcendental phenomena. His photographs of 'Katie King' date from 1874, and to this day are the most reproduced spectral photographs (fig. 97 on p. 217).

That mediums often conjured up attractive young female apparitions like 'Katie King' and 'Kathleen Newton,' especially when the attendees were male scientists, has not escaped the notice of commentators. Both Alex Owen and

Diana Basham[31] have remarked on the limitations as well as the privileges of power that attended female mediumship in the nineteenth century. Essentialist theories of the period dictated that the best (that is, the most 'natural') mediums were women, because their 'passive minds' would better enable them to 'channel' the discarnate spirits' messages.[32] Male mediums, meanwhile, were feminized, and Owen has noted that transgressive gender and culture roles were often played out in the spectacle of the séance, which was beyond the dominance of prevalent moral codes and exempt from possible social reprisals.[33] While the mediums themselves remained models of decorous behaviour, they invoked ghosts of various genders and races who often behaved raucously, swearing, flirting or becoming violent. Eglinton's apparitions, for example, were fond of kissing; both Farmer and Marryat describe scenes similar to the one in which Tissot was able to 'feel the lips' of Newton's ghost.[34] Eglinton even permitted scientists to tie him up and strip-search him, a condition usually reserved for female mediums, who often underwent a gynaecological examination before or after a séance:[35]

> The distinguished naturalist, Alfred Russel Wallace, in a letter. . . , states that he saw Eglinton at a séance in a private house. By his side there appeared Abdullah, a materialized Oriental wearing sandals, a turban, and burnous; Eglinton being visible at the same time sitting in an armchair in evening dress. *After the séance Eglinton was undressed and most carefully searched but neither sandals, turban nor burnous were found.*[36] (Italics mine)

Richet describes these circumstances as if they involved standard scientific methodologies but one cannot help but notice the sexual undercurrents of the séance and the intrusive behaviour of the scientists.[37] The increasingly shameless 'conduct' of the ghosts and the scientists, and the fact that some of those involved in Spiritualism, particularly mediums and spirit photographers, were making money,[38] thrust the whole movement into the spotlight. In France this attention peaked in 1875 when the most important French transcendental photographer, Jean Buguet, was charged and convicted of fraud.[39] Many Spiritualists did not accept Buguet's confession, attributing it to a plot inspired by the Catholic Church to discredit the movement; more extraordinary than the conspiracy theory were the hundreds of letters Buguet received in support of his practise from extremely well-placed citizens, including Maria Caithness, a leading Neo-Catholic Spiritualist. In 1874 Buguet had produced thirteen spectral photographs for Caithness from his London Baker Street studio (fig. 98 on p. 219). Pierre Leymarie, who was indicted along with Buguet for fraud, published

106. Jean Buguet, *Spirit Photograph (Ghost of Madame Dessenon)*, photograph. Bibliothèque Nationale, Paris

a number of Buguet's spirit photographs in *Revue spirite*, France's most important Spiritualist journal (fig. 106).

Scientific spirit photographs were documents taken by scientists for studying ectoplasm, the nature of materializations, and for determining mediumistic fraud. Even as the authenticity of commercial spirit photography was being questioned, the camera was being taken up by parapsychologists. Scientific spirit photographs, although identical in construction to the commercial examples, were published in reputable scientific books rather than in Spiritualist magazines, and were thus taken more seriously. In this period the camera was considered to be an unequivocal tool of empirical science and its perceived ability to reveal the truth meant that it was given more credibility than 'natural' vision. As Didi-Huberman has stated, to capture the 'invisible' became 'the new "ideal" of scientific photography at the turn of the nineteenth century.'⁴⁰ Crookes, Aksákow and Flammarion were some of the earliest scientists to photograph mediums and their work was continued by Richet and Schrenck-Notzing. Their goal, simply put by Schrenck-Notzing, was to use the camera to provide 'positive proofs' of the supernatural.⁴¹ It is in these scientific spirit photographs that the discourses of Spiritualism and science overlap. Outlandish as these images appear to our late twentieth-century sensibilities, we can only assume from the frequency with which Spiritualist images were reproduced, and the testimonials regarding their authenticity, that for a nineteenth-century audience notions of the supernatural were more acceptable then they are today.

The 'Scientization' of Spirituality

> One perceives — one can presage — that the religion of the future will be sci-entific, will be founded on a knowledge of psychical facts. This religion of sci-ence will have one great advantage over all that have gone before it – *unity*.⁴²

There has been much scholarship regarding the critique of Positivism that devel-oped in the Western world at the end of the nineteenth century, resulting in the revival of hermetic philosophies and unorthodox religious sects.⁴³ As Goodrick-Clarke has pointed out, behind these 'New Age' philosophies 'there lay a strong desire to reconcile the findings of modern natural science with a religious view that could restore man to a position of centrality and dignity in the universe.'⁴⁴ The desire to legitimize religion through science is evident in the burgeoning of quasi-religions, such as Spiritualism, Vitalism, Monism, and to a lesser degree Theosophy, that utilised contemporary scientific research.

One of the most influential projects in late nineteenth-century science was that of the German biologist Ernst Haeckel (1834–1919). Haeckel's world view, which was both Vitalistic and Monistic, updated nineteenth-century German nature-Romanticism (*Naturphilosophie*) with two current scientific principles: the notion of a vital process which animated all of nature, and Monism which posited that all forms in nature are united by a common process of evolution.⁴⁵ Kurt Bayertz coined the phrase 'the spiritualization of matter' to explain Haeckel's Neo-Romantic philosophy which 'saw nature as a single universal sub-stance that was both matter and spirit — a universe of animated matter.'⁴⁶ The biologist appropriated the term 'soul' (*Seele*) for the 'vital force,' thus spiritualiz-ing the whole of nature, living and non-living. By 1906 Haeckel had founded the Monist League, which he envisioned as a type of church which would mediate between science and religion. This 'scientific pantheism' recapitulated the basic principles of other fin-de-siècle, 'New Age' religions.

Vitalist and Spiritualist doctrines shared the concept of an animating principle, as well as a populist pantheistic attitude, which for some believers developed into a more sophisticated holistic outlook regarding humanity's place in the cosmos. Haeckel's notion of a single universal substance is analogous to Spiritualism's concept of ectoplasm in that they were both considered to be all pervading, possessing a kind of 'intuition.'[47] Henri Bergson further codified the vital impulse, the *élan vital*, in his 1907 *Creative Evolution*, which postulated that this force directed evolution. Similar Neo-Lamarckian notions were held by Flammarion, and were accepted by Richet and Geley. It was not at all unusual for Vitalists to be associated with the Society for Psychical Research (founded in 1882 by Frederick Myers), whose stated goal was to study 'various physical phenomena commonly called spiritualist: with an attempt to discover their causes and general laws.'[48] The Society benefited from some of the best thinkers of the early twentieth century, including Bergson and the well-known Vitalist biologist Hans Driesch, each of whom was president for a year.[49] Parapsychologists were often antagonistic towards those who uncritically accepted the Spiritualist belief in ghosts. But they did not exclude all romantic or idealistic interpretations; this is true in the cases of Crooks, Flammarion, Geley, Frederick Myers and Cesar Lombroso,[50] as well as in the case of Maeterlinck, whose acceptance of survival after bodily death centred on a directed vital force: 'It would be more reasonable to admit once and for all that matter and spirit are fundamentally merely two different states of a single substance or rather of the same eternal energy.'[51] Others, such as Richet and Theodore Flournoy, promoted more materialistic explanations regarding supernatural phenomena. As implied by Richet, whose *Our Sixth Sense* was dedicated to his 'illustrious friend Henri Bergson the most profound thinker of modern times,' the principle of the vital force had enough scientific credibility to make it popular with both materialists and idealists.

The spectacle of the séance embodied a populist pantheism in that spirits, animal or human, often chose to communicate by animating inanimate objects—table levitation, rapping, and telekinesis (fig. 96 on p. 216). Diana Basham has suggested that Spiritualism was 'more or less independent of the concept of God.'[52] But the avoidance of a (monotheistic) Judeo-Christian approach to religion did not negate transcendental notions. In this regard, the Neo-Romantic philosophers who studied Spiritualism—of which Camille Flammarion is one of the most important—played a key role.

Flammarion's project was no less ambitious than Haeckel's: 'the *début* of a new science . . . [t]his religion of science.'[53] Symbolist scholars have pointed out that Flammarion's romanticization of astronomy was attractive to artists such as Redon and Van Gogh, who were engaged with both science and religion. Redon's stated goal, to seek 'the logic of the visible in the service of the invisible,' and Carrière's oft-repeated phrase 'visionnaire du réel' reflect the blend of empiricism and idealism that permeated this period.[54] These statements could well serve as mottos for fin-de-siècle metaphysical researchers such as Haeckel and Flammarion who relied on the latest technical imaging advancements to foster their Neo-Romantic viewpoints. Haeckel published *Kunstformen der Natur* (*Art Forms of Nature*), which aesthetized microscopic images of natural forms, as a source book for artists in 1899. This book was immensely popular and there is evidence that Haeckel's ideas may have been known to Carrière and Redon.[55] The telescope and the microscope made it possible finally to 'see the invisible,' that is, the similarity between macrocosmic and microcosmic patterns. This recognition of parallelism, belief in a vital, animating principle and an attitude of anti-anthropocentrism, are basic principles of a Haeckelian Vitalistic Monism, which has been referred to as 'Biocentrism,' a late nineteenth- and twentieth-century biologistic, Neo-Romanticism.[56] Flammarion summarized this attitude:

> The sun . . . shines on the orbits of the planets, and he himself moves in a sidereal system that is vaster still. We have no right to deny that thought can exist in space, and that it directs the movement of vast bodies, as we direct those of our arms or legs. The instinct which controls living beings, the forces which keep up the beating of our hearts, the circulation of our blood, . . . may they not have parallels in the material universe, regulating conditions of existence incomparably more important than those of a human being, since, . . . if the sun were to be extinguished, or if the movement of the earth were put out of its course, it would not be one human who would die, it would be the whole population of our globe, to say nothing of that of other planets.[57]

As a philosophy, Neo-Romanticism — Romanticism updated by quasi-scientific theories — was more widespread in nineteenth-century France than has been previously noted by art historians.[58] Tissot and Besnard's appropriation of Spiritualist images, which were sanctioned by scientists, set the tone for a theory and style of Symbolist art which sought a reconciliation between science and

107. Albert Besnard, *Life is Born from Death*, 1896, mural in Sorbonne, Paris, from photograph in *Revue encyclopédique* (1896), p, 434

religion. In Tissot's case his commitment to mystical Catholicism dominated his final oeuvre, anticipating the growing interest in Neo-Catholicism within the Symbolist movement by artists such as Maurice Denis, Emile Bernard and Louis Anquetin. Besnard's views, however, shifted from Spiritualism towards the more scientific discourse of Vitalistic Monism. The dematerializing, indistinct forms of his ectoplasmic drawings are analogous to the emergent Symbolist style represented by Carrière's vaporous figures and by Redon's nature-centred cosmology.

Scientific Symbolism

Qui possède l'art et la science possède la religion.[59]

Camille Mauclair's monograph on Albert Besnard describes the artist as developing myths for the new 'religion of science,' creating a style called 'scientific symbolism.'[60] Besnard's aestheticization of science went beyond allegory to reflect 'les forces de la nature,' the same forces which the vitalists and parapsychologists were codifying during this period. The artist embodied his scientific pantheism with a style which is most often described as nature palpitating 'sous les vaporeuses vibrations du soleil.'[61] The nebulous quality evident in the séance drawings is clearly expressed in his most famous mural *Life is Born from Death*, 1896 (fig. 107) designed for the chemistry amphitheatre at the Sorbonne. Debora Silverman has correctly posited that this mural reflects a 'secular version of Catholic religiosity, infused with a particular kind of organicism called transformism, a fin-de-siècle

French scientific theory that assumed the continuum of being and the unity of all matter.'[62] It is possible now to be more accurate in identifying Besnard's world view with that of Vitalistic Monism or Biocent-ricism. Transformism, a biological–evolutionary theory important for French Monists, developed from the work of Jean-Baptiste de Lamarck and Etienne Geoffroy Saint-Hilaire, who hypothesized that all species evolved organically from an elementary form, or a few simple forms, into complex and differentiated beings. Gustave Geley, a philosopher who helped disseminate Haeckel's ideas in France, explained the Transformist precept this way: '*Tous les êtres vivants . . . descendraient d'un petit nombre de formes primitives ou même d'une seule forme primitive.*'[63]

'Transformist' was the adjective which was used to describe the work of Besnard by Mauclair and Georges Lecomte; the work of Carrière by Gabriel Séailles, and by Elie Faure. It has also been applied to Redon's hybrid creatures.[64] Besnard illustrated nature's creative derivation in *Life is Born from Death* by depicting a primordial, vaporous mist evolving over three panels into an earthly paradise:

> Au centre, un cadavre de femme est renversé parmi des germes de plantes. Un enfant tette une des ses mamelles, tandis que de l'autre s'échappe un lait qui, serpentant au travers de la Nature, forme comme un fleuve de vie. Autour de la bouche errent les papillons, compagnons de toute pourriture et porteurs de germes. . . . A droite, le couple humain dominant la Nature, son future domaine, descend vers le fleuve qui, remontant vers la gauche, charrie au travers des cataclysmes, les débris des plantes et des hommes, et vient se perdre dans les entrailles de la Terre, au fond d'un gouffre de feu, véritable creuset d'où ressortira à nouveau la Vie.[65]

The juxtaposition of the human species with plants emphasises — perhaps awkwardly — the unity of forms. The pantheism of the scene is indicated through the 'vibrant fluidity' of nature represented by 'les forces de la Nature, l'eau et l'air, la terre, le feu, principes de la chimie organique, qui ont créé la plante, l'animal et l'homme sous l'influence du Soleil.'[66] Besnard's panel for the Pharmacy College in Paris, which I only know from Mauclair's description, is a scene — increasingly interesting to nineteenth-century artists — of aquatic hybrid creatures, 'half-fish half-birds,' reflecting evolutionary stages of 'transition,' when evolutionary intermediate creatures such as 'poissons osseux' and winged reptiles, developed.[67] Besnard's and Redon's fascination with primordial sea creatures reflected not only advancements in the technology of underwater research but also new

108. Odilon Redon, *Germination*, pl. 2 from *Dans La Rêve*, 1879, lithograph, 27.3 x 19.5 cm. The Stickney Collection, The Art Institute of Chicago

attitudes about terrestrial and marine flora which, as Larson, Sandström and Silverman have suggested, were closely tied to evolutionary theories, such as Haeckel's recapitulation theory and, I would add, the transition of forms.[68] Transformism also fostered research into plants and animals, which at a very basic level of development are indistinguishable. This parallels the work being done by Haeckel with micro-organisms he called '*protista*',[69] and by the botanist Armand Clavaud, whose studies Redon described this way: ' He searched . . . at the edge of the imperceptible world, that life which lies between animal and plant, . . . this mysterious element which is animal during a few hours of the day and only under the effects of light.'[70]

From the botanist, and from scientists such as Flammarion and Haeckel, Redon learned about the remarkable similarities of form within the macrocosm and microcosm. This knowledge is reflected, for example, in his print *Germination* (fig. 108), which in its purposeful ambiguity may represent either planets or microscopic cells. This image reflects an instance of parallelism, and by adding faces Redon symbolizes nature animated with life. Redon saw himself similar to a scientist, studying nature with great care:

> After the effort of copying minutely a pebble, a blade of grass, a hand, a face, or any other objects from the organic or inorganic world, I experience mental elation: I then need to create, to allow myself to move to the representation of the imaginary. Nature, thus scrutinized and infused, becomes my spring, my yeast, my ferment.[71]

If Besnard's Neo-Romantic work did not capture the imagination of his contemporaries, the art of Carrière and Redon certainly did, and it is evident that they too were developing an avant-garde Symbolist style that echoes Monist tenets.

Carrière, who knew Besnard,[72] is said to have done a series of Transformist drawings in approximately 1895 which seem to have been similar to Redon's hybrid creatures. These drawings are lost, but they have been described by Séailles: 'Carrière se plaît à une sorte de transformisme, qu'il illustre de dessins étranges, où des formes de la fleur, du fruit, par degrés on s'élève à celle de la femme.'[73] The evolution of these images from one category into the other 'by degrees' does embody Transformist tenets, and Carrière's writings are suffused with Monistic statements regarding the unity of all forms, even while they reflect the prevalent gendered view of 'nature':

> Dans la nature, . . . les formes sont sympathiques, d'une même famille, les expressions d'une même idée qui peu à peu s'affirme et se précise. Il y a quelque temps, je revenais de Saint-Maur, je regardais par les vitres courir le paysage, et j'admirais l'ondulation des collines, à laquelle se mariait la courbe des feuillages; je me retourne, et en face de moi je vois une femme à la bouche d'un dessin fier et pur, et dans cette bouche comme répété clairement tout ce que je venais de voir et d'admirer. Il y a ainsi une hiérarchie des formes qui s'expliquent l'une l'autre; dans la nature, rien n'est dépaysé, parce que tout est parent, la colline et la plaine, l'arbe, la terre et l'homme; aussi, que dans un beau paysage apparaisse une belle femme, vous ne voyez plus qu'elle, mais en elle vous revoyez tout le reste.[74]

As this quotation demonstrates Carrière's convictions were not a general 'fin-de-siècle 'salade russe' of scientific and philosophic hypotheses', as Hirsch and Bantens suggest, but rather reflective of fin-de-siècle Biocentrism.[75] In his oft-quoted speech about the wonders of the skeleton, given at the Natural History Museum in Paris in 1901, Carrière insisted that nature be the source for art, '[e]n vérité, le Musée des squelettes est un Musée d'art' indicating a possible knowledge of Haeckel's *Kunstformen der Natur*.[76] As in Besnard's mural, the principle of evolution is expressed in Carrière's art through his recurrent imaging of mother and child, which illustrates the continuity of life and forms, and in his flowing arabesques, which signify the forces of life, as his friend and biographer Elie Faure explained.[77] Carrière also appropriated the liquescent, dissolving forms of ectoplasm in his work, evoking comparisons to spirit photographs and apparitions.[78]

It has long been noted that there were two avant-garde Symbolist styles: Synthetism, best represented by Gauguin's art, and the 'other' Symbolist style typified by the dream-like images of Carrière and Redon. Most scholars have recognized the importance of the latter artists within Symbolist circles, yet their art has been consistently marginalized due to its naturalism—an approach they retained in order to better express their nature-centric philosophy. Albert Aurier's rejection of Positivism and his decision to canonize Synthetism over the 'other' Symbolist style was accepted uncritically by later scholars. Critics contemporary with Aurier such as André Mellerio and Jules Bois however were better able to evaluate the Neo-Romantic elements in Symbolist art. An important source regarding Carrière and Redon's Symbolist style is a little-known article of 1897 written by Jules Bois entitled 'L'Esthétique des esprits et celle des symbolistes.'[79] In this article discussing the theatre programmes that the Nabis produced for Paul Fort's *Théâtre d'art*, Bois articulated the formal elements of the 'Spirit aesthetic,' a style which attempted to effect the 'unconscious' realm through the use of 'equivocal lines,' 'asymmetry' and 'excessive detail.' As Elizabeth Prelinger has noted, Nabi playbills utilised this 'indeterminate' effect 'reminiscent of the style of Redon or Eugène Carrière.'[80] These two Symbolists were on the periphery of the *Théâtre d'art* but their influence on the Nabis print style was strong. The relatively indistinct images of Carrière and Redon evoked a fluid immateriality which fit perfectly with the Symbolist dramas that Fort was producing, such as those of Maeterlinck, Edouard Schuré and Jules Bois.

During the last part of his life Tissot concentrated on imaging his visions of Christ, and thus placed himself in a tradition of high artists working mediumistically, in an altered state of consciousness. By the 1890s, according to Bois, other artists such as the Nabis were interested in this method: mediumship and automatic art had become signifiers of originality. Despite the style he adopted, which can in no way be described as avant-garde by the standards of the day, Tissot knew how to be modern. By participating in the scientific examination of Spiritualism, he anticipated by several years the investigation of the unconscious that formed the basis of the Symbolist aesthetic. The fascination with altered states of consciousness continued into the twentieth century, in which painting the unseen, the unseeable and the unconscious propelled the emergence of both Surrealism and Abstraction.

I would like to thank Dr. Katharine Lochnan for inviting me to contribute to this collection of essays. This article is based on a chapter of my forthcoming dissertation for the University of Toronto. I thank my supervisor Professor Bogomila Welsh-Ovcharov for her continued support. I would also like to thank Oliver Botar and James Bugslag for reading this article.

1. Oration Delivered at the Grave of Allan Kardec by Camille Flammarion (Paris: Didier, 1869) quoted in Camille Flammarion, *Mysterious Psychic Forces: An Account of the Author's Investigation in Psychical Research, Together with those of other European Savants* (Boston: Small, Maynard, and Co., 1907), 31.

2. Christopher Wood suggests that it is embarrassing to read Tissot's descriptions of his religious works in *Tissot* (Boston: Little Brown and Company, 1986), 148. Michael Wentworth remarks that Tissot behaved irrationally after Kathleen Newton's death in *James Tissot* (Oxford: Clarendon Press, 1984), 175, 183. For a discussion of the conservative elements within Neo-Catholicism see Michael Marlais, *Conservative Echoes in Fin-de-Siècle Parisian Art Criticism* (University Park, Pennsylvania: Pennsylvania State University Press, 1992).

3. For example, Jackson Lears, *No Place of Grace: Antimodernism and the Transformation of American Culture 1880–1920* (New York: Pantheon Books, 1981); Jeffrey Herf, *Reactionary Modernism: Technology, Culture and Politics in Weimar and the Third Reich* (Cambridge: Cambridge University Press, 1984); Stephen A. Mcknight, *Science, Pseudo-Science and Utopianism in Early Modern Thought* (Columbia: University of Missouri Press, 1992).

4. Michael Wentworth, *James Tissot*. See chapter 7, 'God and the Blessed Spirits,' and *James Tissot: Catalogue Raisonné of his Prints* (Minneapolis: The Minneapolis Institute of Arts, 1978), 294–9, 334–7.

5. J.G. Keulemans executed a series of colour lithographs after his original watercolours, which were produced 'from life' at one of the two recorded séances he attended with Eglinton in February 1884 and again on 29 September 1885, as John Stephen Farmer reported in *Twixt Two Worlds: A Narrative of the Life and Work of William Eglinton* (1886; 2nd ed., London: E.W. Allen, 1890), 163–7, 159–60. Keulemans is variously

described as an 'investigator' of Spiritualism and as a 'well-known scientific draughts-man' of the paranormal by Farmer (163) and by Frank Podmore in *Mediums of the 19th Century* (New York: University Books, 1963), 2:298. Wentworth mistakenly attributed Keulemans' prints to Tissot in *James Tissot: Catalogue Raisonné of his Prints*, 298–9.

6. Yveling Rambaud [Frédéric Gilbert], *Force Psychique* (Paris: Ludovic Baschet, 1889), 7–9. Besnard's illustrations are dated to 1887 and were transferred to wood engravings by Florian. I have found little evidence to substantiate a friendship between Tissot and Besnard. Tissot painted the two 'ghosts' which made their appearances at the 20 May 1885 séance in London, England. Besnard's illustration (fig. 94) depicts the same event, which suggests that both men attended it. However, neither Rambaud nor Farmer mention that Besnard was in attendance that day. Jacques-Emile Blanche describes a séance held at Besnard's home in London with the Besnards, Tissot and a medium in attendance, which Anne Saddlemyer accepts as the 20 May 1885 séance. Blanche claims that this same séance ended with the medium being exposed as a fraud, resulting in him being jailed. However Eglinton, despite accusations of fraud was never jailed, and I can find no other source suggesting that this séance turned out badly. Blanche's description is either inaccurate or, as Farmer hints, Tissot attended two different séances with Eglinton. See Jacques-Emile Blanche, *Portraits of a Lifetime, the Late Victorian Era, the Edwardian Pageant, 1870–1914* (London: Dent, 1937), 65–6. Besnard may, of course, have illustrated the séance without actually having attended it.

7. Neither Fred Gettings nor Wentworth realized that Alexander Aksákow is the author of this photograph (fig. 95). I do agree with Wentworth that the 'ghost' photographed with Eglinton is meant to be 'Ernest.' See Wentworth, *James Tissot*, 177 n8. Gettings misdates this photograph to 1878, in *Ghosts in Photographs* (New York: Harmony Books, 1978), 49–51, fig. 31. Rambaud states that the photograph of Eglinton is one of eight photographs which were taken in London on 22 April 1886 (*Force Psychique*, 43). The photograph was taken by Alexander Aksákow and reproduced in *Animismus und Spiritismus* (1890: Leipzig: Druck und Verlag von Oswald Mutze, 1919), Plate XI. According to Aksákow the results of these photographic experiments were published in March 1887 and the original photograph was published in December 1887, both in *Psychische Studien* (287). Aksákow's book was published into French in 1895 by P.G. Leymarie, the editor of *La Revue spirite*.

8. Jules Bois, 'L'Esthétique des esprits et celle des symbolistes,' *La Revue des Revues* (January–March 1897), 405–20. This article was republished in a longer version in Jules Bois, *Le Miracle Modern* (Paris: Societé d'Éditions Littéraires et Artistiques, 1907), chapter 3, 140–64. For an analysis of Bois' article see Janis Bergman-Carton, 'The Medium is the Medium: Jules Bois, Spiritualism and the Esoteric Interests of the Nabis,' *Arts-Magazine,* 61 no.4 (December 1986): 24–9.

9. Robert Galbreath 'A Glossary of Spiritual and Related Terms,' in *The Spiritual in Art: Abstract Painting 1890–1985*, ed. Maurice Tuchman (New York: Abbeville Press, 1986), 384–5.

10. Clarke Garrett, *Spirit Possession and Popular Religion: From the Camisards to the Shakers* (Baltimore: Johns Hopkins University Press, 1987), 2.

11. Henri Ellenberger, *The Discovery of the Unconscious: The History and Evolution of Dynamic Psychiatry* (New York: Basic Books Inc., 1970), 145. See also Adam Crabtree, *From Mesmer to Freud: Magnetic Sleep and the Roots of Psychological Healing* (New Haven: Yale University Press, 1993).

12. Ellenberger, *Discovery of the Unconscious,* 146.

13. Max Nordau, *Degeneration* (London: William Heinmann, 1895), 216.

14. Regarding William Crookes' role in the history of 'Spirit' Photography, see Cyril Permutt, *Beyond The Spectrum: A Survey of Supernormal Photography* (Cambridge: Patrick Stephens, 1983), 19–20. For the story of Alfred Wallace and Frederick Hudson, see James Coates, *Photographing the Invisible* (New York: Arno Press, 1973), 37–41.

15. Farmer's reference is not clear (*Twixt Two Worlds*, 186–7). He may be referring to any one of Marryat's various experiences with Eglinton through the 1870s and 1880s, see 50–7, 60–1, 136–8 and 171–3. Farmer quotes Marryat's published account of the July 1879 séance in full (50–7). Florence Marryat republished this story in *There is No Death* (Montreal: John Lovel and Son, 1891), see chapter 11, 'The Story of the Monk.'

16. Marryat, *There is No Death,* 23, 16. The Catholic Church issued a decree on 30 July 1856 exhorting bishops to employ every effort to suppress the abuses of spirit evocation. As Griffin explains, 'Catholic theologians reject the idea that discarnate spirits can be evoked at will,' they find Spiritualist inclinations to 'pantheism' to be heretical, and believe that the 'Sacred Scripture expressly forbids the practise of trying to summon up the souls of the deceased' which they feel involves 'diabolical influence.' See M.D. Griffin, 'Spiritism,' *New Catholic Encyclopedia* (Washington, D.C.: Catholic University of America, 1967), 13:576–7. For a review of the incidence of spirit possession that occur in the Old and New Testaments, see Garrett, *Spirit Possession and Popular Religion,* 3, 6–10.

17. Quoted in K. Paul Johnson, *The Masters Revealed: Madame Blavatsky and the Myth of the Great White Lodge* (Albany: State University of New York, 1994), 63. For biographical information on Caithness, see Marie-France James, *Ésotérisme, Occultism Franc-Maconnerie et Christianisme aux XIX et XX Siècles* (Paris: Nouvelles Éditions Latines, 1981), 60–2.

18. Kathleen Newton died in 1882. Edmond de Goncourt comments on Tissot's distress after Newton's death, and Bastard adds the information regarding Tissot's brother. De Goncourt, *Journal,* 2:204–5, quoted in Wentworth, *James Tissot,* 155; George Bastard, 'James Tissot: Notes Intimes,' *Revue de Bretagne et de Vendée,* 2nd ser. 36 (November 1906): 264–5.

19. Wentworth (*James Tissot,* 177–8 n8) refers to de Goncourt's and Bastard's descriptions of Tissot's ghostly painting, but he does not mention Besnard's illustration of the event or Rambaud's text. Besnard depicts Tissot holding his paint brushes, leaning over an easel, and this matches Rambaud's description of Tissot's reaction during the séance (*Force Psychique,* 7–9). The painting of Kathleen Newton's spirit remained so

important to Tissot that even as late as 1899 he kept it in a special shrine. The painting was not included in Tissot's studio sale after his death, and it is still missing. See Bastard, 'James Tissot: Notes Intimes,' 278.

20. Quoted in Wentworth, *James Tissot*, 191; F. Hugo d'Alési's automatic drawing (1878) was published in J.-Camille Chaigneau, *Les Chrysanthèmes de Marie* (Paris: E. Dentu, 1880). Caillié refers to this image in *Etoile* (April 1890), 59, and Bois reproduces another image by d'Alési in 'L'Esthétique des esprits et celle des symbolistes,' 406. Had he wanted to, Tissot could have seen automatic drawings and spirit photographs in private collections, including those of Jules Bois, P.G. Leymarie, and Marie Caithness. See Jules Bois, *Le Miracle Moderne* (Paris: Société d'Éditions Littéraires et Artistiques, 1907), 149, and Coates on Caithness' collection, *Photographing the Invisible*, 54–5.

21. Cleveland Moffett, 'J. J. Tissot and his Paintings of the Life of Christ,' *McClure's Magazine*, 393, cited in Wentworth, *James Tissot*, 182, 184–5.

22. Hyppolite Baraduc in *La Force Vitale: Notre Corps Vital Fluidique, Sa Formule Biométrique* (Paris: Georges Carré, 1893) lists the other names of this so-called force: 'dynamisme cosmique, ether, force de vie universelle' (3–4). Rambaud correlates the mysterious force to Eliphas Levis' astral light (*Force Psychique*, 11). William Crookes believed that the vital force was characterized by some kind of intelligence: ' I published an account of experiments tending to show that outside our scientific knowledge there exists a Force exercised by intelligence differing from the ordinary intelligence common to mortals' (1898), quoted in Nandor Fodor, *Encyclopedia of Psychic Science* (1934: repr. London: University Books, 1974), 71. Gustave Geley, *From the Unconscious to the Conscious* (New York: Harper Brothers, 1921), suggested that ectoplasm has an 'instinct,' quoted in Fodor, 114. According to Wightman, Haeckel defined his *Substanzbegriff* as having 'unconscious perception.' See William P.D. Wightman, *Science and Monism* (London: George Allen and Unwin, 1934), 252.

23. Fodor, *Encyclopedia of Psychic Science*, 113.

24. Albert von Schrenck-Notzing, *The Phenomena of Materialisation*, quoted in Fodor, *Encyclopedia of Psychic Science*, 113.

25. Rambaud, *Force Psychique*, 7–8.

26. Wentworth, *Tissot: Catalogue Raisonné*, 298–9.

27. Marryat, *There is No Death*, 126–7.

28. Coates, *Photographing the Invisible*, xi.

29. Permutt, *Beyond The Spectrum*, 12–13.

30. *British Journal of Photography* (11 July 1873), see Permutt, *Beyond The Spectrum*, 17, and Gettings, *Ghosts in Photographs*, 109–11. Figure 105 is by Beattie 1872–3.

31. Alex Owen, *The Darkened Room: Woman, Power, and Sexuality in Late Victorian England* (Philadelphia: University of Pennsylvania Press, 1990); Diana Basham, *The Trial of Woman: Feminism and the Occult Sciences in Victorian Literature and Society* (London: Macmillan, 1992).

32. Owen, *The Darkened Room*, 6–12, chapter 8, 'Spiritualism and the Subversion of Femininity,' especially 209.

33. See Owen on cross-gendered behaviour, *The Darkened Room,* 216–18.

34. Quote is from Bastard, 'James Tissot: Notes Intimes,' 265. In his final paragraph Farmer describes kissing one of Eglinton's apparitions: ' and in our midst the face and form of one whose mortal voice had not been heard for many a month before. She bent her head, her lips touched mine, and a simple but unmistakable sign of recognition was given' (*Twixt Two Worlds,* 196). Marryat also describes a kissing scene (*There is No Death,* 120).

35. See Farmer's description of a séance in which Eglinton was bound, *Twixt Two Worlds,* 9. Regarding examinations of female mediums, see Schrenck-Notzing, for example, *Phenomena of Materialisation,* 37–8, 49, 221, 253, 258, etc.

36. Charles Richet, *Thirty Years of Psychical Research: A Treatise on Metapsychics*, trans. Stanley de Brath (New York: Macmillan, 1923), 536.

37. The relationship between mediums and scientists was complex, see for example Owen, *The Darkened Room*, chapter 6, 'Medicine, Mediumship and Mania.'

38. It was possible to earn a decent living by being a medium during this period. Professional mediums did charge a fee, and private mediums were often supported by wealthy patrons. See Owen, *The Darkened Room,* 49–61.

39. Jean Buguet signed his name as Edouard Buguet which has caused some confusion in the literature. For the minutes of the trial see Madame Pierre Gaetan Leymarie ed., *Procès des Spirites* (Paris: Librarie Spirite, 1875); and Coates, *Photographing the Invisible,* 52–64.

40. Georges Didi-Huberman, 'Photography – scientific and pseudo-scientific' in *A History of Photography: Social and Cultural Perspectives,* ed. Jean-Claude Lemagny and André Rouillé (Cambridge: University of Cambridge Press, 1987), 71–5, quote on 71. Also see Linda Dalrymple Henderson, 'X Rays and the Quest for Invisible Reality in the Art of Kupka, Duchamp and the Cubists,' *Art Journal,* 47 (Winter 1988): 323–40.

41. Schrenck-Notzing, *Phenomena of Materialisation,* 12.

42. Flammarion, *The Unknown* (New York: Harper and Brothers, 1900), xii.

43. See footnote 3, and Shearer West, *Fin de Siècle* (London: Bloomsbury, 1993).

44. Nicholas Goodrick-Clarke, *The Occult Roots of Nazism: The Ariosophists of Austria and Germany 1890–1935* (Wellingborough: The Aquarian Press, 1985), 29.

45. My introduction to Haeckel's philosophy came from my husband's dissertation. See Oliver A.I. Botar, 'Prolegomena to the Study of Biomorphic Modernism: Biocentrism, László Moholy-Nagy's 'New Vision' and Ernö Kállai's Bioromantik', Ph.D. diss., University of Toronto, 1998. In chapter two Botar defines Biocentrism as a world view which privileges 'Leben' over 'Geist' and which foregrounds the 'concept of our inseparability from and dependence on nature.' He sees Biocentrism as having its origins in Romantic *Naturphilosophie,* biologism, and neo-Lamarckism. Specifically Botar describes fin-de-siècle Biocentrism as an amalgamation of the anti-anthropocentric, psycho-biological, Vitalist–Monist and holistic aspects of neo-Romanticism. Botar has provided a general template with which to recognize nature-centric philosophies, which I have applied here to French fin-de-siècle art.

46. Kurt Bayertz, 'Biology and Beauty: Science and Aesthetics in fin-de-siècle Germany' in *Fin de Siècle and its Legacy*, ed. Mikulas Teich and Roy Porter (Cambridge: Cambridge University Press, 1990), 278–95, quote on 285; and Alfred Kelly, *The Descent of Darwin. The Popularization of Darwinism in Germany, 1860–1914* (Chapel Hill: University of North Carolina Press, 1981), 27.

47. Wightman, *Science and Monism,* 252.

48. Fodor, *Encyclopedia of Psychic Science,* 351.

49. Henri Bergson was President of the Society for Psychical Research in 1913, and Hans Driesch was president in 1926 and 1927. Regarding Vitalism, both 'critical' and 'naive,' see Frederick Burwick and Paul Douglas, eds., *The Crisis in Modernism: Bergson and the Vitalist Controversy* (Cambridge: Cambridge University Press, 1992), 80.

50. See Schrenck-Notzing's summary, *Phenomena of Materialisation,* 28–9. On Geley see Fodor, *Encyclopedia of Psychic Science,* 114.

51. Maeterlinck, *The Great Secret* (1922; repr. New Hyde Park: University Books, 1969), 219.

52. Basham, *The Trial of Woman,* 113.

53. Flammarion, *The Unknown,* xii.

54. On the influence of Flammarion's romantic philosophy see Douglas W. Druick and Peter Kort Zegers, 'In the Public Eye' in *Odilon Redon: Prince of Dreams 1840–1916* (Chicago: The Art Institute of Chicago, 1994), 146–9, quote on 137; Albert Boime, 'Van Gogh's *Starry Night*: A History of Matter and a Matter of History,' *Arts Magazine,* 59 no. 4 (December, 1984): 86–103; and Sven Sandström, *Le Monde Imaginaire d'Odilon Redon: Etude Iconologique* (Lund, Sweden: Gleerup, 1955), especially chapter 3, 'Symbolisme Evolutioniste'.

55. Haeckel is listed as a source for Carrière's art by Eli Faure, *Formes et Forces* (Paris: Floury, 1907), 29. Barbara Larson mentions Haeckel in relation to Symbolists and Redon, 'La Génération Symboliste et La Révolution Darwinienne,' in *L'âme au Corps: Arts et Science 1793–1993,* ed. Jean Clair (Paris: Réunion des musées nationaux, Gallimard/Electra, 1993), 322–41. Haeckel's influence on the art nouveau movement is better documented; see Erika Krausse, 'L'influence de Ernst Haeckel sur L'Art Nouveau,' in *L'âme au Corps,* 342–50, and Siegfried Wichmann, *Jugendstil Art Nouveau* (Boston: Little Brown, 1984), especially 6–7, 13, and 46–108. Haeckel, as a popularizer of Lamarck and Darwin, was well known internationally. His Monist philosophy was mentioned in the 'New Age' Symbolist journal *Le Coeur* (May 1893) 8, to which the Nabis, Emile Bernard, and Emile Schuffenecker regularly contributed. Gustave Geley, one of France's leading evolutionary theorists and parapsychologists, gave a series of lectures in 1900–1 which summarized Haeckel's philosophy for a general audience. They were published in Gustave Geley, *Les Preuves du Transformisme et les Enseignements de la Doctrine Evolutioniste* (Paris: Felix Alcan, 1901). Haeckel's work was translated into French early on, for example, *Les Preuves du Transformisme: Réponse a Virchow,* trans. Jules Soury (Paris: Germer Baillière, 1879).

56. Botar has referred to the recognition of similar structural patterns found in the macrocosm and microcosm as the topos of self-similarity. See the Introduction of his thesis and footnote 45 in this essay. Sandström describes these vitalistic, monistic fin-de-siècle tendencies using the terms 'panthéisme' and 'parallélism', *Le Monde Imaginaire d'Odilon Redon*, 87–9.

57. Flammarion, *The Unknown*, xi.

58. For more information on the French Idealist movement, see Dorothy Knowles, *La Réaction Idéaliste au Théatre depuis 1890* (Paris: Libraire E. Droz, 1934), especially chapters 1 and 2. According to Marlais (*Conservative Echoes*, 11), Alfred Fouillée argued that science and faith could be reconciled in 'Le Mouvement Idéaliste en France et la réaction contre la science positive,' in *Revue des Deux Mondes* (15 March 1896), 276–304.

59. Goethe, quoted in Elie Faure, *Formes et Forces*, 137.

60. Camille Mauclair defines 'le symbolisme scientifique' as, 'c'est à dire l'incarnation plastique et chromatique des notions scientifiques en allégories décorative', see *Albert Besnard: L'homme et l'oeuvre* (Paris: Delagrave, 1914), 29.

61. Georges Lecomte, 'Albert Besnard,' *Gazette des Beaux-Arts*, 33 (1905): 153–67, quotes on 162, 156.

62. Debora Silverman in *Art Nouveau in Fin-de-Siècle France* (Berkeley: University of California Press, 1989), 226.

63. For the history of Transformism see Geley, *From the Unconscious to the Conscious*, 45–51, quote on 21 (italics are in the original). See the *Dictionary of the History of Ideas*, vol.1, 'Continuity and Discontinuity in Nature and Knowledge.' (New York: Charles Scribner's Sons, 1973), 492–504, in particular 499–500. Haeckel's definition of Transformism can be found in *Naturliche Schöpfungsgeschichte* (Berlin, 1879), quoted in Wichmann, *Jugendstil Art Nouveau,* 8.

64. For Besnard, see Mauclair, *Albert Besnard*, 28, 30, and 41–2, and Lecomte, 'Albert Besnard,' 161–2. For Carrière, see Gabriel Séailles, *Eugène Carrière: l'homme et l'artist* (Paris: Edouard Pelletan, 1901), 37, and Elie Faure, *Eugène Carrière: Peinture et Lithograph* (Paris: H. Floury, 1908), 140. For Redon, Sandström, 86.

65. The descriptions of the mural are by Besnard, quoted in Gabriel Mourey, *Albert Besnard* (Paris: Henri Davoust, 1906), 77–8, and Lecomte, 'Albert Besnard,' 162. Some of Besnard's passage is translated in *French Symbolist Painters* (London: Arts Council of Great Britain, 1972), 25–6.

66. 'Vibrant fluidity' is quoted from Lecomte, 'Albert Besnard,' 162; the rest of the quote is from Mourey, *Albert Besnard* , 78.

67. Mauclair, *Albert Besnard,* 36. On 'formes de transition' see Geley, *From the Unconscious to the Conscious*, 203–11. Larson makes this point regarding Redon's hybrid creatures, 'La Génération Symboliste et La Révolution Darwinienne,' 329.

68. Larson introduces Haeckel's recapitulation theory to help explain Redon's work, 'La Génération Symboliste et La Révolution Darwinienne,' 334–6; see Silverman, *Art Nouveau,* 226–7, 275, 290–1 on Transformism. Regarding Haeckel's well-known phrase 'ontogeny recapitulates phylogeny,' see William Coleman, *Biology in the*

Nineteenth Century: Problems of Form, Function and Transformation (New York: John Wiley and Sons, 1971), 47–9. Regarding Redon's interest in Darwin, evolutionary theories, and natural history museums, see Druick and Zegers, 'In the Public Eye', 137–45.

69. As defined by Wightman, *Science and Monism*, 227 and 222; Wichmann, *Jugendstil Art Nouveau*, 48.

70. Quoted in Odilon Redon, *To Myself: Notes on Life, Art and Artists* trans. Mira Jacob and Jeanne L. Wasserman (New York: George Braziller, 1986), 14–15. Also see Larson, 'La Génération Symboliste et La Révolution Darwinienne,' 333–4, and Druick and Zegers, 'In the Public Eye', 152–4.

71. Quoted in Maryanne Stevens, 'The Transformation of the Symbolist Aesthetic' in *Odilon Redon: Prince of Dreams 1840–1916*, 196–214, quote on 211.

72. Carrière made a speech in honour of Besnard in 1905, published in *Eugène Carrière: Écrits et Letters Choisies* (Paris: Sociètè du Mercure de France, 1907), 96–8; Besnard's speech about Carrière from 1904 is published in Mourey, *Albert Besnard*, 117–19. The two men also corresponded.

73. Séailles, *Eugène Carrière,* 37, translated in Robert Bantens, *Eugène Carrière: His Work and His Influence* (Ann Arbor, Michigan: UMI Press, 1983), 70. Elie Faure also mentions a similar premise which he compares to the theories of Herbert Spencer, *Eugène Carrière: Peinture et Lithograph*, 129–31.

74. Séailles, *Eugène Carrière,* 36–7. Also in Charles Chassé, *The Nabis and their Period*, trans. Michael Bullock (London: Lund Humpries, 1960), 33; and in Bantens, *Eugène Carrière,* 65.

75. The quote is from Richard Teller Hirsch, *Eugène Carrière 1849–1906: Seer of the Real* (Allentown: Allentown Art Museum, 1969). Bantens accepts this view, although he goes on to discuss affinity between Lamarck's vitalism, the aboriginal cell hypothesis and Carrière's art, *Eugène Carrière,* 69–70.

76. See 'L'Homme Visionnaire de la Réalité: Conference faite au Muséum d'Histoire Naturelle,' 1901, published in Carrière, *Écrits et Lettres Choisies*, 27–37, quote on 34. At this point we may also consider other fin-de-siècle artists. The architect Réné Binet came to the same metaphysical morphological conclusions as Carrière when he stated that: 'one can recognize 'the vertebrae of the dinosaur in the porch, the cells of the beehive in the dome, the madrepores in the pinnacles", quoted in Silverman, *Art Nouveau*, 291. Compare this to Carrière: 'la massivité du Rhincéros, qui rappelle les cintres trapus de l'architecture romane' ('L'Homme Visionnaire de la Réalité,' 29). On Binet see Erika Krausse, op.cit. footnote 55. Silverman astutely noted the common interest of Besnard, Émile Gallé and Réné Binet in applying the theory of Transformism to their art (Silverman, 290–1). Regarding Émile Gallé's notions about nature, she correctly links him with Vitalism (232). On Vitalism and modern sculpture see Jack Burnham, *Beyond Modern Sculpture: The Effects of Science and Technology on the Sculpture of this Century* (New York: George Braziller, 1968).

77. Faure, *Eugène Carrière: Peinture et Lithograph*, 128–9, and 123–6. Also see 130–2, 140–1 for Faure's Monist interpretation of Carrière's art which is based on evolutionary

principles, as well as Faure, *Formes et Forces*, 29, which he dedicated to Carrière. For excellent illustrations of Carrière's maternities, paternities and landscapes, see Rodolphe Rapetti et al. *Eugène Carrière 1884–1906* (Paris: Réunion des musées nationaux/Musée de Strasbourg, 1996). Especially interesting in the above catalogue is the article by Jane R. Becker, 'Carrière, Bergson, la durée et l'élan vital,' 27–33, where she points out that Bergson and, I would add, Carrière and Haeckel were influenced by a Lamarckian theory of evolution. For the importance of Lamarck see Peter J. Bowler, *The Eclipse of Darwinism: Anti-Darwinian Evolution Theories in the Decades around 1900* (Baltimore: The Johns Hopkins University Press, 1983). In his chapter 'Anti-Darwinism in France', Bowler explains how Haeckel's recapitulation theory helped revive Lamarck's evolutionary theories in France. He also lists Elie Metchnikoff, Carrière's friend, as one of the important French evolutionary theorists.

78. Paul-Jean Toulet, *Oeuvres Complètes* (Paris: Robert Laffront, 1986), 894, and Fauve, *Eugène Carrière: Peinture et Lithograph*, 126–7.

79. Bois' article was first brought to light by Henri Ellenberger and was then discussed by Janis Bergman-Carton. As Bergman-Carton has noted, Bois was closely allied with the Symbolists and, I would add, in particular Redon, Emile Bernard, and Emile Schuffenecker. See footnote 8.

80. Quoted in Elizabeth Prelinger, 'The Art of the Nabis: From Symbolism to Modernism,' in *The Nabis and the Parisian Avant-Garde* ed. Patricia Eckert Boyer (New Brunswick: Rutgers University Press, 1988), 96: Larson, 'Microbes and Maladies: Bacteriology and Health at the Fin de Siècle' in *Lost Paradise: Symbolist Europe* (Montreal: The Montreal Museum of Fine Arts, 1995), 385–93.

Notes on Contributors

Caroline Arscott is Lecturer in the History of Art, Courtauld Institute of Art, University of London.

Margaret Flanders Darby is Assistant Professor of Writing/Rhetoric, Department of Interdisciplinary Writing, Colgate University, Hamilton, New York.

Tamar Garb is Reader in the History of Art, University College London.

Serena Keshavjee is Senior Instructor in the Department of Fine Art, University of Manitoba, Winnipeg.

Katharine Lochnan is Senior Curator, Prints and Drawings, Art Gallery of Ontario.

Edward Maeder is a costume historian.

Nancy Rose Marshall was the 1998 Paul Mellon Post-Doctoral Fellow at the Yale Center for British Art, New Haven, Connecticut.

Elizabeth Prelinger is Chair in the Department of Art, Music, and Theatre, Georgetown University, Washington, D.C. and Wright Family Distinguished Professor in Art History.

Ann Saddlemyer is Professor Emeritus of English and Drama, University of Toronto.

Carole G. Silver is Professor of English, Stern College for Women, and Chair, Humanities Division, Yeshiva University, New York.

DATE DUE

GAYLORD			PRINTED IN U.S.A.